ITIOUS] BECAUSE I WANT TO MAKE
ENCE, IN A NOTICEABLE WAY, AND
NIZED FOR MY WORK. I'M TIRED OF
G BEHIND THE VELVET CURTAIN."
UCATOR, COACH, CREATIVE, ADVOCATE, 48

"AMBITIO
FIRE FOCUSED ON THAT WHICH
MOVES MY HEART."
—SOCIAL WORKER, SINGLE MOTHER OF THREE, 40

"I TRY MY BEST TO FULFILL MY HOPES AND DREAMS —
MY GOALS FOR HAVING A FULFILLING LIFE."
—THEATER DIRECTOR, ACTOR, 69

LESS AFRAID TO SAY I HAVE HIGH
TIONS. I WILL GET THE THINGS I
D NOT FEEL GUILTY OR ASHAMED.
MAKES ME AMBITIOUS.]"
S REP AND ACTRESS, 26

"[I AM AMBITIOUS BECAUSE] I
AM DRIVEN TO MAKE THE
WORLD A MORE JUST PLACE."
—PHYSICIAN, 46

SATISFIED WITH THE
OF MY LIFE OR THE
SOCIETAL DYNAMICS
I KNOW I DESERVE A
THAT I DEFINE AND
FOR MYSELF."
DUCT DESIGNER, FASHION DESIGNER,
IMPACT ENTREPRENEUR, 33

"[THERE IS] NO EXPIRATION DATE ON AMBITION!"
RETIRED TEACHER, 84

"AMBITION: BEING A WOMAN FARMER, WHO
RAISES AND CARES FOR HER LIVESTOCK 365
DAYS A YEAR, AND A WOMAN [WHO] CAN
ALSO BUTCHER AND SELL HER ANIMALS."
—FARMER, CHEF, GRAPHIC DESIGNER, WIFE, ACTIVIST, 54

HIEVE CERTAIN GOALS FOR
ORDER TO LIVE WELL AND BE
WHAT I HAVE TRIED TO DO."
HER OF THREE, AUTHOR, 43

MBITIOUS, AS I
HE BEST I CAN."
MENT MANAGER, 62

"EVERYONE WANTS TO BE THE BEST AT
WHAT THEY DO. WHETHER IT BE CAREER
ORIENTED, BEING A PARENT, OR JUST
BEING A GOOD FRIEND TO THOSE IN NEED."
—MARKETING PROFESSIONAL, 56

"AMBITION IS PROBABLY IN MY BLOOD. I COME FROM A LONG
LINE OF SURVIVORS OF WARS, FAMINE, POVERTY, AND CULTURAL
REVOLUTIONS. TO SURVIVE THESE CATASTROPHES, MY ANCESTORS
HAD TO HAVE SOME FIRE IN THEIR BELLIES AROUND SURVIVAL,
GROWTH, AND A WILL TO REPRODUCE."
—PHYSICIAN (HIV SPECIALIST), GRAPHIC DESIGNER, MOTHER OF ONE REALLY INTENSE KID, 40

DOUBLE BIND

DOUBLE BIND

• • • • • •

WOMEN ON AMBITION

EDITED BY ROBIN ROMM

LIVERIGHT PUBLISHING CORPORATION
A Division of W. W. Norton & Company
Independent Publishers Since 1923
New York   London

"On Impractical Urges," Copyright © 2017 by Ayana Mathis. All rights reserved.
"No Happy Harmony," Elizabeth Corey: A version of this essay previously appeared
in First Things. "The Price of Black Ambition," Roxane Gay: A version of this essay
previously appeared in Virginia Quarterly Review. "The Chang Girls," © Lan
Samantha Chang. "Original Sin," Copyright © 2017 by Francine Prose. All rights
reserved. "Know Your Place," Copyright © 2017 by Ringwald, Inc. "Escape
Velocity" © 2017 Claire Vaye Watkins

For information about special discounts for bulk purchases, please contact
W. W. Norton Special Sales at specialsales@wwnorton.com or 800-233-4830

Manufacturing by LSC Communications, Harrisonburg, VA
Book design by Helene Berinsky
Production manager: Anna Oler

ISBN 978-1-63149-121-4

Liveright Publishing Corporation
500 Fifth Avenue, New York, N.Y. 10110
www.wwnorton.com

W. W. Norton & Company Ltd.
15 Carlisle Street, London W1D 3BS

1 2 3 4 5 6 7 8 9 0

For Jacquelyn and Sylvie, my mother and daughter.

CONTENTS

DOUBLE BIND

How one's life might turn out, even after heroic effort, is anyone's guess. It's like this: a door opens, perhaps just a fraction of an inch. There's no telling if the door will open at all, or for whom, but if it does, you push push push until it is wide enough for you to squeeze through.

—AYANA MATHIS

My heart says, get up, get back in the game, this isn't just about you.

—THERESA REBECK

I was overcome with weariness, and I thought: Fuck it, I give up. *But of course that's not true either. Nope! Not at all. Onward.*

—ELISA ALBERT

Introduction

● ● ● ● ● ● **ROBIN ROMM**

When I first asked successful women to write about ambition, I received enthusiastic responses. *Yes! Great topic, very rich, very current—so much to say.* But invariably, a few days later, I'd receive a clarifying follow-up email: "I just want you to know that I'm not sure I'm ambitious. Lucky, yes. Hardworking, yes. Disciplined, very. But I'm not sure about ambitious."

This happened not once, but numerous times. Most of these women—best-selling writers, tenured professors, doctors, lawyers, scientists—were working at the top of their professions. They lectured at universities, raised children, wrote books, and navigated mercurial careers with fearlessness and grace. Were they really going to argue that their accomplishments had nothing to do with ambition?

This discomfort with the term *ambition* and all it suggested made me even more eager to commission essays. My own experiences with ambition were fraught. I've always been goal-oriented, motivated by the desire for mastery and achievement. (I define ambition, per Anna Fels, as the desire to do good work in the world and have that work recognized by people who understand it.) But by the time I got to college and became increasingly self-aware, this quality felt more complicated than it had felt as a girl, not only something to be proud of but also something to cloak. In my twenties, I inherited what so many young women inherit, the pervasive sense that striving and achieving had to be approached delicately or you risked the negative judgment of others. The ideal was achievement with an air of self-sacrifice or gentleness. As I moved on, into the world, I continued to feel a tug between two desires: to be the best student/investigator/writer/editor/professor that I could possibly be and the desire to be seen the way I saw myself, as motivated and curious, not "aggressive" or "strident."

I didn't always recognize this for what it was—the perpetual double bind of the gender, success paired eternally with scrutiny and retreat. Until I began to edit and compile this book, I only suspected how this conflict pervaded the lives of other women, how thoroughly the desire to succeed in their work complicated their careers, family planning, childrearing, art-making, friendships, and families. As I got deeper into the project, I not only found my tribe of conflict-ridden, energetic, interesting, thinking women, but I also realized that this central topic had never been addressed with the nuance and detail I craved.

For the past couple of years, every time this book has come up at a dinner, at a party, at an artist's colony, on the airplane, it has inspired passionate dialogue. *Isn't ambition about ego? Can doing good or living a good life be an ambition or is ambition solely about career? Are you fetishizing career with a book on ambition? It's a problem that women go to part time when they have kids; it leaves men in all the management roles and so the work culture never changes. It's a problem to leave your kids with sitters—sets off a spiritual crisis. I gave up on ambition, I don't see myself as ambitious, I have always been ambitious, my husband thinks I am ambitious but . . . I want my daugh-*

ters to be ambitious but I also want them to be selfless . . . My mother never got to do the things she wanted and so I feel called to do them. I am wildly ambitious and only recently realized people find that ugly. Is being wildly ambitious seen as ugly? I don't like the idea of selfishness, so I don't like the word "ambition." I prefer the word "passionate." I prefer the word "fortunate." I prefer the word "engaged." More and more people joined the conversation, argued or swapped tales from the trenches. I marveled at just how deep this issue cut and through how many layers.

I'm a writer and a reader, a believer that stories do what no statistic or graph can: humanize dilemmas that often feel intellectual or abstract. A slew of groundbreaking business and sociology books have recently tackled the subject of women and striving, but I wanted the nitty-gritty details, the actual ways striving affected individual lives. Women said they breastfed while being CEOs but *how*? Women switched careers midlife or defied their families' expectations, but what did that look like? Why is the word so difficult to embrace? Who else out there felt conflicted when they sought success, when they achieved success?

These stories were hard to write. Ambition, for many of my contributors, felt connected to deeply private impulses and actions that made them too vulnerable, that exposed things that felt less pretty or tidy than the façade they wanted to project—or felt they needed to project to stay in their roles. Frequently, I received essays on loss or faith or childhood or forgiveness, but not on ambition. Back to the drawing board.

But this challenge and the triumph of the resulting essays are what make the book so strong. There's no recipe here for how to get a raise, or wardrobe tips for looking like the corporate warrior. The contributors, through bravery and discipline and many, many drafts, have created a striking book about struggle and failure and achievement and identity and everything in between. It's a validation that women's ambition is tricky to navigate but entirely worthwhile, and that no young woman should feel, as I did, confused and silenced by all that is unspoken about it.

Of course, the deeper I got into the compilation process, the more I wanted to include. Every essay inspired me to think of another topic, equally crucial. We had one on balancing motherhood and career, but did we have one on giving up a career for motherhood? We had one on writing, but what about engineering? Everyone I spoke to had a wish list: *What about a woman in the clergy? What about an essay by a woman who failed? What about an Etsy entrepreneur? What about a woman in banking?* I spent months trying to find women who could write with nuance and precision about every single facet until I realized there are infinite facets. That's what makes this topic truly compelling. I couldn't possibly represent them all.

So this book isn't every story—it's a way to ignite conversation, to inspire women of all ages and walks of life to consider the role of ambition in their lives, to embrace it with more confidence, to define it and own it and understand why it feels uncomfortable. I hope this book will help them live at the far reaches of their abilities and talents.

It's an entry point. The rest is up to you.

Ebenezer Laughs Back:
Confessions of a Workaholic

● ● ● ● ● ● **PAM HOUSTON**

My beautiful mother ran away from Spiceland, Indiana, at the end of the eighth grade. Her Aunt Ermie, who had raised her to that point, had bet my mother fifty dollars that she could not get straight Cs on her final report card. But she did get straight Cs, took the cash, and got on a bus bound for Broadway. Once in New York City, she got plucked off the streets by two young actors—who, thirty years later, became my Uncle Tommy and my Uncle Don. For the next several decades, she danced and sang and told jokes and did handsprings and cartwheels across stages in countless theaters, nightclubs, and cabarets in New York and elsewhere. During World War II, she went overseas with Bob Hope's USO touring show. After that she became Frank Sinatra's opening act in Vegas, and after that, she returned to New York and acted in supporting roles both on and off Broadway with some of the best of that time—Jackie Gleason, Walter Pidgeon, Nancy Walker. She never made it big, but she always had work and she was proud of that. And though she never said it to me precisely this way, I believe she loved her life in those years with a ferocity approximating the love I have for my own life as a writer and traveler and teacher of writing.

Then, somewhere in the neighborhood of forty-two (she always lied about her age and my father lied in her obituary, so now we will never know for sure) for reasons that are utterly inexplicable to me, she married my father and got pregnant. In that order—I have checked the dates a hundred times. He came backstage one night, so the story goes, after her performance at the Bucks County Playhouse in New Hope, Pennsylvania, with a dozen roses and an invitation for the pretty actress to take a spin in his cream-colored Buick convertible. She got so drunk on their first date she threw up all over his milky leather seats, and he said, "You better get your act together because we are going to get married."

Six weeks later they wed, and so began the miserable, conventional, ambitionless rest of her life.

⚬ ⚬ ⚬ ● ● ●

From a very early age, I wanted to grow up to be someone who wrote, traveled, and lived, as much as possible, surrounded by animals. Even before I had ever been there, I had a strong desire to live in the American West. The first time I stood in front of a classroom, I found out I loved to teach. All of those things together formed what we might call my ambition.

Now I am fifty-two. I have written six books and countless stories and articles. I teach creative writing in graduate programs at two universities, and in several other venues around the country and the globe. I have been to seventy countries and counting (Cuba will make seventy-one later this year), and I live on a ranch at nine thousand feet in Colorado with two dogs, two horses, five sheep, two miniature donkeys, and a formerly feral cat.

We can conclude, therefore, that I am ambitious, perhaps even wildly so. If I were a man, someone might call me a lucky bastard. I'm not sure what the female equivalent of a lucky bastard is, but I do know luck has been on my side often enough in my life that some people call me blessed. Other people call me an asshole. But I don't think I actually *am* an asshole. Perhaps assholery is like ambition or luck or even color blindness, where, the more you have of it, the less likely you are to recognize it in yourself.

• • • • • •

I will say straight out that I gravitate toward people, especially women, who are ambitious. I was going to say that I don't have much respect for people without ambition, but then I thought of a monk I met who was living in a cave in the mountains of Bhutan, for whom I have a world of respect. But now we are swimming in the deep water of abstraction because surely the monk has ambition, even if his primary ambition is to be ambitionless.

And like all abstractions, the word *ambition* is built to cover some pretty wide territory, from insidious social climbing to nose-to-the-grindstone dedication to flights of artistic, or even capitalistic, vision. The harder I think about ambition as a thing, isolate from other things, the more it collapses in on itself. In fact I don't even know whether to write that I have ambition *to*, or that I have ambition *for*. In the first version, ambition is like a *drive*, and in the second it is more like a *jones*.

• • • • • •

I used to believe I could do without sleep. I more than believed it; I actually put my theory into practice. For roughly twenty years, between the ages of twenty-five and forty-five, I didn't go to bed at all two nights a week on average, and the other nights I felt pretty good as long as I closed my eyes for three or four hours. I used to count the hour I spent showering, dressing, and drinking coffee toward my sleep total because they all seemed like relaxing activities. Needless to say, I got a tremendous amount of work done. I never had to turn down any professional opportunities, because if things got tight I would just stay up for a night or two or five and get everything done by the deadline.

"I'll sleep when I'm dead," I used to say, appalling my friends and loved ones. I thought, because I wasn't partying in the wee hours of the night, only writing essays and grading papers, staying up all night probably wasn't that bad for me. I still don't know if it *was* bad for me, though recent science suggests it was.

By the time I turned forty-five, I had to admit I felt better if I got at least five hours' sleep a night, but I could still get enough work done to maintain my seven or eight various paid occupations that add up, I always figure, to something like three full-time jobs. Now, at fifty-two, I need six hours a night and do better when I have seven. When this first started to happen, I thought it meant I was dying of some dreaded disease, until somebody pointed out that I was simply becoming a normal person. But I have not learned to say no with a normal person's frequency.

• • • • • •

"I gave up everything I loved for you," my mother would say to me almost daily, to get me to clean my room or part my hair on the side or wear my retainer. And I would want only to find a way to give it all back, to restore her satisfying working life before being saddled with the burden of me.

"But *why* did you do that?" I wish I had had the wherewithal to ask her.

Alcohol addiction notwithstanding, my mother had the strongest will of anyone I have ever known. She barely ate and she never perspired and she did not grow body hair. I am fairly certain if her biological clock had ticked one time she could have willed it silent with her mind or smashed it with her fist.

My father was charming, but she had had forty-two years,

plus or minus, to learn to see through his kind of charm. Had thirty years in the ups and downs of show business simply worn her out? Did she marry my father because she saw a future rushing toward her where the fact of her age would make it harder and harder to land roles? Or did some Indianan idea of conventionality sneak up out of the cornfield and grab her from behind?

If it did, it lied to her about how it would feel once she got there. Her mother had died in childbirth with her, so it stands to reason that my birth would have killed her at least a little. She lived on until my thirtieth birthday, an honorable life that included fundraisers for the United Way, work with the developmentally disabled, devotion to the altar guild, good friends, and lots of tennis. But it seemed to be only a half-life, a shadow of the thirty years that had preceded it, and when a combination of vodka and Vioxx took her out at seventy (give or take), I was, alongside my sadness, glad she didn't have to witness herself losing any more than she already had.

• • • • • •

It is still nearly impossible for me to turn down a job. For a long time, I thought this was because my father was a child of the Depression and was so afraid of being poor that he often couldn't keep himself from putting his finger down on the disconnect button of a total stranger's long-distance phone call; his favorite piece of life advice was "one day you will realize you spend your whole life lying in the gutter with someone else's foot on your neck." And it's true; I accept nearly every job, large or small, that comes my way—partly out of fear that each one might be the last offer. But I have been at this life for decades now and the work opportunities have never abated. Furthermore, virtually every professional prospect still sounds interesting, and/or rewarding, and/or fun.

I write literary fiction and nonfiction, and I teach others to do the same. That means I am in a subset of a subset of a subset of anything that matters on any large world scale. I am not curing cancer or even making shows for network television, and perhaps as a result, I have come to understand that ambition's real payoff is less about being loved for the work you do and more about getting to do the work you love.

·   ·   ·   ·   ·   ·

While I was growing up, I assumed everyone had ambition in equal amounts. But then I got older and met people that didn't have as much, or really, any. That was shocking to me, as ambition never felt like anything I cultivated, but something I came with, prepackaged. I can't imagine what it would be like to be lazy, or metaphysically exhausted or disinterested or aloof—I simply don't have those speeds—but I do know how I am is not all good news. I do know enough to ask where ambition ends and workaholism begins.

·   ·   ·   ·   ·   ·

There are so many ways to divide the world, but sometimes I think the demographic with which I have the least in common is women who don't work, with women who had ambition, for instance, to marry well instead. I know we are supposed to pretend those women don't exist anymore, but they do. I know some. For instance, I have a friend, let's call her Q, who used to like to work in an artistic field—and she was good at it—but then her ambition became to snag a rich guy, and it turned out she was good at that too. At her wedding, she announced, without irony, "I have arrived." I found the moment chilling and was not surprised to see that, before too long, Q lost nearly all of her interest in making art.

I am trying to write about Q without any judgment whatsoever, because what feels important to me is not whether Q's choice is more valid than mine or vice versa. What feels important to me is my absolute clarity that if I married a rich guy and stopped making art (not that any rich guys are banging down my door or ever have), I would become suicidal. If you took away my artistic drive, I am not even sure there would be any *me* left to become suicidal. What I am saying is I work hard, therefore, I am.

• • • • • •

I know the suggestion driving this anthology is that women are afraid or embarrassed to be ambitious, or that they are socialized not to be ambitious because it reads less attractive on them than it does on men. Like many things that are blamed on men these days, I don't doubt the truth of the phenomenon because I have experienced it in the world. But it is definitely not the whole truth, and even if it were the whole truth, it would not make me feel personally let off the hook in the ambition department. Also, too much ambition of the most ruthless, thoughtless kind is ugly on everybody, men and women alike.

• • • • • •

Here is a bit of a koan. The richest people I know well, without exception, are the unhappiest people I know well. And yet, all of the people I know well who are struggling financially believe they would be happier if they got rich. But ambition and money are two separate things, you say—and I say—certainly, but then again, nothing is ever completely separate from anything else.

• • • • • •

It is not precisely true to say that my mother stopped working after she married my father. For a while, she kept doing summer theater. When she gave that up, she landed roles in TV commercials and bit parts on soap operas: the long-lost cousin, the visiting aunt. For several years, she was Betty of Betty's Roadside Stand in a series of Post Raisin Bran commercials, and she pre-dated Jane Russell as the face of "I Can't Believe It's a Girdle." Yet, for every day she went off to New York for an audition or shoot and came home glowing and singing, there were ten other days when her task list read: laundry, dinner, dry cleaning, Pam to dentist, cat to vet.

And then there is this. Even in the "Betty's Breakfast" years, when her residual checks added up to more than his income, my mother handed her checks directly over to my father. He gave my mother $200.00 for household money every two weeks to buy groceries, clothes, and every single other thing the fam-ily needed from the time I was born till I left for college with no adjustment for inflation. My father carried more than that $200.00 in his wallet at all times, bought Cadillac convertibles and Italian suits while my mother made our clothes on the sewing machine and scoured magazines to find interesting things to do with leftovers. The song that was on continuous repeat in my childhood kitchen was my mother reasoning or flirting or begging for an advance on next week's money, and him shaming her, no matter what the circumstances, for spending it too fast.

⬦   •   •   •   •   ●

My fifth-grade teacher, the wonderful Mr. Kashner, looked me in the eye one day and said, "You have the smarts to get the hell out of here." I don't know if he really said *hell* to a fifth grader, but that is the way I heard it. There were a whole lot of things Mr. Kashner did not have to say out loud for me to hear them. Like, "I get how bad things are at your house." Like "I know how it feels to get straight As and win every prize and excel at every extracurricular activity and still invoke your father's wrath."

Like, "One day not so long from now this place is going to be in your rearview mirror, and I will be standing in the middle of the road cheering."

Oh, Mr. Kashner. Was it you who created this tailwind of good fortune that I am still somehow riding on? If so, I want to pay it forward a thousand times. I want to say to my students every day: *I see you. I see your suffering and also see all that you are capable of.*

For all of my childhood and some of my adulthood, I believe that if it were possible and relatively painless, I would have sucked myself right back up into the ether if it would have given my mother her ambition back, and with her ambition, her hopes and dreams and joy. In lieu of that I got straight As forever (never a single A minus), I learned to mix a martini very dry (you just pass the bottle of vermouth over the top of the glass without actually letting any spill out), and I rode my bicycle every single place I needed to be.

Eventually my own ambition made itself known to me, and I stopped wanting to trade my life for hers. But it would be years before I stopped trying to be perfect. Decades, even. Probably still am.

When I say I love to work, what I mean specifically is that other than walking down a dirt trail behind the butts of a couple of Irish wolfhounds or sitting in a baseball park on a hot June day, work is the only thing I can count on, 100 percent, to make me feel better. Like Ebenezer Scrooge. Except unlike Ebenezer Scrooge the biggest reward for me isn't the money, it is the work itself.

Work is my pleasure, my refuge, my comfort, my challenge, my driver, my definition. And by work, I don't mean just the sexy work of writing a short story or a novel or reading at the Library of Congress. I mean reading a ten-inch pile of student manuscripts in an intro to creative writing class. I mean writing a semi-positive review of a book I didn't love written by someone I'll have to see at a conference later in the year.

When the shit hits the fan emotionally, when a houseguest becomes radically problematic, or my partner's ex is driving us crazy, or when I have a sick animal that has been treated and now we just have to wait, all I want to do to is turn on my computer. When the work is going well, or even if it is just going, it is a little hammer tapping me on the shoulder saying everything is going to be okay.

. . . . . .

But of course everything is not going to be okay. First, there is climate change, and then, there are super bacteria outsmarting our super antibiotics right and left. There is the fact that the rich are getting richer and the poor are getting poorer and any armchair economist will tell you where that plan invariably winds up. And what place will books even have in the apocalypse, more and more of them foretell? When Manhattan disappears into the Atlantic and we start killing each other over aquifers and penicillin reserves, will I wish I had spent more time rubbing the donkey's heads and sitting on the porch watching the cloud shadows move across the mountains? Will I wish I had had a little less ambition and a lot more fun?

"But what could ever be more fun than work?" I ask.

And Ebenezer laughs back, "Nothing!"

. . . . . .

If the question is "where does ambition end and workaholism begin?" I think the answer is "somewhere around my thirtieth birthday."

My mother did not appear in the first draft of this essay. In fact, this essay has been in so many drafts that it has taken me twenty thousand wrong words to get to four thousand right ones. Because my mother mostly stayed at home and my father mostly went to work, I began writing with the hypothesis that I had gotten my ambition primarily from him. But then I realized my father's feelings about work were tepid, really, compared to the arias my mother sang daily to her bygone showbiz days. If your mother runs away from Spiceland, Indiana, to Broadway at thirteen, if she spends the last thirty years of her life asking—begging, really—her husband for the money *back* that she earned to pay for his freshly starched shirts, if the single most powerful and omnipresent emotion in your family's home is her soul-shattering grief over the absence of meaningful work in her life, that is likely to inform your relationship with ambition. And if most of my striving has therefore been *away* and not *toward*, does that mean I am not, in essence, as different from the ambitionless women as I thought I was? Does this mean that in some Condoleezza Rice–like way that I have drunk the Kool-Aid too? Did my mother drink the Kool-Aid? Who made the Kool-Aid? Who sold it to my mother for five cents a glass?

I often tell my students that no matter what happens to them in the publishing world, no matter how much money they make or don't, no matter what literary prizes they win or don't, nothing will feel better than when they nail a scene, when they keep pounding away until the understory finally reveals itself, when they get up from the computer wrapped in that cloud of giddy joy and self-satisfaction (even if they read it the next day and think it sucks).

Not every good thing has happened to me in the world of publishing, not by a long shot, but enough good things have happened to allow me to understand them for what they are: momentary flights of fashion. I know this to be true: ambition's greatest reward is to do the thing you love most, and do it, at least momentarily, well enough to satisfy yourself.

.   .   .   .   .   .

There are still things I have ambition for. I want to be kinder, smarter, bigger, broader, more compassionate, more generous. I'd also like to sail the entire coast of Turkey, and go to the Arctic on an icebreaker. I hope to have a stage play produced in a reasonably sized city. I want, most embarrassingly and perhaps more than anything, to be chosen to edit *The Best American Short Stories* before I die.

.   .   .   .   .   .

My first book, a collection of short stories called *Cowboys Are My Weakness*, was unexpectedly successful. My publisher printed five thousand copies as a first run, and they went back to press eight times before the book was even a month old. My biggest dream at that time was getting a book of my stories out into the world. I had no ambition regarding what would happen to it once it got there: selling hundreds of thousands of copies or being on *All Things Considered* and *Good Morning America*. I didn't understand what was happening to me, even as it was.

My editor, Carol Houck Smith, asked me to call her every night I was on tour so I could tell her my good news (how many people came to the reading, how many books sold), and she could tell me her good news (which lists the book had popped up on, which magazines wanted to do a profile)—it was a sweet and heady time.

One night, two weeks after the publication date, I was in

Seattle giving a reading at the old Elliott Bay Book Co. in Pioneer Square. So many people came that they were packed into the window wells and doorways, pressing into the reading room from the café next door. I called Carol and told her how they had held up their lighters for an encore. People holding up lighters for an encore would not have made my very longest list of ambitions.

Carol told me the paperback auction had been that day. She told me she had very good news and that I should go to the minibar and get out the bottle of champagne. My tour had already been extended several times by then, and I was using the American Express card—the one I had wisely applied for as a college student to establish my credit rating—to buy new plane tickets and to check into the kinds of hotels I had only seen on TV. To say I was setting an American Express personal best record that month would be a grotesque understatement. I was a graduate student making $4,500 a year when *Cowboys Are My Weakness* came out. I knew W. W. Norton would reimburse me, but I didn't know how that worked or when it would happen, and there was just no way I was going to add a thirty-six dollar hotel champagne split to the burgeoning, stultifying amount.

"Do you have the champagne?" Carol asked.

"Yes," I lied.

"I want to hear the cork pop!" she said, and I made a noise I had learned to make in summer camp by pulling out my thumb quickly from the inside corner of my cheek.

She told me the amount the paperback sold for. It was $121,000. Half of that would go to W. W. Norton, the other half to my agent, and after she took 20 percent commission, the rest would come to me. I mention the amount partly so you will know it was not $5 million, but also so you will understand that it was more money than a graduate student making $4,500 a year could contemplate. (Months later, when the check finally came,

the amount was, poetically, within single digits of the amount I had borrowed to put myself through college, an amount that because I was finishing graduate school, was about to come due.) A silence hummed on the line that I hoped Carol would take for shared satisfaction.

"You know what this means, don't you?" she said, finally, and I said, truthfully, that I had no earthly idea.

"It means that if you want to, you can be a writer for the rest of your life."

I don't think ambition ever gets any better, or purer, or more satisfying than that.

What Came Next

● ● ● ● ● ● **THERESA REBECK**

So I'm walking to a rehearsal in Midtown, and my agent calls me.

He runs me through one thing and another, and then he gets down to it. Had I heard that Steven Spielberg had set up a project at Showtime, a TV series about backstage at a Broadway musical?

"They want you to write it," he informed me. "Mr. Spielberg read one of your plays over the weekend, and he called this morning to say that he is infatuated."

Let me tell you something. When Steven Spielberg calls your agent to say he is infatuated with your writing, that is a good day.

The saga of what came next is so long and complicated it would take a book to write it all out. Sometimes I think of writing that book and sometimes I think that writing that book and reliving the whole thing would be somewhat akin to shooting myself in the head. But we'll get to that.

So I took the job, I wrote the pilot, I created all the characters, I nurtured it through a transition from Showtime to NBC, I produced the pilot, and the show got picked up for an order of seventeen episodes. I was the show runner of the first season, which got terrific numbers and established itself immediately as an international sensation. The show was called *Smash*.

At the end of the first season, I was fired without cause. No one likes being fired, and guess what, I am no exception. As the dust settled, it became clear that at the management level a lot of dastardly stories had been invented about my character. Sometimes I try to parse them and fit them all back together; I have been, at times, desperate to figure out what actually happened. There was a destructive and incoherent madness to it that resists interpretation.

Mr. Spielberg, to give him much credit, called me the day I was fired and apologized. He told me that he blamed himself. He felt that the politics had gotten way out of hand, and they wouldn't have if he had been around more. He was probably right.

And, of course, as soon as I was fired, all the men who had conspired to have me removed from my post realized that the show wasn't going to survive without me and so they slunk away and went off to do other things.

The network then hired a whole bunch of other people to run it in my stead, and it fell apart, and one year after I had made that show into a bona fide hit, it was canceled.

Everyone told me the best thing to do was ignore it and put it behind me.

Then I couldn't get hired for three years.

Then I fired my lawyer and I fired my manager and I fired my agent.

And then my new agent and new manager and new lawyer all sat me down and explained to me, in no uncertain terms, that I had to take a step back, accept a demotion, and take a job below my skill set and pay grade. At this new job, I had to say yes to everything, and I had to prove that I played well with others.

The whisperers had run around and told everyone that I was a lunatic. So this is what I had to do, if I ever wanted to run a show again: I had to keep my head down and prove that I was smart and hardworking and a team player.

God knows I had plenty to do during those years. I wrote two plays. I finished my third novel. I directed *All My Sons* for a major regional theater, and I wrote and directed an independent movie. My son started college; my daughter finished middle school.

But I was convinced that I had to return to television. I felt cheated by what had happened on *Smash,* and I was determined that the men who had cheated me would not have the last word on my talent and my character. It pissed me off that the men at my level who had been fired in similarly ridiculous circumstances somehow managed to bounce upward. I felt like what had happened to me was yet another version of the recklessly hideous way so many talented women are treated—silenced, kicked to the curb. I didn't want to just slink away and disappear. I wanted to fight my way back into the game.

To successfully run a television show, you have to be a general. I was an excellent general. But in order to prove I could do it again, I had to be a good girl.

•   •   •   •   •   •

My ambition is wearing me out.

I've been on many different television shows over the years, and my husband is frankly enraged by the way people behave in this environment. He threatened to leave me, a couple of times, if I ever went back on staff of another TV show. He was kidding, but only sort of. He wants me to take my ambition out of the game and stay out of it.

He's not necessarily wrong. I tell stories about the shenanigans that go on in writers' rooms, and my friends outside the business roar with laughter or cringe in disbelief. Most of the shows I've worked on have at their center an institutionalized despotism so entrenched it truly is both silly and terrifying. The executives at the networks and the studios, none of whom are writers themselves, insist upon a systemic strangulation of the writing process called "note giving." Sometimes, after they have shredded your work with hundreds of notes, they might just decide that the whole thing doesn't work at all, and you have to throw the script out and start from scratch. They call this "blowing up a script." You are expected to do every note you are given, no matter how inane, no matter how much they are blowing things up. You are also expected to be really cheerful and appreciative while you do it.

You are not allowed to mention that hundreds of millions of dollars are wasted every year on this process. If you think that corporate capitalism is not the best systemic structure to put in charge of storytelling in America, you really need to keep that to yourself.

In the worst of these environments, the show runners behave like tin-pot dictators. They change their minds relentlessly. They rewrite everybody and act like they're the ones being put out by the terrible writers who work for them. If you go into your show runner's office and say, "I hate the way you rewrote this scene. Can we go back to what I had?"—well, you would never do that. You could seriously get fired for doing that. The show runner is allowed to do whatever he wants *all the time* and any brushback whatsoever is off the table. Your job is to tell him he's brilliant while he destroys your work.

Over the years I've been through it all, but so many writers have. One show runner made me sit in the room and watch him while he rewrote my script. One guy could never remember what he had told anybody to write; he was also a screamer. It was, as one might imagine, an exhausting combination. (He turned out to be a cokehead.)

One guy I worked for would rewrite my outlines, and then put my name on them when he handed them into the network. Then I'd end up on phone calls with people who would say things like, "Well, Theresa, this outline doesn't quite work for me." And I'd think, *Well, it doesn't work for me either. The other thing that doesn't work for me is having someone putting my name on something I didn't write.* Having your name on things you didn't actually write is the sea that everyone in television swims in. Unless you're the show runner, your writing is treated like raw material for anyone and everyone to mess with.

One time I got fired from a show because the show runner put poop jokes into one of my scripts, and it offended the star of the show. No one ever told the star that I hadn't written any of the offensive material. I just got fired.

The misogyny is beyond anything that people believe when I tell these stories. On my first job in television, when I was in my twenties, I would sit, dazed, while a roomful of men sat around and told fist-up-the-ass jokes, roaring with laughter. In another room, the guys would sit around and pitch stories, and then write everything down in great detail on little white cards. Whenever a scene with female characters showed up they would write a card that said, "girl scene here." Then they would look at me and say, "You're a woman, you write this." When I said, "You know where I come from, we write both women *and* men," it was considered provocative.

One time, I was in a room where one of the guys was pitching a beat in a story. He said musingly, "Two people walk into a bar. No wait. Two people and a woman walk into a bar."

One time, after a number of seriously offensive jokes were told in succession, I said, "Come on, you guys, am I going to have to leave the room?" Instead of apologizing, one of my male peers said to me, "If you think that's rough, you haven't been in enough writers' rooms."

"Don't tell me where I've been, asshole," I replied.

Okay, I didn't really say that, I just thought it. But the rest of those stories are true.

Why would any writer with curiosity and brains and a simple will to tell a decent story put up with bullshit like this?

Well, they do pay you a lot of money. Writers of all other genres—fiction, theater, poetry, nonfiction, independent film—generally don't make much money at all. By contrast, television writers are quite well paid, although many of them don't think so because if you spend too much time in Hollywood, you inevitably end up comparing yourself to people who make even more than you do.

Back in the day, writers like Clifford Odets, F. Scott Fitzgerald, and William Faulkner went out to Hollywood to make money, and the system treated them like this as well. And they complained, drank too much, fell into despair, and went back to their "real" writing.

I don't know why I put "real" in quotes; they actually *were* leaving this nonsense and going back to doing real writing. And that sort of thing is still going on: We all howl about it and write novels and plays and movies like *Barton Fink*, excoriate Hollywood, and then go back for more money.

I personally had given up on all that nuttiness by the time I got that phone call from my agent, so many moons ago. Truth be told, I was in a healthier headspace back then. I was living where I wanted to be living, doing what I wanted to be doing, and hanging out with the people I wanted to be hanging out with. I didn't have any fierce need to run my own television show. At least, I wasn't chasing it.

Why didn't I stay there? When I think back to that day when I was just walking to rehearsal for a play that paid me next to nothing in a lousy space in Midtown, before my agent called to tell me Mr. Spielberg was infatuated, mostly what I remember is that I was happy.

But I don't know one person on planet Earth who would have turned down that offer. Everyone wants their own show. I recently found out that one of my favorite novelists wasn't writing novels anymore because he was trying to get his own show on Showtime. Apparently he needs the money, but trust me, it's not merely about the money. The thought of having your own TV show is a big promise to a hungry little ego.

My friend Lisa cops to the hungry little ego. "Twelve to fifteen million people hearing my words and seeing characters who they love, and I love expressing my values and my empathy and my humor, I fucking love that. I really like being one of the people who has the privilege of pouring stuff out into the world and hoping it lands and sticks and resonates with whoever's watching and listening. Full of myself a little? Yeah, I think you have to be, to think that your work is worth the many millions of dollars to film it, and the attention of the audience."

Her position, I think, really is swell. I also think that Lisa's hungry little ego is a sort of pleasant and respectful version of the breed. Most egos don't behave as well as hers does. Add to that fact this: The apprenticeship of television writing is all about having your own ego kicked in the head so many times it develops a revenge fantasy. Television is a training ground for fucking up people's characters just enough to make them truly dangerous when they are finally given power over other creative souls.

And the truth is, everyone in the industry knows it.

"I can't say I enjoy writing for television," another friend told me. "It's unhealthy in general. The system is a killer. You sit in a room with other writers eight hours a day, then the show runner comes in and makes all the decisions. And that's the part before you get notes, do rewrites, more notes, more rewrites, then get totally rewritten anyway." But she started as a playwright and couldn't get her plays done. When she's not writing for a television show, she doesn't have decent health insurance.

In the face of this, we all sit around and tell apocryphal stories about shows where the network left you alone, where the show runner had a good heart and a light hand. There's always a mythic show out there, where they treat the writing staff with respect and shoot the scene the way you wrote it, and it came out great, and the lowly but talented and decent staff writer is vindicated.

The heart remains hopeful. Every show actually seems like just a great job at the beginning. Everybody likes each other. The network notes haven't gotten too crazy; the boys haven't started acting like jerks yet. The excitement is heady. Money! Health care! Telling stories for a living! It's truly all you know, and all you want to know.

· · · · · ·

Freud writes eloquently about the ego's need to return time and again to the same pattern of behavior, repetition compulsion, a drive so strong it overrides the pleasure principle and sends us back into traumatic situations that we know are traumatic. That mysterious thing called the Self seems to want to go through the same pain over and over and over again, mystifying itself with the belief that next time, I'll master it, I'll control it, I'll get it right. Mircea Eliade writes of the Myth of Eternal Return. The Buddhists call it samsara. I felt the reality of these definitions strongly once when I was stuck in a traffic jam on Sunset Boulevard going to a meeting. *Holy shit*, I thought. *How did I get here again?*

Although, endlessly indulging in repetition compulsion might also be tagged as perseverance. Or ambition. Women are told they have to be better, smarter, tougher, and more resilient than their male counterparts because, well, that's just the way the world is. Men tell us this. I cannot count the number of men—including my new agent and my new manager, who are great and on my side—who blithely announce that this is just the way things are. So maybe we've just been programmed this way.

Who knows. One time I asked my daughter Cleo why she was doing something that was getting her in trouble over and over again. She was about four years old. With tears streaming down her face, she said to me, "I'm a stubborn girl." My husband had to stop himself from laughing. "I wonder where she got that?" he said.

I am a stubborn girl.

I am also a talented and hardworking girl, and the truth is I do play well with others. But in corporate culture, "play well with others" has come to mean absolutely agreeing to everything that gets thrown at you. It is a given: You have to say yes to your boss all the time. And that means all the time, and cheerfully—that, I'm not as good at. And the men who I've seen attain success in this world are salesmen, charmers; they know how to manage up.

That's another phrase I learned: manage up. Basically that means making your bosses love you, whether or not you are doing a good job.

Here is another phrase that I learned: comfort level. When I was fired from the show I created, my soon-to-be-ex–agent told me that the president of NBC had a "comfort level" issue with me.

Comfort level, I came to learn, is Hollywood code for men who don't want to work with women. So women, who are suspect because there is this comfort level issue have to work extra hard to play well with others and manage up, in addition to sucking everything up and understanding that things are going to be handed to the guys, and then they're going to tell a lot of sexist jokes and tell you to your face that you're supposed to be writing the girl scenes because they're too busy writing about shooting people and blowing things up and other utter bullshit.

Ooops, did I say that? This is another thing that "play well with others" means: Keep your mouth shut.

In television, we have to be very stubborn girls indeed.

• • • • • •

I loved running a television show. I was really good at it. I liked that I had to write so much, I liked working with the actors and the directors, I liked production meetings, I liked going all over to location shoots, I loved editing. I loved my postproduction supervisor and my line producer; both of them taught me life lessons about graceful professionalism, taking care of your collaborators. I ran a clean set, so the people who worked there were happy. I was a good general.

I also have to admit that it was fun rewriting my whole writing staff on *Smash*. "Fun" might be too strong. Because I hated having it done to me so much, it was not something I took on lightly; I actually tried *not* to rewrite everything egregiously just because I could. But for that first season at least, it was my show and I had the last word and I understood the thrill of that, and the responsibility. So I did my job, and I stand by it.

But no matter how hard I tried—and trust me, I'm not a lunatic, and I did try—the boys didn't want me running that show. One of the other executive producers kept saying, "But who is in charge?" He had never worked on a television show before so I assumed this was just informational, and I would tell him, point-blank: I am the show runner. That means I am in charge. This struck him as more than slightly insane. I had to keep explaining to him how television shows work: You stand with the show runner. You don't keep attacking the show runner; it will bring the show down. It was a truth he did not want to understand.

There was also an architectural problem in the power structure above me. How to "manage up" was never very clear. Mr. Spielberg is an enormous force and a great storyteller. He and the head of the network both believed that *they* were in charge. There was a strange dysplasia. They seemed to think that I was some kind of factotum, or typewriter even. No matter how polite I was, it rocked everyone to the core when the typewriter talked back.

Was it gender based? It sure felt like it. The power structure included ten men and one woman, and, in spite of all their second-guessing and wrangling, the show was terrific until they fired the woman in charge. I was explicitly told, during my firing, that the show was "too important to the network," and so they were taking it out of my hands. The person they gave it to had virtually no credentials and no experience in the theater. His television credits were nowhere near as comprehensive as mine. The show died under his watch. Two years later, another network gave him another show to run. Meanwhile, I was still being told that I was unemployable because everyone knew that I was a lunatic.

The whole thing was dreadful. And I do want to do it again. Is this like childbirth? You think, *Oh god, it's so great having a kid, I don't remember the pain.* No, it's actually not like that. The memory of the pain is pretty vivid.

Woody Allen has famously admitted the heart wants what it wants. But what does that mean? Is that just a way of excusing inappropriate desire?

I tell myself that it's not just enraged ego; I have stories to tell. My heart wants to tell stories. Women should be telling stories. And the earth will not survive without women claiming their voices and their partnership for its people. It may not survive even so. So my heart says, get up, get back in the game, this isn't just about you. Stand up, you stubborn girl. If I have an ambition, it is to change the world. So yes, I am ambitious. And while I do believe in playing well with others, I ultimately don't know how to keep my mouth shut. What storyteller does?

I wish this were not the story I have to tell today. I have other stories. I am anxious to get on with them.

On Impractical Urges

● ● ● ● ● ● **AYANA MATHIS**

I.

It is October 2012. I am in Paris. In May 2011 I graduated from the Iowa Writers' Workshop. In July of that same year I sold my first novel. A few months later, I sold the first European rights to a small French publisher. In celebration of these events, my then girlfriend and I rented a little apartment in the Passage du Grand Cerf, one of those stunning nineteenth-century covered shopping arcades, with a glass and wrought iron roof arching over the marble-tiled walkway below. The Passage is more beautiful than we'd anticipated. At night a grainy yellow light shows from the fixtures above the locked boutiques, a sexy ambient light that illumines our walk to the apartment door, our steps clicking on the marble floors and echoing through the deserted passage.

I have one professional obligation. A popular magazine has decided to review my novel—we are three months from its publication—and they would like a quote to include in their article. They will call me at 2 PM on a Thursday on the rented apartment's telephone. Thursday dawns brilliant and blue. I get up early and have a pastry and coffee at a café on Rue Montorgueil. I walk to the Tuileries and then to the Place des Vosges.

At 1:30 PM, I rush across town to the apartment and sprint up the stairs. I was told the call from the magazine would be brief. I pick at my fingernails and hope they'll call on time because the gorgeous afternoon is going on without me, and the forecast calls for rain the next day. It is two o'clock, and then five past and then nearly ten past and, really, I am getting a little huffy and have begun to search for the number to call my publicist's office when the phone rings.

"Hello," I say briskly. There is a delay in the connection, and then a voice says, clear as day, clear as though it were sitting next to me, "Is this Ayana?"

"Yes," I say.

"This is Oprah Winfrey." There is a long pause.

"No," I reply. "It isn't."

"It is. It's Oprah Winfrey."

My head buzzes and my heart feels as though it has grown dangerously large in my chest. Its beating might crack my ribs. I look around for a bottle of water, but there isn't one. I think I might like to smoke a cigarette, but I can't do that either because I am on a landline sitting on this couch in this apartment in Paris talking to Oprah Winfrey, and a cigarette would not be appropriate because, somehow, she might see me. I take a deep breath and start over. "Hello," I say.

A great many things are said during our conversation, about my novel and literature in general. Oprah quotes Toni Morrison from memory. My goodness, I think, she really does read all of those books. On we go talking, and I might even sound a little bit natural because I am a good mimic and I can mimic "natural." It's all going very well until my girlfriend returns to the apartment and something in my tone (perhaps I didn't sound as "natural" as I thought I did) makes her pause. She stands in front of me with her head cocked, listening. After a minute or so, she jabs at me with her index finger and starts waving her hands around and mouthing, exaggeratedly like a silent film actress, "Is that Oprah Winfrey? *Is that Oprah Winfrey?*"

Oprah says I shouldn't tell anyone about being the Book Club pick because it's all a huge secret until it's announced. She also tells me that instead of publishing the book in January as planned, she's going to have them move it up so it can be available for the holidays. Then she's gone, and I am out on the street standing near a little playground bent at the waist with my hands on my knees to steady myself. My girlfriend is lying on the asphalt kind of laughing/crying. The French passersby are not particularly amused.

When you are a writer, people will always ask, "When did you know you wanted to be a writer?" I have an answer for that question: I starting writing when I was a kid. When I was nine, I filled a marble notebook with short stories about a little girl named Blue. When I got a little older, I wrote poetry and wanted to be a poet. I like this answer because it is true and also because it is neat and satisfying. I had an aspiration, and with some luck and hard work, it was realized, a sure sign of an intact American Dream, an assurance that merit does indeed determine success. Any other answer raises the specter of randomness, or worse, the uncomfortable truth that there are a great many people who work very hard for all kinds of things and never, ever get them.

We have a cult of success in America. We believe that if we just work hard enough, we will achieve. It is certainly better to have these beliefs than a fatalist vision of the world in which fortunes are determined entirely by factors outside of oneself (social position, nepotism, economic status, for example). Nonetheless, there is something naive about our way of looking at things, and cruel too, in the way children can be cruel because they are too young to have anything but an absolutist vision of the world. It isn't always true that failure has direct correlation to insufficient grit or ambition. We resist the fact that race and class play a significant role in what we want and whether we have the tools to make an attempt at getting it. The humbling, and unsettling, reality is that all obstacles are not surmountable. And in any case, is the sole objective of our lives the surmounting of obstacles so that we can come in first, like dogs in a race? This seems an impoverished vision of our human experience, more tragic and empty than any failure could ever be. But I have wandered into questions about how we might characterize a life well lived, and that is not the subject of this essay.

With regard to "wanting to be a writer": when I was nine, writing the stories about the little girl named Blue, my mother was very sick and was hospitalized. My grandparents took me to see her once. To get to her, we had to pass through several heavy doors that each opened with a loud buzz and then a click. The doors slammed behind us: Bang! Bang! Bang! After the last bang, I saw my mother sitting on a couch behind a glass window with tears streaming down her cheeks. She asked my grandmother to please, please take her home.

I wrote poems throughout my high school years. My mother was still ill. We lived a transient, pillar to post, paycheck to paycheck kind of life. Sometimes there were no paychecks. My poems were not ostensibly about any of those things. I wrote about a kind of general disaffection, about loneliness and being very angry, enraged really, with the world. I kept journals in which I recorded my discontents in capital letters with red ink. I had a great many female friends, but I was angry with them because they were thin and I was fat. I had a lot of male friends with whom I found greater kinship, though I was secretly in love with half of them (in retrospect this may also have been the case with my female friends). This unrequited love was a confirmation of sorts. I was a relatively popular girl but despised myself a little. That my infatuations were not reciprocated reified my self-assessment. Why should anyone return my fat, black, poor affections?

I should mention here that I was a teenager in the 1980s. Reagan was president. Black people were on television all of the time. For thirty minutes a week those black people were the Huxtables, being middle class and wearing sweaters. But most of the time the black people on TV were being arrested, selling or doing drugs, or wandering around the ghettos in which they all (except the Huxtables) lived. Sometimes they were prostitutes. Frequently they were some iteration of Reagan's favorite societal scourge, the Welfare Queen. She was usually sitting on a bench in a public housing project surrounded by the brood of unkempt, unruly, criminals-in-the-making children she'd birthed as a result of her uncontrollable libido, children she could not provide for because she was too lazy to get a job. She had no husband to help her because black men don't get married; they just impregnate women and go to jail.

The damage done by those images of black people is inestimable. Why would the nation rally against a government that didn't support public schools, social programs, or make any attempt at improving the conditions of poor and black folk when every available representation of those people showed them to be irremediably degenerate? And what were we—young black people raised on a steady diet of images that showed us as unworthy, ugly, peripheral—to think of ourselves? The lucky among us didn't break. But every last one of us took a beating politically, economically, and psychically.

What I am getting at in all of this is that I did not have a moment in which I fixed upon writing as an ambition. I couldn't quite name my ambitions. They had something to do with not being the Welfare Queen, with being a person that would not be disdained or dismissed. I wanted to be understood as a distinct self, my distinct self—inviolate and individuated, in the way I saw the not-poor, not-black other was granted its selfhood. So overwhelming was this desire to be, and so bewildering any specific course of action to achieve it, that all the things I most wanted took on an unqualified and non-goal-oriented character. "Being a writer" meant that I was a person who wrote and wanted to write, but that sensibility was uncoupled from tangible outcomes, like the publication of a book, or building a professional life. The notion that my writer identity could concretize into goals or achievements was farfetched, maybe even a little ridiculous.

I was suspicious of all of the things I wanted, writing or otherwise, simply because I wanted them. And so my desires were reduced to beautiful dreams that floated through my adolescent and young adult life, only acted upon in half-hearted fits and starts. Five or six months of furious writing were followed by a year or two in which I didn't pen a single line. I never made any real attempt at publishing my work. Better a dream deferred, than hopes dashed.

II.

It is Wednesday, December 5, 2012. I get up at 8:00 and make some coffee. I walk the dog. When I get back I open my laptop. The headline on Oprah.com is "Ayana Mathis, Oprah Book Club 2.0," followed by an image of my book and a giant picture of Oprah and me. My head is thrown back in a wide, toothy smile. I am a happy Tyrannosaurus rex in an orange blouse. The phone rings. It is my publicist. At 8:15 AM the Oprah empire sent a press release to all of the country's major media outlets. I was told this would happen, but I didn't understand what it meant. I imagined that an email would be sent and someone in the bowels of "the media" would file it away, or something.

I Google my name. Pages of hits appear: *New York Times, New York Daily News, Philadelphia Inquirer, Washington Post, Boston Globe, People, USA Today,* and on and on. By 10:00 AM, the phone rings nonstop. I do a phone interview with the *Daily News* for a feature in the next day's paper. Arrangements are made for photographers from the *New York Times* to come to my apartment for a photo shoot that will accompany a profile. My editor calls, weeping, to tell me that she wants to read me Michiko Kakutani's review of my book. "Michiko Kakutani!" I say. My stomach lurches. "Oh no." The review is a rave. I cry between interviews.

I have not eaten or changed out of my pajamas and it's nearly 3 PM. My mother calls, and we sit in silence on the phone together, both too stunned to speak. Here is what has happened, though I do not yet know it: On December 4, I had one life. On December 5, I had another life, and it wouldn't ever go back to the December 4 life.

I received a great many emails and phone calls from well-wishers during that period. When they asked how I felt, I said I was shell-shocked. This was true. It's still true, perhaps. Thankfully, I was aided by my provenance. I am the product of manner-minding, nose-to-the-grindstone aspirant (but poor), middle-class black folk. I managed my surreal new existence by thinking of all the publicity and attention as work. Work I could do! My job in this period, I told myself, is to publicize this book. I told the well-wishers as much. Everyone told me to "enjoy it." I tried to do that, though once my book tour started, I was so sleep-deprived and jet-lagged that in the evenings, after I had finished the day's duties, I would lay in the hotel room darkness with the blankets up to my chin watching movies on HBO. For all it may seem pathetic, this was as profoundly soothing as a bowl of chicken soup when it is raw cold outside and your throat aches.

The well-wishers also said: "You deserve it!" This presented a number of problems, which I resolved outwardly by simply saying thank you. (When people first began saying this, I would look startled and then reply in some self-deprecating way. Various parties repeatedly and vigorously explained to me that self-deprecation and fright are not the appropriate response to heartfelt congratulations.)

"You deserve it!" is just one of those things people say, I realize, but it unsettled me. That anyone deserved outsize success, that I deserved a success beyond every fantasy I'd had about the fate of my book was incongruous with my sense of myself, what I knew about the nature of lived experience and the experience of the people I love most. Those lives are bound up in struggle. Struggle isn't tragedy. It is necessary to say this because too often the former is conflated with the latter. And too often we create false narratives around struggle; we say that people have "overcome" their circumstances or "overcome" their struggles, when in reality people often manage to survive their circumstances by way of the very mettle or knowledge gained through the circumstance itself. It is not ever possible to entirely leave behind any aspect of ourselves; we cannot step out of history, personal or otherwise. I come from strugglers. For us, the measure of a life is survival by means of elegant improvisation and wiliness; grace and dignity in the face of difficulty.

My grandparents were born in Virginia near the turn of the twentieth century, my grandmother in 1910, my grandfather in 1908. They migrated to Philadelphia, where they married and raised nine children with a good deal of pragmatism and a lot of hard times. They were poor people, in my mother's sense of the word, by which she means anyone for whom a utility bill has caused a crisis, or who has eyed the steaks at the butcher counter knowing all the while she'd end up with a bag of navy beans and a package of ham hocks. My grandmother cleaned white people's houses and worked in a munitions factory during WWII to save enough money to buy the family's first house.

For some thirty years most of my grandmother's dinners consisted of whatever was left at the bottom of the pot after she'd fed her children. When my mother was a girl she saw Grandmom, as I called her, licking drying food from the tines of one of the children's forks when she thought she was alone. She would never have admitted to being hungry. My grandparents were not the sort of people who talked about how they felt about things, or what they yearned for or were heartbroken by. Their children grew up and had decent enough lives and didn't have to clean white folks' toilets. I don't know if this outcome was sufficient to them. I used to believe their silence on these matters implied an absence of desire, or a repression so great it mimicked absence. This was a lazy and insulting conclusion. What did I know about their inner lives? Or what they dreamed in their privacy?

My mother inherited my grandparents' reserve, but she was prone to whimsy and restlessness. Her life was marginally easier than theirs in sociopolitical terms. She was not born into Jim Crow at the turn of the twentieth century. Despite the vicious, entrenched racism of the Philadelphia of her youth, she was freer than my grandparents. Freer to want things and express those wants, whether she could act on them or not. In high school my mother's drawing teacher encouraged her to apply to art colleges. She was desperate to go, but my grandmother, who did not see the sense in sending her black daughter to art college in 1952, forbade it. My mother finished high school with a secretarial degree and went to work in an office. She went on dates and had boyfriends and did all of the things young women her age and generation did—except get married and have chil-

around or under or over. I'd scratch those pages out and start again the next week, with less conviction and energy. Each day, sometime toward evening when the light turned orange and slanted through the high windows of my writing room, I would feel as though I had dissociated from myself and was looking down at this Ayana, this writer at work in her studio in the house she bought. Whose life is this? Then, I would think, put away those notebooks. The first book was a fluke. You can't write another. This was the voice of paralyzing doubt, doubt of the kaleidoscopic variety continually morphing into new and convincing iterations of itself until it arrives finally at futility: Why do this writing thing at all? It doesn't matter.

IV.

It is January 17, 2016. I am in Iowa City, Iowa, where I come in the coldest part of the year to teach for a semester at the Iowa Writers' Workshop. The temperature is negative one. The sun is bright and high, but if I go outside for more than sixty seconds, my fingers ache. This does not stop me from putting on a thick pair of gloves and smoking a cigarette on the steps outside of the apartment I am renting for the semester.

I have a recurrent fantasy. At the end of the term, having written fifty pages of my new novel, I give a small reading in the glass-walled library in the building where our classes are held. My work is enthusiastically received. As I read aloud, I hear that the language is powerful and resonant and the characters are moving. I am restored to the self I was when I was a student here. At that time, in 2011, my novel was only a computer document to which I returned daily in my privacy. There were no reviews or interviews, no accolades. There was no career. After a time, the novel in progress took on its own momentum and became a kind of a propulsive force urging both of us forward.

I was exhausted during that time. But it was exhilarating. I had named my ambitions at last. I would be a writer. I would finish my novel. I would not be stopped.

Now we have arrived at the heart of the matter: the legitimization of desires. In order to write the novel, I'd had to first acknowledge that I wanted to write it, that I could and would write it. Why had it taken nearly forty years for me to understand that I had the right to my ambitions? This is not a question for the lean-in crowd. That conception, useful though it may be to some, is the province of the entitled classes. Women who come to the big boys' table with education and privilege; perhaps just not quite enough to make more money, to have more power, to be more successful. This is an inadequate model that implies that the old hierarchies, the old systems of inclusion and exclusion, the old distribution of power and wealth is perfectly acceptable, it's just that the ladies have to sit at the big table too.

I and mine are not lean-in women. Mine is a long and illustrious heritage of elegant survivalists and creative realists. We made our way without a road map, or even a road, as is the case for those of us who were, by virtue of race and class and gender, barred from the paths to success. We have dreams aplenty, some realized and some not, but the manifestation of our ambitions is not a given. It isn't even a given that we will recognize our right to have them.

The evening temperature drops to negative ten. Too cold for another cigarette, too cold for anything but bed. Tomorrow I will teach my first class as a member of the permanent faculty. There's no going back to my student days, no magic restoration to a former self. It occurs to me that perhaps this fear and sadness is also a crutch. If I am crippled with doubt, I don't have to write. I don't have to risk disappointing myself with a bad novel or discovering that it is in fact true that I can't write another book at all. In order to continue after these first jarring and sudden successes, I must find some way to understand ambition on my own terms.

I could spend the next three years as I've spent the last three: stuck. I might, as I have in the course of writing this essay, arrive at some truths about the mechanisms of my tangled relationship with my dreams and accomplishments. This might get me moving again, or it might not. If my grandmother, an elegant survivalist if ever there was one, were still alive, she'd shrug at my dilemma as if to say: all of that might be true but you still have to get on with things, a sentiment my mother echoes nearly every time I talk to her. They're right. If I'm honest, what I want is a neat answer to all of my questions, and instructions about the way forward. I won't get those things, of course. Nobody does. But I have my mother and grandparents and their parents, their lives and labor and the ways they kept going through the worst, and the best. In my scramble to get a foothold in this new life, perhaps I can borrow their strength for a while. That's enough being scared, they'd say. We didn't do all of this struggling so you could just give up. Get up now. Take a step. Then another. Then another, like we did.

Girl with Knife

● ● ● ● ● ● **CAMAS DAVIS**

"All right. Are you ready? Why don't you try on this dress and we'll see how it looks on you," the stylist says.

It's a black number, the kind worn to cocktail parties, with a modest cut just above the knee, and a gauzy, translucent back.

"And why don't you try on these boots while you're at it." The boots are black too. Leather. Knee-high. Three-inch heels.

She points me to a dressing room that has been fashioned out of a sheet hung from the ceiling by clothespins. I step out of my jeans and T-shirt and into my costume.

The dress is meant for someone who is more well-endowed than I am, but my stylist works her magic with a few safety pins attached to the dress at the back. The boots are too small for my big feet, but I only have to stand in them for a half hour or so while I pose for the camera.

"How do you wear your makeup normally?" the makeup artist asks me.

"Natural."

"Ok. We'll make it look natural then."

I look like a drag queen.

Another dusting of powder on the nose, some mousse worked into my curly hair, another safety pin, and then the photographer.

"Wow. You have *got* to be the *sexiest* butcher I have *ever* met," he says and then laughs and then I laugh and then everyone in the room—his assistants, the stylists, the PR people for the knife company that have chosen me to be a spokesperson for their new ad campaign—laughs too, in the way that well-meaning people laugh when a well-meaning joke is told to simultaneously call attention to and distract from the fact that something out of the ordinary nags at us from the periphery. It's a gentle, communal one-of-these-things-is-not-like-the-other laugh.

"So I was thinking you could hold this cleaver up near your face like this," the photographer says, demonstrating. He wants me to hold it so that the sharp edge is pointed straight at my face. I grip the cleaver—it's heavy. The pose feels awkward and dangerous, which is maybe the point, but I can't be sure.

"Like this?" I ask, tentatively.

"Okay. Maybe not. How about if you grip it with your hand like this, and rest the back of it on your shoulder?"

"You know, I don't even really use cleavers," I tell him. It's true. I don't. Not really. I've only been studying to be a butcher for a little over a year at this point, and I don't yet have the confidence it takes to be able to cleave a straight line, say, through a rack of ribs, with a few deft swings of my arm. If I need to get through bone, I use a handsaw, or if all I have is a cleaver, I use a dead blow mallet, hitting the top of the cleaver with it as I would a hammer to the head of a nail.

Besides, while cleavers have become the most iconic tool of butchers, the butchers I'd been learning from in France and Oregon didn't use them much. I'd learned that the bulk of butchery—the process by which animal carcasses are transformed into edible cuts of meat after an animal has been slaughtered and eviscerated—could mostly be done with a short, thin, flexible blade that more closely resembles a paring knife than a cleaver. The butchery I'd witnessed dwelled more in the realm of subtle finesse, tiny flicks of the knife that separate fascia from muscle, muscle from bone. Dramatic, demonstrative, sweeping arcs of the cleaver are an occasional part of the equation, sure, but that particular image is more folkloric than anything else. Despite knowing all of this, I'd bought into the folklore too, and so my not yet being able to use a cleaver with confidence meant that I felt, almost constantly, like a fraud.

I had anticipated this moment, and fretted over it, earlier that morning, while on the 6 train headed down to Astor Place, where the shoot was to occur. The knife company had flown me from Oregon to New York City—where, in my former life, I'd been a magazine editor, mostly covering food and drink. They'd put me up in a fancy hotel and planned to photograph me before they came out to Oregon to film me further. I'd been chosen alongside two men, both seasoned chefs, to take part in their new ad campaign, which would feature people in the culinary world who were, in the campaign's words, "defining the edge." They had agreed to pay me a small amount of money for the work, but it had felt like a lot to me after spending six months surviving on unemployment checks, maxing out my credit card to learn butchery in France, and then spending a year working for just above minimum wage at a restaurant and then a butcher shop. After that, I'd taken a chance and launched my own meat school, the Portland Meat Collective, with the mission to inspire everyday people to make more responsible choices about the meat they eat, by way of hands-on, experiential education. It was a project for which I'd recently received an increasing amount of media attention, thus the knife ad. As the subway hurtled through the dark tunnels underneath Manhattan, I'd worried that if I posed with a cleaver, the image would convey that I was indeed a butcher. A bona fide, skilled butcher. The genuine article. How could I subtly convey to them that I wasn't really a butcher? I was an educator. A thinker. A writer. An organizer. The founder and owner of a unique meat education program. A former lifestyle magazine editor. But not a butcher. Definitely not that. Not yet anyway.

"Okay," the photographer says, "that's great. Now just turn the cleaver a little bit toward me. Gooooood. Great. Beautiful. And now look at the camera, but keep your head facing to the side. Look intense. Look like a butcher!"

•   •   •   •   •   •

When the story of the last eight years of my life started appearing in newspapers, the headlines usually went along these lines: "Woman leaves job as magazine editor, runs away to France to learn butchery." In magazines, it became a little more nuanced. In a publication like *Woman's Day,* the headline might read something like, "The New Mrs. Cleaver: One Woman Trades in Her High Heels for a Life in Meat." *Esquire* might strike a cheekier tone. Perhaps, "Fresh Meat: A Woman, a Pig, and a Six-Inch Boner." (In the meat world, "boner" is shorthand for "boning knife," the kind of blade most often used to remove meat from bone.) Here's a sensational headline that actually appeared in *Vice* recently: "This Ex-Vegetarian Is Teaching Portland How to Cut Up Cows."

None of these headlines are false, per say. In fact, I *was* once a vegetarian. I *did* leave my ten-year career as a magazine editor to learn butchery. I *did* in fact trade in pen and paper for a boning knife, although I prefer the five-inch variety.

But in each headline, we also see the power of spectacle hard at work. A *vegetarian* who now teaches people how to kill animals? How'd *that* fall from moral grace happen? A magazine editor turned butcher? What kind of person makes *that* kind of career change in *these* modern times? Indeed, not only is a magazine editor probably not well suited for the job of butcher, but also our culture has decided that hardly anyone is well suited for it, save for automated machines and underpaid migrant workers.

The spectacle perhaps hardest at work in these headlines, of course, is my gender. Because, before industrialization took over our food system, we *did* think some people were well suited for the job of butcher and those people were, and still are, largely men. But "The New Mr. Cleaver: One Man Trades in His Penny Loafers for a Life in Meat" just doesn't have the same ring to it. The fact that I'm a woman in this context makes me doubly out of place, doubly unusual, doubly a spectacle. However, this very fact—and the accompanying possibilities for clever headlines—has also, curiously, garnered me much recognition and success.

And that recognition and success have given me the opportunity to meet and learn from smart, talented people I would not have otherwise met or learned from. It has brought lucrative grants, a book deal, the chance to be a spokesperson for a food movement I strongly believe in. It has taken me into communities working hard to reform our country's meat production system. It's even pushed me onto a red carpet with Martha Stewart who, as cameras flashed, told me the best way to harvest a turkey is to feed it vodka first.

But when I left my career as a magazine editor eight years ago and set out to learn how an animal could be transformed into food I had no such ambitions to be recognized publicly as a butcher. I wasn't even sure I wanted to be a butcher. I wasn't sure about much of anything, really. I did know this: that I'd spent ten years prior to that diligently working my way up the masthead at various lifestyle publications, translating the world around me into perfect story angles, cheeky captions, spectacular headlines. I'd been wholly engrossed in mediating the lives of others, working twelve-hour days for a decade to tell readers how to eat, where to hike, and what to drink. And then, a new editor-in-chief at the city magazine I'd been working at decided she didn't like me, and so she got rid of me—although the official story was that they couldn't afford me anymore. I was shocked. Disappointed. Clinically depressed, actually. But I was also done. Done thinking about every single experience that unfolded in front of me as a potential magazine story. Done coming up with clever headlines. Done working for dysfunctional bosses. Done.

I was ready to reinvent myself and, given my bleak financial situation, I needed to do so rather quickly. I craved, on the most basic level, the opposite of what I had done for the last ten years. I wanted to do something unmediated, something that, at the end of the day, kept me fed or clothed or sheltered, but which did so in the most direct way possible, and not because I'd come up with a clever headline and gotten paid or praised for it. The work I began looking for, that I felt better cut out for, was the kind of work I'd originally come from: carpenters and mechanics, scratch bakers and cooks, people who fixed and assembled things, people who hunted for their own food, who gardened and canned their own tomatoes, people who worked with their hands.

What I really wanted to do, what I'd started thinking about even before I'd lost my job, was to learn a skill. A *skill* skill. The kind that could, at least theoretically, keep me alive by putting food in my mouth, even if I had no job. The kind of skill no one could take away from me. A skill that would help me survive no matter what situation I found myself in. Magazine writing had come to feel very much the opposite of that.

"But why meat? Why not learn how to grow vegetables? Why not become a yoga instructor instead?" I am often asked.

I'd spent much of my magazine career writing about food, and one of the big mysteries that remained for me was meat. I knew, more or less, having grown up hunting and fishing, how it got to our tables the old-fashioned way, and I'd read plenty about how it got to our tables the industrial way, but I'd never fully taken part in the basic, pre-industrial processes by which it got there. I didn't *really* know, not in any intimate way. And I had a hunch that the loudest people in the morality debate over meat in America didn't *really* know either. I wasn't sure I wanted to *be* a butcher. But, at the very least, I wanted to learn, in the most intimate and direct way possible, how an animal went from being alive to being dead and then to becoming a steak on the table. I wanted to grapple with that. I wondered whether, by inserting myself into the process, I might land somewhere new inside the argument. I'd already been a vegetarian. I'd already blindly eaten whatever meat the grocery store provided me. Was there a choice somewhere in the middle that would feel right? In order to find out, I was willing to jump right in and learn. It seemed as direct and unmediated a skill as I could possibly pursue.

But I did not, at the time, have much of a clue as to what I would do with this particular skill or whether I would ever turn it into a job or career, or if I would even like doing it. I certainly didn't imagine that I would be acknowledged publicly for it, even if, as a former magazine editor, I knew quite well that it all made for a very good story.

•   •   •   •   •   •

It didn't seem like a tall order to me, but it was: I was looking for a mentor or two who wouldn't blink an eye when I asked them to teach me, who would gently and patiently guide me in the ways of knife and bone, and who wouldn't ask me too many questions about why I was there.

I ended up going all the way to France to find those mentors. They were four French brothers in white meat smocks with thighs and calves as thick as prosciutto hams and two of their wives with personalities just as sturdy—a family who owned every part of getting pork to people's tables. They grew the grain to feed their pigs; they ran a cooperatively owned slaughterhouse; they did all the butchery and charcuterie themselves; and they sold all the meat at local outdoor markets. Their operation was far from the factory-farm model that was so common back in the States. Two days a week, I stood in the cold *sal de coupe*, or cutting room, in white rubber boots that were two sizes too big for me, cutting up shoulder for brochettes and trimming belly for *ventrèche*. When I did something wrong, they told me. When I did something right, they told me. They were busy and tired, but they were patient teachers. One day a week I worked the market, watching customers haggle over blood sausage and pig ears. I also visited the abattoir and witnessed the swift and hopefully painless, but nonetheless totally visceral, slaughter of animals for food.

Not an easy thing, that. But not a hard thing either. Not exactly. It was something else completely, something I had no vocabulary for. Each day I stared down these massively complicated concepts of life and death and sustenance and yet, somehow, the whole equation felt quite simple. My teachers taught me how to understand what killing an animal for food meant and how it would change my place in the world forever. By the end of the first week, I felt, for the first time since my childhood, rooted in the real world. And for just a little while, before I returned home and started my meat school and began to field calls from the *New York Times* and *Martha Stewart Living*, before I found myself posing in a little black dress with a great big cleaver for a billboard in Times Square, before people started to call me a butcher even though I wasn't one, before I found myself in court staring down a crowd of angry vegans, before I launched a nonprofit and got a book deal and started speaking publicly about meat reform, my life, my very existence, finally, felt elemental. I had no money and no job and no specific purpose, but in setting about to learn this one thing—the very definition of ambition, I suppose—I felt supremely proud and satisfied. Learning felt delicious. Not knowing what I was really doing felt totally acceptable. I remember saying to a few friends, "I can actually feel my brain *growing.*" I imagined brilliant red and hot pink new pathways twisting and turning their way through the tired, bored, overused gray matter of my brain.

· · · · · ·

When I returned home to Portland, Oregon, by no means a confident butcher, I landed a job at a restaurant that did some whole animal butchery and then I tried my hand working at a butcher shop. I was eager to keep learning—I had *ambitions* to keep learning—but I quickly discovered the men at the shop had no interest in teaching me, or even talking to me. "You're not a butcher," one of them—a sweaty, resentful, judging young man—made sure to remind me. "You'll never be a butcher." He was like a little boy, pouting and crying, because he had not been given the red truck he had wished for at Christmas. His rage seemed laughable and old-fashioned to me. I would be lying, however, if I didn't say that he was one of the main reasons I quit the butcher shop and started my own meat school. I called it the Portland Meat Collective. The idea behind the Portland Meat Collective, as I have always told it publicly, is to bring the kind of hands-on education I had in France to my community in Oregon. But I also started the Portland Meat Collective so that I could keep learning. The sweaty, resentful, judging man certainly wasn't going to help me.

Portlanders are known for being obsessed with the provenance of their food, which meant my idea for the Portland Meat Collective was successful almost immediately. I asked whole animal butchers, retired meat science professors, slaughterhouse workers, chefs, and self-taught backyard meat producers to teach the classes and they said yes. I sourced whole, half, and quarter animals from small, local farmers who were raising their animals in a thoughtful, sustainable, humane fashion. I offered hands-on slaughter classes, whole animal butchery classes, sausage classes, pâté classes, charcuterie classes. And, without having to do much marketing at all—in fact, in the seven years that I've been doing this, I've never once sent out a press release or purchased an ad—all manner of people signed up as students: young, old, female, male, Republican, Democrat, doctors, lawyers, bike mechanics, truck drivers, college students, and everyone in between. Classes sold out within hours of announcing them. In each class the students learned how to transform an entire animal into food. They picked up knives and cleavers and inserted themselves into the process by which meat—not just any meat, but clean, fair, local meat—got to their tables. Just as these experiences had changed me in France, so too did they change the students. They began to think more critically about where most of the meat we eat in America comes from. They began buying from better sources. They ate less meat. They questioned our industrialized meat system. I'd not only created a business that changed others, it also changed me. I'd managed to create a business that allowed me to make a living *and* keep learning, the reason I'd gotten into this in the first place.

But before I even felt comfortable teaching classes, before I felt comfortable calling myself a butcher, or, simply, even saying I knew *how* to butcher, I began to gain recognition and praise *as a butcher.* I wasn't labeled an activist or an educator—titles that would have been more fitting at the time, and which are, perhaps coincidentally, titles more traditionally predictable for women. I was labeled a butcher—a much less likely label for a woman, and therefore, in an interesting modern twist, the more appealing label to those around me. It happened first at parties and other social situations—"Have you met my friend, Camas, the lady butcher I told you about?" Then, in a few news stories. Then the knife company came calling, and there I was posing in that little black dress with that cleaver trying to look like a butcher and not really feeling like one.

When the ad campaign appeared in national food magazines across the country, when my mom called because she'd seen a huge poster of me in the window of a kitchen supply store in my hometown, when an old friend from my magazine days in New York texted me a photo of my drag queen face on a billboard in Times Square—"Looks like you finally made it in New York," she'd joked—I felt sheepish. In the ad, the two men had been dubbed "The Rebel" and "The Believer," respectively. I'd been dubbed "The Poet." I found some comfort in this. I didn't write poetry, but I felt I was more of a poet than a butcher, and they'd rightly picked up on the fact that my greatest strengths lay in my ability to write and speak about butchery and meat reform. Although they called me a butcher—nay, "a master butcher"—they also said this: "As a woman in a traditionally male dominated profession, Camas is challenging expectations, breaking stereotypes and bringing intellectual depth to the art of butchery."

They were right. It was a fair and good assessment, but at the time, all I could think about was that I was the only female poet-poseur-butcher in the whole world in a little black dress holding a cleaver even though I didn't use cleavers and wasn't a butcher, and not even really a poet. It was lonely, that fact.

Whether I was right or not, I couldn't shake the feeling that the spectacle of my gender, of my particular choice to study butchery, was the reason I was getting the attention, not my actual skill (or even my imagined skill). It was as if everyone had assumed that because I'd gone and done something so out of the ordinary as a woman, I was also extraordinary enough to master all of butchery in just over a year. I was simultaneously a spectacle and an imposter. I felt *looked at* but not *seen*. It's not that I wasn't searching for recognition—when any of us set out to master a skill, having others recognize, out loud, our own progress toward that mastery can be quite helpful. It's that the recognition seemed premature, misguided, even empty. Increasingly, all I wanted was to be seen for who I really was: a woman who chose to learn butchery and wanted to continue to learn. I wanted to be seen as someone in the process of becoming. But where's the sexy headline in that?

At the same time, the sexy headlines are precisely what allowed me to do what I had set out to do: learn. They brought me into contact with teachers and mentors I might not have otherwise had access to. It would be false to say I was simply a victim of those headlines or to suggest that people should not have written about me. I knew exactly how the spectacle of my story benefited me *and* my cause. I could have refused the interviews, the knife ads, but I didn't. Simultaneously, the attention felt largely unwarranted. I was afraid of being accused of hubris—in fact I *was* accused of hubris, mostly by male butchers who weren't getting their own headlines—which is maybe a very female concern, or maybe it just reflects the way my parents raised me.

Even as I improved as a butcher, and began teaching a few classes, as I began to cut meat in front of large groups of people, and in front of the camera, I never knew how to judge my own abilities. I recently read an article about what happens to children who are told they are great at something before they have been given the time to actually master the task they are being praised for. It makes them less likely to actually achieve mastery, because, regardless, they'll still be praised. It makes them stop learning, essentially. This is what it felt like for me. Was I good at butchery? Was I terrible? Was it okay to remind people I was still learning? I couldn't be sure.

After the knife ad, more media outlets called. The *New York Times*. *Martha Stewart*. *Bon Appétit*. *Food & Wine*. *Time*. More requests for butchery demonstrations in front of hundreds of people. And on and on.

"You can do this," I kept telling myself. "Just run with it. Fake it until you make it." Was I really faking it, though? At some point, didn't I actually know what I was doing? Notice I say this in the form of questions, not answers.

That I had, maybe, of my own volition, gotten myself here, that I was being recognized because I'd done something interesting and worthy of note did not occur to me. That I'd taken a risk, dropped everything familiar to me and set out to learn a totally new skill just for the sake of learning, that I'd been changed by that learning, and that my story of that transformation appealed to people, didn't occur to me until quite recently. Nor did it occur to me that it was actually quite rare to find someone who knew how to butcher *and* could articulate the bigger picture, and that I was that kind of person. That it was maybe even acceptable to just be *okay* at butchery, to not yet have mastered the skill *and* receive attention didn't sink into my brain either. The only thing that mattered to me for so many years was that I was not really a butcher, at least not the kind everyone wanted me to be, the kind that wielded a cleaver with confidence.

It was meant to be flattering, this attention, this recognition, this modern, postfeminist, you-go-girl praise—I understood that—but ultimately it felt like a setup, like a rigged game. What I really wanted most was for someone to appreciate what I'd learned so far, what I'd actually mastered, and to help me figure out what I might still have left to improve upon. What I want still is to not be held to a standard of immediate perfection before I have actually had the time to perfect. It has occurred to me recently that maybe that standard of immediate perfection went both ways—that I held myself up to it as much as everyone else around me did.

"I'm not really a butcher. I'm *learning* to butcher," I often say to anyone who introduces me as a butcher.

And the thing is, it's true. I'm not lying. I'm not really a butcher. Not bona fide anyway. Not a professional one. I look back at some of the early videos of me roaming around online (with astoundingly insulting comments to boot), videos in which I'm cutting up a whole pig or a chicken, and I think, *Wow, I wasn't very good back then. I'm a lot better at butchery now.* But I still don't like to call myself a butcher. Maybe because unlike all the real butchers in the world, who work day in and day out, unrecognized, never photographed, whose profiles never appear next to a single headline, who spend their days stuffing pig intestines with ground pork shoulder or trimming the mold off of dry-aged rib eyes, I am the one who gets to pose with a cleaver for the camera. I get to pose as a butcher. I'm assuming there are at least a few butchers who are disgruntled by that fact. Should I care? Maybe not. But I do. Should they care? Maybe not. But they probably do. I know Mr. Sweaty Resentful Judgmental Butcher Man sure cares.

A female friend recently said to me: "Why can't you just own it? You've done something amazing." Sure, I told her. I can do that—it's the example I, of course, want to set for other women trying to break into the industry in whatever way they want to—but it doesn't mean I'm ready to ignore everyone else who has also mastered butchery and not been recognized. "That's very female of you," my friend told me.

Since I went to France and started the Portland Meat Collective and shook Martha Stewart's hand and posed holding a pig head on a silver platter for the *New York Times Magazine*, there are several men and women who have also posed with cleavers for the camera. Whole animal butchery, knowing where your meat comes from, thinking more consciously about how much meat you eat, it's a *thing* now, a *movement* I helped start. Some of the people posing with pig heads and cleavers for the camera now are in Carhartts rubbed with oil and paint, made to look more worn than they actually are, some are in black dresses, some are in stark white chef jackets. They are men *and* women. I have often wondered if they also consider themselves butchers, or if they, like me, wish no one would ever call them that.

Recently, at a conference about meat reform, I met a young woman who is the head meat cutter at a butcher shop in New York (there are so many more of these women now than there were when I first embarked on this journey) and asked, "So when people started referring to you as a butcher, did you feel like you actually were one? Or did you feel like people were just calling you a butcher because it made for a good story, you being a woman and all. . . ."

"I don't really understand what you're asking," she said. "I'm a butcher because I know how to cut meat."

I admired her confidence. I felt a little embarrassed for even asking. I too know how to cut meat, so why am I hesitant to call myself a butcher? Maybe because once I left France, no one ever bothered to fairly and squarely assess my skills out loud. My *skills*. Not the spectacle of my unusual story. My skills. Maybe someone did bother to assess hers.

◦ ◦ ◦ ◦ • •

I recently did a butchery demonstration at a hunting and fishing convention. I stood behind a table covered with cutting boards surrounded by a sea of people who looked like the people I come from. Hunting caps. Wrangler jeans. Camouflage vests. Work boots. The organizers had wanted me to butcher veni-son. I'd never butchered venison, even though my father and grandfather had been deer hunters, but I knew that it would be just like butchering lamb and it was. I was nervous, but I did okay. I could have done better, which is usually how I feel after these things—I am always trying to improve, which maybe means I don't actually believe in total mastery after all. But no one had stood up and left in the middle of my presentation— whether because of my being a woman, or because of my skill or knowledge, I can never be sure. People came up to me afterward and asked more questions. And as I was packing my knives, an older gentleman—square, stocky, with an intimidating perpet- ual scowl and the sort of thick, ham-like arms and legs that the French brothers had sported—approached me.

"I used to run my own meat processing facility," he told me in a gentle voice that contradicted his stern expression. "Worked it for fifty years. You did pretty darn good. A lot of great infor- mation. Next time, remember to keep your elbows in near your torso when you're cutting. You'll be less likely to get tendonitis that way."

"Thanks for the advice," I said. And I'd meant it.

"Pretty darn good," he'd said. And he'd meant it.

"Next time," he'd said, with encouragement in his voice, because he believed there would be a next time. Because he rec- ognized in me room for improvement. He did not seem fazed by my looks. He had not concerned himself with my headlines, my story, my anomalous narrative, my gender. It was a relief, how- ever fleeting, to finally be seen.

Reply All

● ● ● ● ● ● **ROBIN ROMM**

'm fifteen weeks' pregnant as I write this essay. On the ultra-sounds, I have seen the baby move her hands, suck her thumb, and do a few early dance moves. It took me a long time to get pregnant—five years. I'm forty years old. I've published books, traveled, won awards, been a professor, fallen in love . . . but being pregnant with this baby is the best thing I have ever done. Is that regressive? Well, I don't really care.

When you are nearing forty and struggling to have a baby, people assume a lot of things about you. They think you put off having kids when nature intended, intent on having a career, and you made your own bed. They think you are a desperate woman, unable to find love until late, a sad cliché. It feels, any-way, that this is the ticker tape running at the bottom of the screen. There's a pathetic quality to all of the intervention, to draining one's life savings to buy hormones and surgeries, to create the late-in-life offspring. Doctor after doctor looked at me and said, in a voice hushed with either concern or conde-scension, "Women over thirty-five have diminished egg quality." The takeaway: You should have had kids in your twenties.

In my twenties, I had not been thinking about children. Who thought about children? My mother was a civil rights trial attorney who had an illegal abortion when she was eighteen. She was passionate about a woman's right to choose, about a woman having a real career and making an impact on the world. She ran me around to political rallies and ballet class and museums, prepping me for this important life I was to have, a life with a fulfilling career, intellect, and purpose. Never mind that she was eternally stressed, working full time, then running back to cook dinner, do chores, help me with my homework, and finally collapse in front of the television, eating snacks and growing ill while my father tended to his own demanding career. I could have it all!

At eighteen, I went to an Ivy League university where I never had a single conversation with a girlfriend about either marriage or children. We talked about Derrida and Greek mythology, feminism and literature, boys, our parents, where we wanted to live. I went directly from graduation to a job as a federal investigator, investigating discrimination complaints in San Francisco and beyond. I rose to the top, often the best investigator in my district. I loved the work—getting in the government car, traveling to prisons in northern California, to sweatshops in Saipan. I looked into racial layoffs and forced abortions and, once, the sexual mistreatment of corpses at a funeral home. I loved to learn, to work. Work gave me proximity to the heartbeat of the world. Kids felt like a distant reality, something I'd do later, much later, when I had done that abstract thing: figured myself out.

And I was good at my job, sufficiently absorbed. My life in San Francisco felt thrilling. One quarter, I settled two very large cases—a disability case against a grocery chain for almost $100,000 and a class action gender bias case against a nonprofit for a quarter of a million. My boss, an ambitious woman herself who appreciated and mentored me, sent a note out to the head of the legal department about my accomplishments. That quarter I'd settled cases for more money than all the lawyers combined. I was twenty-four years old.

The older white man who headed up the legal department wrote an email back, to which I was accidentally cc'd. "Obviously Robin's numbers are very impressive. But she's so aggressive when she's on a case. Her assertiveness is off-putting."

My boss rolled her eyes. I marveled at the sexism of the email. Was I supposed to be soft-spoken and pretty while in the civil rights trenches? My mother was a hard-ass. She wore silk shirts and had a Brooklyn accent when she was mad. She won her cases and wept if she lost. And anyway, did this guy, this senior Equal Opportunity Employment Commission lawyer, even understand the spirit of Title VII of the Civil Rights Act? What a joke! Jesus. He was a chauvinistic fart with the self-awareness of a gnat. At least he'd be dead soon, my young self reasoned. I deleted the email.

I thought it was water off a duck's back, but actually, I still remember it with absolute clarity fifteen years later. The water hardened into a little prism.

But I didn't modify my behavior all that much. I worked. I continued to be the top investigator in the district. I wrote elaborate legal recommendations to my director.

"You know, some people write a four-page outline of the case," my attorney advisor told me. "You write thirty pages with dialogue and a plot climax that results in a legal argument. You're a writer. You should leave this job and write."

*　*　*　*　*　*

In my MFA program, which I attended the following year, I earned a coveted teaching appointment and fell in love with my students. Getting people to think about things I deeply cared about, having them create art where moments ago they had only blank paper . . . it seemed like a magic trick. I marveled at the growth of my students—the punk rocker who fell hard for Gertrude Stein. The sorority blonde who finally, after weeks of writing terrible poems about her boyfriend, wrote a rage-filled play about her mother coming out as a lesbian. I loved teaching, I realized. I loved writing, too. The combination felt intoxicating. I wanted to be like the women professors I had had in college and graduate school—C. D. Wright with her quick use of metaphors and deadpan grace; Michelle Carter with her deep intelligence, warmth, and light editorial touch. I wanted to teach creative writing, and I wanted to write.

I won a publication prize in graduate school and published a chapbook. Two years later, at thirty, I landed my first book deal. A year after that, I got my first tenure-track job at a small, funky college in Santa Fe. This was no small feat and involved hours upon hours of learning how to apply and interview for these positions. It required beating hundreds of applicants. It was a dream job—great colleagues, meaningful work. But it didn't last. Two years later, due to a bad bond gamble, the college went out of business and the entire faculty lost their jobs.

That was unlucky, but I was even less lucky in my next job. Though I had plenty going for me—my second book came out to critical acclaim and I'd started writing regularly for the *New York Times Book Review* and other places—there were startlingly few jobs. I landed only one: a tenure-track position at a far-flung university in the middle of a hostile desert. The department was embroiled in a battle over ego and position. The hostility felt alive, like the hallways were teeming with beasts. My partner Don and I couldn't make the friends we'd always made everywhere. The impoverished city didn't have the small luxuries we yearned for—bookstores, restaurants, ways to relax if things got hard. And it was at this point that I started to realize how badly I wanted a baby. Everyone around me waited until tenure to have them and I was thirty-four. I had three more years of tenure-clock ticking to wait out. Then I would be thirty-seven.

Eventually, with so much job misery plaguing us, Don and I threw caution to the wind and tried for that baby anyway. If I got pregnant before tenure, whatever. Maybe I'd still pull it all off, despite the fearful chatter of all the junior women I worked with.

But the baby didn't come. We were both so deeply miserable, the kind of miserable that doesn't fit in an essay, that is too dark and saturated and fucked up. My ambition had led us straight into a snake pit. We were barely getting along. Who am I kidding? We were not getting along. The job stress had put a crack right through our long relationship. Who could blame a baby for staying away?

It took a couple of years for that crisis to work itself out, but by thirty-seven, I'd left the job for a much less stable life of freelancing and teaching part time. Don and I reconciled. We moved first to Portland, then to Iowa City where Don got a fellowship. We lived in a darling house by a creek and I wrote and he taught and we fell back in love and ate big meals and hung out with our dog and made friends. My career looked nothing like I had wanted it to—that life of a professor teaching in a university with her pens and her papers and her purpose, but we had the happiness, time, and sanity to try again for a baby. My mother might have shaken her head at my formless days, but my mother had been dead almost ten years. Still, though, no baby came. The doctors bowed their heads. Thirty-seven, they said. Poor, misguided dear with her books and jobs and no baby.

I began fertility treatments back in Portland one year later. They failed. For two years, we cleaned out our savings. We spent any extra money we got on attempts. Over and over again, doctors explained to me, their voices soft and stern, as though talking to a wayward child, that my ovaries basically belonged in a nursing home, spitting out their geriatric eggs. My chances of success, every day, were diminishing.

When I was thirty-nine, we took the big financial leap and tried IVF. I floated on a sea of hope. My baby, my baby—what did it matter if I got to her on a raft of cold cash and colder doctors? If I got to her, it wouldn't matter. But all the embryos were abnormal. Seventeen thousand dollars later, I was back where I started, but instead of hope-tinged desperation, I was filled with terrible, unending grief.

It turned out that it was not my age or my geriatric eggs causing our infertility. In fact, after years of feeling like my career had ruined my chances of motherhood, our problem turned out to be a rare genetic abnormality, unrelated to my eggs. How many times had my age been blamed and, covertly, my ambition? Thousands, it seemed. We made substantial adjustments to our plan. We got creative. Just after my fortieth birthday, fifteen weeks ago, I got pregnant through a more elaborate version of IVF.

When I got the voice mail with the blood test results, I was walking through downtown Portland during a break in the rain. December, the world out shopping. "You're pregnant," the voice mail message said. I began to laugh, the tears of relief hovering inside that laughter the way my tears often do. I collapsed against the brick wall of a building. A woman in a fake fur coat shot me a look like I was insane.

I had it all, didn't I? Sure, I still mourned for that lost vision of myself as a professor teaching creativity with intelligence, deadpan grace, and warmth. But if you couldn't have it *all* all the time, then you could have it all in moments, and I felt lucky.

•   •   •   •   •   •

Then, at thirteen weeks' pregnant, I was offered yet another academic job, a one-year visiting appointment in Eugene, the city where I was born, two hours south of my home in Portland. I'd been wanting to return to a stable teaching job and had been eyeing this program for a few years; it had a solid reputation and was nestled in a familiar and beloved landscape near family. The catch, of course, was that the position began in September. This baby, my baby, my hard-won happiness catcher, was due August 31.

That really seemed impossible to pull off. What if the birth was hard? What if I had a cesarean? Who would I be right after her birth? Who would the baby be? I drove to the university and spoke with the chair, a man in his seventies in the traditional university attire: rumpled shirt and plastic glasses. I explained my concerns about the possibility of surgery, a hard labor, and he barely met my eyes. But he had three children, daughters, and though he seemed a little exhausted by the effort, he offered to move all the classroom teaching from the first quarter to the third. So, though I'd still have academic duties, I wouldn't start the majority of the classroom teaching until the baby was four months old, and then, to make up that early modification, I'd need to teach a double course load when she was six months old. At that point, I'd be so frantic at work that I'd barely see her. But my potential cesarean scars would have healed.

What did I want to do? Did I want to teach and hope to make a good impression, to be able to compete for the very competitive full-time position that would open the following year? How much of the baby's development would I miss, and would it affect her ability to form healthy attachments? I could afford to keep living the makeshift life I'd constructed. But the job would mean a year of security and benefits and a deeper sense of purpose. I would get to do what I felt I was meant to do all those years ago: teach creativity, while simultaneously having the blessing of actual creation in my arms. It involved compromise, but what in life didn't?

I flew to New York for a trip I'd planned with the job offer in hand, uncertain how to proceed. On the plane, I sat next to a mother and father and their four-month-old baby. I watched the mother (who told me she had stopped working to stay home) nurse the baby, watched her kiss her head and coo. The baby nestled into her. The baby smiled at me. The baby grabbed my finger.

I can't feel my baby yet, but she's there in all the ultrasounds, the beginning of life. When the baby on the plane grabbed my finger, I felt a pull so intense, like God herself was in the air right around me, like my dead mother was hovering with all my grandmothers, with all the dead women I hail from. Could I leave a tiny baby to go teach for a chance, a tiny chance, of making it a career again? Could I leave a helpless baby, a baby I worked so hard to bring into this world, when all that the baby wanted was to be held and nursed by me?

"Take the job and put the baby in a childcare service," said a friend of my father at dinner in New York, a man without kids.

"You should take the job," said my father's girlfriend. "I was a doctor full time when my kids were babies, and I don't feel like I missed out on anything." *Nothing?* I thought. Huh.

"You'll go crazy staying at home with a baby all day," said a friend.

"I wouldn't do it," said my friend Maud, the mother of two. She gave up a job as a therapist to stay home. Her kids are the most well-adjusted kids I know. "Those first years are precious. I mean, I see what people are saying—people put their kids with sitters every day and their kids are fine. But do you want that? I didn't want that. It's a personal choice—and obviously not everyone can make it. A lot of women have to work. But, I mean, if you can do something else that requires less moving, less commuting, less stress, I would."

"That job sounds like hell, honestly," said my friend, Dahlia, the mother of two. "The only job worth having with small kids is a job that is flexible, where people fall in love with you and get the job to work for you."

· · · · · ·

I couldn't sleep. Night after night I lay in bed, staring into the dark. Should I take it? Should I let it go? Would they really give me a shot at the permanent position the following year if I excelled at the juggling act? Or was I just a convenient one-year fill-in who would get tossed out for a sexier candidate with a fancier book after I'd potentially missed out on major motherhood milestones? There wasn't a way to know. Everyone really wanted me to come, said a young woman in the department. They had their fingers crossed.

Finally, I decided to send a note asking for reduced duties and reduced pay, a schedule that would be lighter and allow me to teach while also spending time with my baby. I still might miss her painfully when I was on campus, and we'd still need to live in some kind of temporary arrangement two hours from our house so I could make it all work. Don would need to compromise his work life to help pick up more slack. But I'd read *Lean In*. Sheryl Sandberg cautioned women to stop dropping out of their careers: "Career progression often depends upon taking risks and advocating for oneself—traits that girls are discouraged from exhibiting," she wrote.

I crafted an email that explained what I was asking—a 75 percent appointment, fulfilling all the most important duties of the job, but avoiding that crazy, overloaded spring semester when my baby would be six months old. Why not ask? The worst thing they could do was say no, right?

You'd think a former civil rights investigator would be less naïve.

I received an email back asking if I would still do all the

university service duties for the reduced pay (give a lecture, a reading, advise students, give exams), and noting that such a job might be categorized as just a hair over half time. I wrote back, saying that I would do the service duties, of course, but that I thought the job I proposed was 75 percent of the listed job and should be paid closer to that. "But let me know what you think," I added. Also, I mentioned that my book on gender and ambition (this book) would come out in the spring of that teaching year. I suggested that it might be of interest to the larger academic community and be a nice perk for the department, and maybe even the deans, as universities always like it when faculty publish.

That night, a male professor on the search committee, a man about my age who'd been keen on hiring me before he found out that my pregnancy meant I might need adjustments to the workload, sent out an email. The email wasn't supposed to go to me. It was yet another accidental *reply all*. It said:

> I am not very encouraged at all by this email of hers. This is not really my sense of the person I thought we were dealing with. If I were in her position, I would realize that we are not dealing with a buffet. She cannot expect the salary to exactly track the amount that she wants to reduce the job. . . . It's great she has a book—she told us that already. But she seems to suggest, by bringing it up in this way, that we should cut her a better deal because she has a book coming out—about gender issues . . .
>
> I think we need to move on right away.

I felt ill. Of course, the department had the right to say no to my request for the ideal accommodation to nurse my newborn and balance my life. This is the United States, and, unfortunately, maternity has no protection under the law. But I wasn't prepared for such hostility to go on behind my back simply because I requested what I felt would be a win-win. It felt like a joke, like a too-extreme example from Sheryl Sandberg's book.

I wrote back, apologizing for being misunderstood— apologizing! Ugh. I'm embarrassed I did something so gen- dered, that I let myself be bullied into that behavior. I reiterated that I was only trying to find a way to make the job work with a newborn, that my motives were completely pure. I received a response from the author of the ugly email. The note had a cur- sory apology that ended: "I have some concern that with a new baby, a new book coming out, and maybe still teaching at [your part-time job], this job might be too much for you."

It was so nice of him to help me see my limits, wasn't it? It's great when men do that.

Maybe it infuriated him that I advocated for a salary that matched the duties. But wouldn't a man stick up for himself with regard to salary? Wasn't that basic self-respect, Negotia- tion 101? I felt well within my rights. And why should asking for something—a pay reduction to spend time nursing and estab- lishing a bond with my newborn while still maintaining most of the duties of the job—mean that my character got called into question? I wanted to do right by this baby, this baby I had worked for years to bring into the world, this Hail Mary pass. But I also wanted to work a meaningful job, doing one of the things I love best. I owed it to myself to try and make it work. That is all I had done, and yet there I was again, marveling at an awful email. This guy was in his forties. He wasn't supposed to be a chauvinistic old fart. My young, plucky self had nothing to say to my older self; this dude wasn't about to die.

•   •   •   •   •   •

These two emails from white men in positions of power hap- pened about fifteen years apart in very different fields, but they both exposed the sexism many men—even educated, "feminist" men—feel toward women but wish not to say to them directly. Yeah, she's good at her job, but it makes her less appealing. How dare she try and honor motherhood with a request for fewer duties and less pay? What does she think this world is, a buffet? She's not the person we thought she was.

Well, who did they think I was? What was I supposed to be? A doormat?

No woman should be a doormat. And yet, to try and do well, to try and achieve—even to achieve *balance* is seen as suspicious behavior and opens women up to scorn and discomfort. That's a sad reality. For all the work we've done, for all the education women have received, for all the degrees we've racked up and books we've published, no matter how polite and self-effacing our emails, we still wind up dealing with acres of crap.

•   •   •   •   •   •

Thanks to the powers of genetic testing, I happen to know that I am pregnant with a little girl. I don't know who she will be become. My sole hope right now is that she will be born healthy with all of her brightness intact, that no ill befalls her before she can grow into a young woman. Will she have ambitions? Maybe. Will she be a mother? I can't see the future. I want to be able to tell her that I did fight the fight toward making the world a place where women could thrive and be whole in all ways—as creative people, as smart people, as professional people, as activists, as mothers, as any combination of those things. I may not have won this fight for her. I may not have gotten it all right. My own mother fought, too. She made plenty of mistakes—sacrificed way too much, leaned in too far. And we both got burned along the way—several times.

But what choice do you have? You have to try and do the fulfilling things, all of them. You have to try and fend for yourself. You have to be strong but also openhearted, willing to take risks. And though I am tempted to curl up in a ball and obsess about how I might have played my cards differently, the truth is, I played my cards fine. The game is rigged, and not in women's favor. But at least I tried to play.

Baby girl, if you want to play the game, any game involving your mind and talents, then I wish you the strength to withstand the bullshit that will sometimes come back at you. Because along with great rewards, there will inevitably be bullshit. I wish you the strength to dust yourself off and stare back, to understand that you did nothing wrong by aiming high, by taking risks. I wish you the courage to know the world is unfair and not to take it personally, but not to be complacent either. I hope that with your bravery and guts and gumption combined with the bravery and guts and gumption of all the women who came before you, we will make the roads for your daughter, if you choose to have one, a little less fraught.

Nature and Nurture

• • • • • • MARCIA CHATELAIN

Lately we have been having rousing conversations about the "nature vs. nurture" debate in my house. What makes us who we are? Are humans the sum total of cellular material and endless strands of DNA? Or, are we all simply blank canvases when we are born, stamped by how well we were cared for in our formative years and colored by our experiences?

My husband Mark and I don't usually engage in such deep thinking at the dinner table, but it's a new season in our life— we are in the waiting period of an adoption of two girls. A major part of our adoption preparation included parenting education classes, and the curriculum can take your mind and heart to a number of places. I've read about rare pediatric diseases on medical websites, with tears streaming down my face. I know of every food additive and preservative that exacerbates a child's behavioral problems. I have become an Internet-credentialed child development expert on attachment disorders and discipline. When I can't take any more worst-case scenarios, I have to soothe my anxiety borne out of overeducation via the parenthood dark Web. I turn to the fantasylands of the Internet, where

I can put virtual pins on pictures of ironic onesies, mid-century modern baby furniture, and endless lists of parenting life hacks. Yet, regardless of how many articles I read or outfits I organize in online folders, I think about what my children will take from me—what is my nature and how was I nurtured?

Everything Mark and I have been or done or felt or seen feels like it needs to be named, processed, and categorized as either valuable for our future family or incompatible with being the parents we want to be. In this cataloging of who and what I am, I think about my ambition, and I wonder if its origins are subcutaneous or if it is rooted in my subconscious. I wonder if my drive—my relentlessness that has gotten me so far from where I started—is something that must be passed on, like the carefully crocheted baby blanket my husband's grandmother made for us before she died. Then I worry if our accolades—the external proof of two ambitious souls in one marriage—will make our children feel stifled, unable to define themselves apart from Mark's business success and my academic achievements. I again can't keep thinking about all of it, so I retreat back to the comfort of articles that provide "26 Ideas for Traveling with Kids," order some feminist storytime books, and I convince myself I'm just overthinking it again.

Considering I hail from an immigrant family, you could argue that ambition is in my blood. The very act of leaving behind all that is familiar to you in order to re-create a life in an unknown context means that you are at the very least brave. As a first-generation American, I was raised knowing that my life was inflected with the sacrifice of others. The act of leaving was ambitious, yet my family's need to simply survive often masked it. The opportunities available to them rarely matched their capabilities and their intellect. We regularly heard about how our uncles, family friends, and acquaintances were "big-time doctors" or "well-educated" back home in Haiti, but we knew them as taxi drivers and maintenance workers in America. Even if no one ever said it to you directly, every night shift worked or second job acquired screamed: "We came to this country because of you!" The weight of that knowledge, being made aware that their parenting was about a fundamental disruption of comfort in the service of the possibility of success, was never lost on me. There was no choice but to be good, be better, be an outward contestation of and tribute to the indignities that my family endured. For every racist employer, for every news story that cast Haitians as a plagued people during the AIDS crisis of the 1980s, or exasperated listener too impatient to understand heavily accented English, I felt that I had to do and be something.

My ambition started small—a flicker really—because of my shyness. My parents' acrimonious breakup when I was nine, which plunged us into financial instability, is what made my ambition intensify. My mother gathered our belongings one day, and we had to move in with my aunt and her daughters; at times we lived seven to a two-bedroom, one-bathroom apartment. With little privacy or space for myself as a moody preteen, school became my workplace, my refuge, my laboratory for creating a potion to turn a quiet girl into a force of nature. At home, there were too many people, all older than me, and it was difficult to stand out. My sister and my cousins were natural comrades because of their ages. My mother and her sister were the best of friends. I was alone in a crowded house. But, at school, where everyone was my age, I could assert myself, get noticed, and receive praise for being the best.

•   •   •   •   •   •

I attended Catholic schools paid for by the overtime wages of my mom, her sisters and her brothers, as well as the benevolence of unknown wealthy people I wrote thank-you notes to before summer breaks. I thought I owed all my backers my very best. Strangely, no one ever said I had to achieve. I am certain most people assumed I had a helicopter/stage/coach mom that forced me to get good grades and heap on responsibilities in extracurricular activities, and insisted that I keep focused on collecting every coveted plastic trophy in the Chicago metro area. The reality is that I was my own helicopter/stage/coach parent. My mother worked seemingly endless hours to take care of me. She would wake up and work for a couple of hours, drive me to school, pick me up at the end of the school day, drop me off at home, then go back to work her second job. We would talk in the car or in the half hour she spent showering and getting dressed to work again at her night job. I never felt ignored or unloved, but it was clear to me that love was work—not emotional labor, but intense, exhaustion-inducing work. When you loved someone, you went to work to take care of them. When you worked, you were bringing value to the relationship. I worked hard at school to honor my mother's work. My dream was to one day be successful, so I could have money to help my mom, but I never imagined anything short of all-consuming work. You went to school so you could have a career and work all the time. The logic was simple, and this idea remained with me for most of my life.

By the time my parents were officially dissolved, I embarked on a campaign for attention and affirmation—the kind that my father never cared to provide—and it became clear that ambition was the route most suited to me. Growing up a girl teaches you that you will either be smart or pretty. Smart made more sense to me; it was practical. Trying to be pretty, to remain pretty, was risky and tiresome. If you are a pretty girl, boys and men pay attention to you. In a tight-knit, gossip-fueled immigrant community where a girl talking on the phone with a boy was met with as much concern as an unplanned pregnancy, using ambition to chasten yourself seemed reasonable, smart even. If

I prioritized school, getting into college, and later getting into graduate school—if I remained ambitious as my friends turned boy crazy or simply boy confused—then I could avoid confronting my insecurities about dating and relationships. From my vantage point, women paid for their love lives with their ambition. The proof was on the daytime talk shows I watched while all the adults were at work. I found evidence in the cautionary tales circulated by my aunts, who told tragic stories of the goddaughters who married too early or the children that came before the college degrees. Fortunately, I met someone who showed me something different, and our marriage stands squarely against the tales told to me as a girl and young woman. I've enjoyed most of my professional success with my husband alongside me encouraging me and assuring me that I was the best (in his unbiased opinion). I hope our relationship teaches our children about partnership and how a couple can tend to each other's dreams. I want this to be our legacy.

Although I've settled into a life with as much professional fulfillment as personal happiness, I'm still not sure if my ambition is friend or foe. In order to feed it, nurture it, and maintain it, I've allowed my life to get out of balance more than I like. I've signed up for too much and left too little for myself. The day I found out I got tenure, within hours of hearing the news, I was doubled over on the floor of my bathroom—vomiting uncontrollably for what felt like an eternity. The symbolism wasn't lost on me. It took six years of a PhD program and seven years on the tenure track to finally arrive to that celebratory moment, and I was too sick to raise a glass of champagne or eat the congratulations cookie my husband bought for me after I called him with the good news.

What was this all for, if it only made me sick and exhausted? It was for me, and for my family, and for my future little ones, and for the students whom I teach every year who show up at college the way I did—with this thing they call resilience and label "grit" in studies and in think pieces. We applaud young people—often first-generation college students—for having what it takes to survive. I share stories on my Facebook wall of the kid who moved from a homeless shelter into a college dorm, and I've had more than a few real-life students whose stories of overcoming adversity are shared in confidence. The world of higher education is starting to acknowledge the perseverance and determination not captured on a transcript or the anecdotes edited to comply with the college essay word count. If I were starting college today, my work life starting at fourteen, my responsibilities for paying for school clothes, my needing to contribute because we didn't have enough, would be amplified and applauded. We are in a new era where we don't shame the fish out of water, but we still know that staying afloat takes more than praise.

I'm excited about parenting. Unlike most of my endeavors, there is no opportunity to do it over again, to return to it like a manuscript that can't quite come together or a denied grant application that can be revised for resubmission. I can't merely move "BE A GOOD PARENT" to a different line of my to-do list when I get distracted. I have to be present each and every day, and it will require me to draw from other parts of me, not just my ambition. Will the parts of my life that will make me a role model for our children necessarily make me a good mother?

Now that I'm on top of one professional mountain, I struggle to sit quietly atop it and scan the horizon. I look down too much. I worry about tumbling toward the bottom and hurting myself along the jagged edges. I fix my gaze on the mountaintops on either side of me. I strategize. What will it take for me to scale that one? I hate that I'm not looking at the vista. I don't want to nurture our children to be this way. As a historian of girls and women and an observer of the larger culture, I know the many ways girls are discouraged and shaken and demeaned. I want my daughters to be tough, to never shrink, and I want to do the other things that the books I read about making sure your daughters have a healthy girlhood tell me I need to do. But I don't want them to feel sick from overwork, for their ambition to get in the way of discovering the other things that matter—love, companionship, fun.

Growing your family through adoption disabuses you of ideas that your children will have your nose or your father's brow or your bookishness. Your child gains what you provide—a love of classical music, a taste for spicy tofu, or a penchant for horror films. So, you start to think about how intentional everything must be, or at least I do. I think about this in relationship to my ambitiousness. Good or bad for parenting? I'm never quite sure. What I do know is that I have a lot to offer, to show my children. So, what will I teach my daughters? What is the right way to do all or any of this? I realize that in grappling with this question, I am struggling with the fruits of my labor—my kids will know an economic comfort, privileges that I envied as a kid. They won't know the parental narrative of leaving behind the familiar to seek something better for your family. Is it in my nature to be so ambitious, or was it my mother's circumstances that quietly nurtured these characteristics? In the world of educated parents, very little is left to chance. While my friends bemoan how hyper other parents are about their children's achievements, they are also fretting about the admissions standards of kindergartens, scheduling extracurricular math and language classes, and imploring us to join them in the frenzy. Strangely, my cherished upbringing—in its emphasis on independence above all things—has provided me with a beautiful model that I feel totally incapable of following. I guess I'll try to not overthink it, though that is unlikely. But, as I overprepare for parenthood, I find it strangely liberating knowing that this is one of the few places in my life where I can't expect perfection. I know that it is an impossibility—being the perfect mom. I now take on this new sense of freedom and hope, learn from others, learn from myself, and rest on my desire to nurture. Maybe this sense of freedom will start to become second nature. Perhaps this new sense of freedom is what our daughters will inherit from me.

Crying in the Bathroom

● ● ● ● ● ● ERIKA L. SÁNCHEZ

I t was October, and I had fallen into the worst depression of my life, the darkness outside enveloping me in a crippling and unfamiliar despair. My therapist asked me if I ever thought about suicide. I said no, but the truth was I thought about it several times a day. I'd rent a cabin in Michigan and off myself with a bottle of wine and a fistful of pills. I'd listen to the beautiful piano works of Erik Satie as I slipped out of consciousness and into a peaceful oblivion. I was never able to say it out loud, mostly because I knew how melodramatic it sounded.

At thirty, my life was in shambles. I'd escaped my poverty-tinged upbringing to pursue my dream of becoming a writer, and here I was, a grown woman paralyzed with hopelessness and self-doubt. All I could do was binge-watch *Gilmore Girls*, finding comfort in the idyllic New England town of Stars Hollow, the benign and quirky characters getting into silly capers. I loved watching the interactions between Lorelai and Rory because it was so unlike my relationship with my own mother.

● ● ● ● ● ●

As soon as I hit puberty, my mother and I began to resent each other. Our relationship was nothing like the wholesome white fantasies I saw on TV. I grew up in the working-class town of Cicero, Illinois, which bordered Chicago's west side. My neighborhood was plagued with poverty and violence. Sex workers and their johns loitered in front of a seedy motel at the end of our block. Strange men snorted drugs off our garbage cans.

I struggled to find a place for myself in this harsh environment. I had always been a weird kid—most of my family and peers misunderstood me, disliked me, or both. Nearly all the girls my age looked like traditional Mexican daughters, with their neat clothes and braided hair, or wore "urban" clothes—sneakers, basketball jerseys, large hoop earrings. Meanwhile, I wore combat boots, flappy black dresses, alternative band T-shirts, and dyed my hair funny colors. When I "became a woman" and my sexuality began to flourish, I turned into a serious nuisance. I had opinions and no one liked them. I had feminist inclinations, hated church, enjoyed solitude, and loved to read and write. I was always scandalizing my mother in some form or other.

One of my earliest forms of rebellion was shaving my legs. I was thirteen, and my dark hair was growing in thick as cactus spines. Embarrassed, I secretly used my father's razor in the shower. One afternoon we were at a family party at my uncle's house. It was summer and I was wearing a pair of overall shorts, and as I passed my mother, I felt her hand brush against my leg.

"*Hija de la chingada,*" she muttered, her face flushed with anger and disappointment.

I constantly groused about the unfair distribution of labor in our house. Why did I have to heat tortillas for my brother? Didn't he have hands? Why couldn't it be the other way around? And how come the men always ate first even though the women did all the work? To my mother's chagrin, I was not at all interested in housework. Anytime she tried to teach me how to cook,

I'd end up storming out of the kitchen, exasperated by her criticism and profoundly bored by the minutiae of chopping onions, sorting beans, or frying tortillas. I was not the ideal Mexican daughter. I was a straight-up aberration.

My mother grew up in a cabin in rural Mexico. The daughter of a migrant worker in the Bracero Program and a frequently ill mother, she had to run the household and take care of her seven siblings. She started cooking at the age of five, which would be cute if it wasn't so depressing. Though smart and driven, she was allowed only a few years of schooling in her remote mountain village. This resulted, unsurprisingly, in a very narrow worldview, particularly when it came to gender norms. In 1978, at the age of twenty-one, she immigrated to the United States. Two decades later, when her daughter began to act like an Americanized teenager, she was rightly bewildered, and reacted how any Catholic Mexican mom would: with unbridled repression. She wanted to know my whereabouts at all times, grew suspicious of me whenever I left the house. Though she was only trying to protect me, she always suspected the worst and did everything in her power—mostly through shame—to prevent me from getting pregnant and ruining my life.

In the beginning I just wanted some room to breathe. After a while, though, I did the kinds of things she feared: I experimented with drugs, had sex, pierced body parts, and got my first tattoo. I'd try anything to quell my restlessness. Once after an argument with my parents, I punched a door in frustration. When I was really desperate, I cut myself.

●　　●　　●　　●　　●　　●

To escape the wasteland of my working-class hometown and my tense relationship with my mother, I lost myself in books. I latched on to writing. Writing made me happy. I excelled at it, and I hoped it would offer me a way out. I realize now that it was also, critically, convenient and inexpensive. All I needed was a pen and paper. I had many other interests—particularly art and music—but those required many more resources. My parents once bought me an acoustic guitar from a garage sale, but I soon gave up when we couldn't afford lessons and I was unable to teach myself with library books. Writing was the cheapest way for me to feel free. I was scrutinized and controlled at home, and the blank page offered me endless possibilities, a vehicle to create another reality for myself.

In high school, a few teachers noticed my talent and encouraged me to keep writing. One particularly supportive teacher, Mr. Cislo, would give me mix tapes and books he thought I'd like. Once he even made me a packet of all of his favorite poetry. The work of Sharon Olds, Anne Sexton, and Sandra Cisneros—women who wrote unapologetically about their bodies and inner life—struck me. Writing felt like an emergency. And so I wrote poems about menstruation, sex, and sadness. Writing offered me a way to explore the stigmatized subjects of sex and mental illness.

My sophomore year I got censored in our literary magazine for using the word *cunt*. Another time I was reprimanded for reading a poem with vaginal imagery at a school assembly. Those were some of my proudest moments.

· · · · · •

While I was brooding in my room reading Anne Sexton and writing poems about my vagina, most of my family members were breaking their backs as laborers. My dad got up at dawn to make cheesecakes with my uncles and cousins in a factory on the west side of Chicago. My mom worked the night shift at a paper factory and came home with chapped, cracked hands and melancholic eyes.

Success in my family meant sitting at a desk; it meant you had air-conditioning in the brutal summer months; it meant your boss didn't talk down to you because you didn't speak English; it meant you didn't fear *la migra* would deport your ass while you were minding your own business trying to make a living.

Neither one of my parents made it past sixth grade, so at thirteen, my brothers and I had already surpassed their education level. My older brother and I became our parents' interpreters and cultural brokers. We translated legal documents and important medical information. The power dynamic between immigrants and their American-born English-speaking children can be mystifying for those who've never had to advocate for their disempowered parents. Sometimes we had to be the caretakers, whether we liked it or not. Talking to strangers and asking for things became easy for me. I learned to shed any sense of self-consciousness or intimidation because my parents needed me—at a parent-teacher conference, at the mall, or on the phone with an insurance company.

When I was fifteen, my mom and I were at a diner, and as usual, I was in charge of communicating with the waitress. She scowled as she took our order and then turned around and chatted gleefully with the white people sitting next to us. Enraged, I wrote a note on a napkin: "Mexicans are people too." I now see that these kinds of experiences helped me develop my assertiveness. I learned to stand up for myself. I learned to get shit done.

* * * * * *

People often ask me who my role models were growing up, and the truth is I didn't have any except Lisa Simpson. True story. To me, Lisa was brilliant and utterly unafraid to be who she was. I loved the way she earnestly voiced her unpopular opinions about all sorts of subjects and issues: feminism, literature, animal rights, immigration. Sure, she was occasionally irritating and overzealous, but damn, she had gumption and integrity. Lisa was just about everything I wanted to be, and I related to her in ways that I didn't even understand at the time. I saw myself in her when she ruined Homer's barbecue by destroying his suckling pig in her quest to save the animals of the world. That's exactly the kind of self-righteous shit I would have pulled when I was a teenager. Many years later during a therapy session, when comparing Lisa's relationship to Homer with my relationship to my own father, I suddenly burst into tears. I couldn't believe I was crying over a cartoon, but it made sense. My father loved me but had no idea who I was, and I, too, lacked the compassion and maturity to understand who *he* was.

* * * * * *

Everyone in my family was incredibly hardworking, and I admire them for their resilience and generosity, but nobody, *nobody*, had the kind of life I wanted, particularly the women. My aunt, who worked at a candy factory, looked at my hands when I was a kid and told me I had *manos de rica*. It was true— they were smooth and soft rich lady hands. My mom, most of my aunts, and many of my cousins married young and had children soon after. In addition to all the cooking and cleaning, their jobs involved intense physical labor. Every day my mother came home to never-ending cooking and chores. Who could blame her for being perpetually tired and cranky? Her life seemed like a crushing burden. Her world revolved around us and the factory, and there was little room for anything else. She never did anything for herself, never had the luxury of time or money, didn't even have hobbies or good friends to unwind with after work. When I was eight or so, I used her face cream thinking it was body lotion, and she was so angry and disappointed. "Why?" she wanted to know. "Why would you do such a thing?" At the time I had no idea why she was yelling at me over moisturizer, but now I understand that it was probably one of the few things she ever indulged in, and I had taken it away from her.

What did *I* want out of life? I sure as hell didn't want to work in a factory. That was my parents' worst nightmare. They didn't cross the deadly Tijuana border for their kids to work like donkeys in this country. I know they would have been happy if we simply had white-collar jobs, it didn't even matter what kind, but I always knew I wanted so much more than that—ridiculous, impossible things.

I certainly didn't want to get married or have kids. Judging from what I saw in my family, children sucked all the fun out of life. Most of the women I knew seemed unhappy, so I fashioned together my dream life from various books and movies. If other women were financially independent, traveled alone, and went to college, why couldn't I?

• • • • • •

I got myself through college and graduate school on my own. One fall I couldn't even afford to buy myself a coat. It was a shameful existence at times, but I had pulled through alone, and I was proud of that. After I received my master's degree, I was stuck in corporate America for two grueling years until I was able to cobble together a living by tutoring at a local university and freelance writing for major publications like *Cosmopolitan for Latinas,* NBC Latino, *Al Jazeera,* and the *Guardian.* I was hustling and barely surviving; my income was downright embarrassing for an adult. Though I was successful in many ways, I felt financially disempowered. I was too old to be struggling like a college student. I'd been poor for most of my life, and I was tired. Accolades were nice, but I wanted my success to translate into cold hard cash in my little brown hands. I wanted the luxury of buying a pair of shoes without falling into a spiral of worry and guilt.

I got married the summer I turned thirty. During that time

my writing garnered the attention of a public relations firm, and they offered me a full-time, salaried position as senior strategist. Much of my writing was focused on reproductive rights, which I'd been passionate about for many years, and it was more money than I had ever seen in my life. It was not my dream job by any means—I imagined I'd be a professor or famous writer at this age (ha!)—but I was excited to write about issues I cared about, and I was eager to be compensated for my knowledge and talent. Though I could still live in Chicago, the job would require me to frequently travel to New York. I had always been scrappy, however, and had traveled to many places on my own; I felt like I could do anything.

Nothing could have prepared me for my monumental unraveling.

*   *   *   *   *   *

After my first day, I went back to my work-provided apartment on the Upper West Side shaky and scared. That's all I remember. Every night after, I woke up drenched in sweat. Sometimes I would meet friends after work and cry over dinner. Fortunately, we were in Manhattan and no one cared that a grown woman was weeping into her kung pao chicken. The man walking down the street with a cat perched on his head and the drunk woman stumbling around in fishnet panties were much more interesting.

*   *   *   *   *   *

When I returned home from New York the second time, I began to lose my mind. It was as if some wires got crossed in my brain. I panicked. I was suddenly so tense that I forgot to breathe at a normal pace. "I don't know how to breathe anymore," I told my husband.

This is when I found my saintly therapist, who helped me

uncover the childhood anguish I had so carefully compart-
mentalized and buried deep inside my psyche. I've always been
introspective, often to an unhealthy degree, but some memories
I had unconsciously obscured just so I could go on living my life
without shattering. Suddenly, however, I had a flood of flash-
backs that unmoored me.

•   •   •   •   •   •

The most appalling component of my shiny new job was a
time-tracking system called Time Task. Essentially, we were all
required to account for every minute of the day. If I switched
tasks—say, from a press release to discussing another client with
a coworker—I was expected to stop the timer that kept track
of my work on that project and begin a new one to record the
length of my conversation about the other client. Our timers
were supposed to run all day so management could keep tabs on
what we were doing. Multitasking became excruciating because
every stupid task had to be documented. We were required to
write a description for everything we did throughout the day,
and when we left, we had to account for about eight hours of
work. If your time didn't add up, if there were any gaps, there
was going to be trouble.

Not only was Time Task humiliating, it triggered episodes of
severe anxiety for me. I couldn't sleep. I lost weight. I cried in
the bathroom. I secretly took antianxiety drugs from my husband just to get through the day. I had fought so hard to create the kind of life I wanted for myself—a life of art, freedom,
adventure, and social justice—and now I was stuck at a job that
controlled my every move. It scared me. Though my white-collar
job paid far beyond my parents' meager factory wages, I was, in
some ways, treated like they were—my boss was exacting and
condescending, and I was expected to crank out writing as if I
were a machine. I was consistently required to produce complex

writing products in unreasonable amounts of time, which would fill me with panic. Once, my boss scolded me in front of another coworker for taking notes during a meeting. Another time she forced me to revise a six-hundred-word document eleven times, which amounted to about nine hours of work. And when she made mistakes, she would blame others and expect us to rectify them. She remains the worst person I've ever met, an impressive title considering how many assholes I've come across throughout the years.

When I described the office culture and working conditions to a friend of mine, she very accurately called my job *a sweatshop of the mind*. I had never felt so devalued and disrespected in my entire adult life.

●   ●   ●   ●   ●   ●

I've been a perfectionist since I was a child. Once in kindergarten I made a Christmas tree that involved gluing cereal loops together to make the garland. I didn't like how my tree had turned out—I'd used too much glue, and it was too messy for my taste. I asked my large and sour-faced teacher for the opportunity to start over, but she refused. Though she insisted that it looked fine, I was so ashamed of my shitty artwork that I cried inconsolably. My teacher called my dad and forced him to pick me up.

Because I always understood that I wasn't what my parents, culture, or community expected, that I was, in many ways, a disappointment, I cultivated incredibly high standards for myself. I studied hard and worked on my poetry for hours at a time, fixated on finding the perfect words. Years later in college, I realized that I had to work harder than my white classmates because people automatically thought I was less intelligent. People like me were not expected to succeed.

My grades were excellent until my depression worsened, and

I eventually became suicidal at the age of fifteen. By then I really started to feel that my life, and even my body, were not my own. Even when I tried to conform, because being who I was caused so many problems, I just couldn't do it. My sadness grew more severe, and I didn't know how to ask for help. I was convinced the world would never allow me to be who I was.

• • • • • •

I had trouble functioning several weeks into the new job. I couldn't pry myself off my couch and would often sleep to escape the turmoil of my brain. I kept my family at a distance because I didn't want to alarm them, and I rarely socialized with friends because the mere thought of talking to people exhausted me. I had just married my boyfriend a few months before, and our marriage was already beginning to unfurl. It was one of the loneliest times of my life.

My hypercritical boss and the time-tracking system stirred up my issues with authority and control. I resented the shit out of the situation because it reminded me of being a child. My environment, once again, wanted me to conform.

Fifteen years after my first suicidal episode, here I was wanting to die again. I thought my writing was going to give me the freedom to be whatever I wanted, to live the life I had imagined for myself when I was a girl. But it was just another kind of trap. How could I get out?

I finally understood that until I addressed all the underlying problems in my life—my constant need for validation, the depression I'd left untreated for years, my issues with my family—no amount of achievement was going to make me happy, and this kind of work environment would cause me debilitating anxiety. I tried first to negotiate a better work situation for myself, only to be offered a less advantageous setup. One evening I unleashed all of my frustration and disappointment in an epic phone call with my boss. I paced around my apartment and outlined all the ways in which their family business was completely fucked up. It felt amazing, the kind of thing you fantasize about but never do. Still, quitting felt like a failure. I saw myself as strong and independent, a woman who spoke her mind, but I simultaneously hated myself. *Who the hell do you think you are?* I asked myself over and over again. After what my parents survived to raise us, my inability to handle an office job, no matter how loathsome, felt shameful.

I was afraid to tell my mother that I had quit the highest paying job I'd ever had, but when I did, she was relieved rather than disappointed. She had seen the toll it had taken on my mental health and was worried I would relapse. "*Tu si eres chingona*," my mother said to me when I shared the news. It's only now that I can see the irony of her compliment: *chingona*, a badass bitch—literally, a woman who fucks. I had defied her attempts to shelter me, and she had somehow learned to admire that. I finally understood that I'd never be a failure to my mother. We spent so many years bickering and misunderstanding each other that I hadn't realized how proud of me she had become.

• • • • • •

A few weeks after I left my job, an international organization I'd previously worked with offered me a consulting project in Trinidad. I was sent there to write a report on cervical cancer prevention and interview low-income women benefiting from the lifesaving procedure. I was being paid to travel and write about a feminist issue I cared about; it was one of the most exciting opportunities in my life.

As I stood in the passport line waiting to enter the country, I reflected that only weeks ago I was sobbing on my couch, wanting to die, unable to leave my apartment. And now here I was in a foreign land, not only functioning but also exhilarated by my circumstances, by the life I was able to painstakingly build and rebuild. I was mobile and independent, privileged to make choices my mother could never even fathom. When she crossed that border thirty-eight years ago, she was giving me permission to cross my own.

Both

● ● ● ● ● ● **YAEL CHATAV SCHONBRUN**

The moderate knows she cannot have it all. There are tensions between rival goods, and you just have to accept that you will never get to live a pure and perfect life, devoted to one truth or one value.

—DAVID BROOKS, *The Road to Character*

My two-year-old son announces that he wants to tell me a secret. The secret, "Bonky bonky," is loud and wet. We both giggle, and I kiss his round belly as I lift him from his car seat. But as we enter the door of the family day care where he spends three days each week, his grasp tightens and his smile evaporates. He attempts to merge his body with mine, to delay the breakup he knows is coming. I disentangle from his embrace and place him on the ground; he tries to climb back up. I break his grip as Jeannie, his day care provider, picks him up and tries to distract him. Wise to attempts to break his focus, he twists his neck to maintain eye contact with me and begins to wail.

Even as I feel the tug toward him, I am eager to disconnect and begin the non-mother part of my day. I'm either a modern woman admirably committed to my career at all costs, or a failing mother who regularly sheds her maternal responsibilities in favor of her own, self-interested objectives. Perhaps I'm both.

On the morning of this particular Tuesday drop-off, I'm headed to the university-affiliated psychiatric hospital where I've conducted my research for the better part of the past decade. I welcome the fifty miles that separate my ambitious self from my nurturing self. My gig as a clinical psychologist and research faculty in the medical school of an Ivy League university requires a fundamentally different set of skills than those of mother: stoicism in the face of a relentless barrage of criticism (also known as the peer review process), the ability to sustain logic and high-level reasoning through complex arguments, and a persistent focus on pursuing the next achievement. Truth be told, I'm not close to a perfect ten on any of these traits to begin with, and magnifying my shortcomings is the fact that I spend much of the traditional workweek mothering my two- and five-year-old boys. I rely on the long drive to sharpen the softer edges of maternal me.

I turn "Animal Alphabet Songs" off, switch to NPR, and sip my coffee. I'm feeling more scholarly already. My two-year-old is probably having a great time, and I'm set to have a productive day using my brain to accomplish tasks for which I have spent my adult life training.

While the mother me exists largely in the private world of my home, my professional self has the opportunity to achieve and contribute in a manner that is widely and publicly respected. A day of outstanding parenting, whether that involves staying calm through multiple tantrums or consciously relishing the sight of my two boys racing through the kitchen in superhero capes will bring no accolades. I'm ok with this, because even as it's hard to quantify the meaning of those seemingly insignificant moments, it is those moments that make for a connected and fulfilling life. And yet, I find vast meaning and fulfillment in my professional life. My work as a researcher aims to increase knowledge of how to treat underserved individuals, and my role as a therapist can bring healing into the lives of individuals who are in significant pain. And the less magnanimous part exists for me, as well: the more tangible rewards of professional life—accomplishment, income, recognition—are hard to relinquish. So I haven't.

I tune in to my mental to-do list as I head in to my office. In addition to the ever-present pressure to get moving on scientific papers—the one currently on my docket examines predictors of involvement in sex trading among hazardously drinking jailed women—I have several meetings to squeeze in today. Once in my office, I set up my laptop and get to work on the paper. I'm in a satisfying groove when I realize I'm late to meet a research assistant. I email an "early draft" to my coauthors, some of whom I will be meeting with shortly, explaining that my hope is to have a complete draft available to them the following week.

After a quick update from the research assistant, I'm off to a team meeting in my colleague Linda's office. Linda is a senior professor and researcher. Known for her wide-reaching contributions to psychotherapy and pharmacologic treatment of substance use disorders, Linda is something of a rock star in the world of addictions research. She is impressively successful in the currencies of the academic trade: securing large grants, publishing in top-tier journals, and knowing who to know among the top academic dogs. I am the first one to get to the meeting, so we have a few minutes to chat.

"I read what you sent," she tells me. (How in the world did she have time?) "Why do you think this paper is taking you so long to complete?" I mourn her disinterest in the value of conversational pleasantries as a pink flush climbs up my neck and into my cheeks.

"This topic is a whole new literature for me . . . I have so few hours every week to work. . . . There were so many school closings this winter. . . . The results kept changing because the data aren't well suited for the questions we decided to try to answer. . . ."

She gazes at me quietly, steadily, as she leans back in her swivel chair.

I force myself to be silent for a moment, and try again. "I know. I just need to get it done." I try to put together a collegial smile, which she kindly returns.

· · · · · ·

As an eager college student, I became spellbound by the power of scientific research to understand human behavior. The ability to quantitatively capture abstract phenomena like mood and relationship functioning, and to apply that quantitative knowledge in a way that informed treatment, seemed like a superhero power accessible to the learned; I wanted to be that kind of powerful. Throughout my twenties, I industriously checked off tasks from the traditional to-do list of young academics. Research assistant in a well-known research laboratory: check. Admission to graduate program: check. Match to competitive internship program: check. Early career grant to provide a foundation for later, larger grant awards: check. Despite a few anxieties and predictable blips in my progress, I was on track to become the kind of academic psychologist that I admired—a successful one.

I had no qualms about having a family while I pursued my career. I knew lots of colleagues who did it, and while I knew there would be challenges, I felt confident that I would rise to them. I was all-in, had a flexible career, and had plenty of resources at my disposal.

Then I had my first baby. To my surprise, I discovered that the idea of being apart from my child for the full workweek felt intolerable. It wasn't an issue of quality of childcare or of any other structural, policy, or even marital constraint. It was my own internal psychological and spiritual dilemma: it pained me to be away from his tiny body full of baby smells and sounds. I was familiar with the body of research suggesting that babies are not negatively impacted in the domains of social, cognitive, or emotional development simply because they have parents who work. So it didn't feel logical to feel so torn up about not being able to snuggle that baby all day long.

I hadn't seen it coming. Plenty of professionals, with far more power and prestige than I, had gone back to work after having babies. Among my peers in academia, I knew only of the brilliant women and men who managed to become loving, devoted parents while sustaining their commitment to productive careers. I had assumed I would be in that camp and had planned accordingly. I had no idea how to respond to the intense feelings that were throwing a wrench in my well-laid plans.

The gut wrenching toggling back and forth over what to do lasted about a year. I spent much of that time engaged in a tiresome inner dialogue about my core identity and values and asking myself, *What should I do?* Was it more meaningful to pursue excellence and make civic contributions, or to be devoted to raising one's children? And then there were the practical questions: What would we have to give up as a family, and what I would give up in independence, if I relinquished my income? Would my years of professional training be seen as a waste— by me and by the many mentors who contributed to my professional development—if I backed out of my career? And what would that mean to me?

I'm a psychologist, so naturally I worked to gain insight and resolve my internal dilemma. I began to practice tuning out the pervasive cultural messages about what a highly trained woman in modern society "should" do, and tuning in to what made the most sense for my family and me. But as I sat with all of these thoughts and feelings, it became increasingly clear that there was no obvious answer. Instead, I detected a series of complicated choices, each accompanied by unavoidable costs.

Ultimately, I worked with colleagues to renegotiate my position to allow a much shorter workweek. I reduced my private therapy hours and shifted those hours to minimize the disruption to my family's schedule. I curbed my ambition and got off the tried and true academic path and onto an uncharted path, which would lead to . . . I wasn't really sure where.

No longer on the traditional road to success, I reasoned that surely I could redefine success for myself. I could restrain my ego and find professional satisfaction in a nontraditional way. I knew I wouldn't be able to keep up with the brilliant colleagues who committed to their work full time. Instead, I reasoned that if I could carve out some specific roles for myself, I could still make meaningful, recognizable contributions, and I could still express my ambitious self in my professional life.

But it has become increasingly clear to me why part-time effort is a unicorn among those with my level of training and career trajectory. In academia and academic research, one cannot fit in—let alone achieve conventional success—without an all-in commitment to professional life. Staying abreast of and conversant in advances in research requires ongoing attention. Being available for conferences and talks and other hobnobbing events necessitates your physical availability. The concepts of "ambitious" and "part time" seem to be a schematic mismatch.

•   •   •   •   •   •

Into the discomfort of our awkward exchange, the rest of the research team soon enters Linda's office. We begin reviewing recruitment issues and how well our study is working to link incarcerated women with alcohol problems to volunteers who are doing their twelve-step work. I nod along as we segue from one topic to the next. I'm partly paying attention, but mostly immersed in my internal hamster wheel of worry about my career trajectory and what all of my colleagues must think of me.

After the meeting finally ends, I return to the sex-trading paper, forcing myself to make progress before my coffee date with another colleague.

When I arrive in the hospital coffee shop, Janie is waiting for me, coffee in hand. As usual, she looks perfectly professional and polished, with a dark gray, ironed skirt, heels, and designer glasses perched on her nose.

"Janie!" I call out, and we give each other a warm hug. Janie and I did our postdoctoral fellowships together in the university internship program. But, since having kids, our lives have diverged. Janie also has two children, but unlike me, managed to stay fully immersed in her research career throughout her children's early years.

Janie talks as quickly as she thinks: "I've barely had a moment to breathe in the past couple of months," she tells me. "Florida was recruiting me for a new director position in the research division of their anxiety disorders clinic, so George and I decided to bring the kids along on the interview and make it into a family trip. But, of course, the interview was grueling, and then we needed to rush back so we could have a day home before I headed to a conference in Michigan. A week later I had to go to sit on a review committee in DC. And between all of that, I got word that another investigator had done a small pilot study testing a social phobia intervention similar to my approach, and I needed to get my pilot results out before theirs. I ended up doing several long writing nights after the kids went to bed in order to get that paper out. It just got submitted earlier this week, so I'm relieved it's under review."

I nod with appreciation and murmurs of disbelief at all that she's managed to accomplish. Hearing about the life she leads gets my blood pumping.

She tells me she received an attractive offer from Florida and was being aggressively courted, but that our university was working hard to keep her.

Why are we so different? How is she so prolific and impressive? Would I—*could* I—have become just as impressive and impactful as she is if I hadn't backed down? Am I a better parent than she is, even though she clearly outshines me in the professional world? It's more important to be a parent than a professional, right? *Right?*

Humorist Tim Kreider writes in *We Learn Nothing* that "it's tempting to read other people's lives as cautionary fables or repudiations of our own, to covet or denigrate them instead of seeing them for what they are: other people's lives, island universes, unknowable." I knew Janie's life, because at one point I was living and breathing the same air. But now we live in distinctly disconnected island universes. Yet, as I remind myself not to compare (especially because I know her to be an excellent parent), it is hard not to feel a little inferior.

"What about you? How are things?" she says.

I describe how my five-year-old has turned into Forrest Gump with his passion for running and how my two-year-old has picked up some choice phrases from his older brother. We laugh. And then I confess to her that my productivity has been lacking, but that I feel ready and motivated to start to pick up my pace. She nods empathically. "Well, it's hard to be productive when you're only working part time."

There is no judgment in her voice, yet I feel sheepish, so I turn the conversation to a new project we've been piloting to engage couples in a brief inpatient intervention. Research on couples' treatment has been my particular joy since the start of my career, but it's only recently that I've returned to it. Although I had sub-mitted manuscripts throughout my childbearing years—albeit at a much slower pace than I had previously done—I haven't submitted a grant proposal in almost three years. Since she's far more practiced at it, Janie talks me through some of the grant application bottlenecks that are likely to arise. Soon enough I realize it's time for me to wrap up loose ends and head out of the hospital. We hug good-bye, and I head back to my office.

It's now 2 PM. Still early by most standards, yet my workday is about done. With the meetings I've attended and the tasks I've managed to check off my to-do list, I want to call this day worthwhile. And yet, I'm feeling pretty deflated. I shut down my computer, stuff it in my bag, and head to my car.

My older son's pickup is in an hour, and it takes about that long to get to him. As I turn on the engine, I call my husband to let him know that we are going out to dinner—I am in no mood for cooking. He picks up on the first ring.

"Hiya." I say. "Today stunk."

My husband listens to me recount the day. After a pause he says, "I don't understand why you do this to yourself. No one expects you to keep up with them when you're part time. You *decided* you wanted to be home more with the kids. It's amazing and lucky that you've been able to make it happen while keeping a career like yours alive."

I silently curse him for not indulging my self-pity.

"I guess," I say. "But I just can't figure out how to feel comfort-able with being so much less successful than people like Janie."

My husband sighs. "You *are* successful. You are successful at what you've decided to do."

"I know, I know," I say, cutting his lecture off. "I definitely don't want less time at home with the boys."

When faced with the option of choosing to increase my work

effort and reduce time with my kids, I unfailingly land on the side of restraining my professional goals. But then why can't I stop agonizing?

My five-year-old needs to be picked up by 3 PM. I give up on NPR and change the station. Top 40 hits it is. It's about ten seconds of my trying to unwind and relax before my mind drifts. *What should I order for dinner tonight? I'm famished already. Is that traffic? How was I going to get this stupid paper done this week? Maybe a doughnut would make me feel better. I should have enough time to hit EZ-off doughnut shop now that the traffic is moving.*

By the time I pull into the preschool parking lot, I've downed a chocolate-frosted doughnut and a Diet Coke. I quickly put the car in park and race in. Three o'clock on the nose.

I chose this school partly because it has an optional extended day. Today, as often happens on my workdays, my kid is the last one to be picked up. Seeing me in the doorway of his cheerfully decorated classroom, my towheaded son bounds toward me, but before reaching me, he turns on his heels and runs in the other direction. "Ha!" he says, "I'm Flash Gordon! You can't catch me!"

His teacher smiles patiently. "Time to go home, buddy." She is clearly ready to be done with her day.

"C'mon, sweets," I coax him. "Let's go to the park and swing until it's time to pick up your little brother." He loves to swing, so he bounds back, gives me a big wet kiss, and grabs the latest additions to his paper airplane fleet.

As we head to the playground across from the school, we see his friend and his mother at the swing set. "Jason!" my son squeals. Without another word, they begin a game of tag, which soon transitions into a game of racing paper airplanes. I watch the two boys with Jason's mom, who has become my friend during their year in preschool.

Belinda, with her blonde hair and blue eyes, looks like the

traditional 1950s images of the stay-at-home mother. Of course, she is far more than this two-dimensional characterization, but she looks so effortlessly cute and happy in the mother role.

We sit together on the swings talking about our kids and what we are having for dinner, and it occurs to me that in this moment I've automatically morphed back into my mother self.

I imagine that Belinda has overlooked the fact that I haven't devoted myself fully to motherhood today until she chides me: "Yael, you know I could have picked up your little man today so you didn't have to rush over here!"

Somehow, her generous offer triggers the same twinge of deficiency as Janie's description of her academic prowess. Our achievement-oriented world recognizes and rewards those who are extraordinary at one thing, not those who are pretty good at many things. A wider focus might be more rewarding, but it will likely go unrecognized. For someone who wholly bought into the culture of excellence before kids, being part time every-where and highly successful nowhere has been an unexpected challenge.

"Oh, that's ok." I shrug. "I look forward to picking him up at the end of the day."

As I hear myself say these words, I feel the meaning resonate in my chest. I got to wear both hats today. Perhaps I'm imperfect in each role, but in this moment, I can appreciate being blessed to take part in both. I wouldn't give up either world because there is, indeed, satisfaction to be had in the balance. If I can just slow down a little more often and allow myself to appreciate it.

. . . . . .

Am I lucky, or nuts? Intense engagement in the joys of both motherhood and professional life is a gift that only the truly privileged are able to access.

Still, I have to wonder: If I worked full time, would I feel greater satisfaction? Or might I feel more fulfilled if I gave up on my professional life and wholly devoted myself to mother-hood? Despite years of deliberating my best course, I have con-sistently chosen not to close the door on either world. They each matter too much to me.

Even as I may be less accomplished in either arena, I cherish the exquisite blessing of having a fuller and richer life resulting from being so deeply invested in both.

And that, I believe, is pretty extraordinary.

No Happy Harmony

● ● ● ● ● ● **ELIZABETH COREY**

t least once a semester, a young female student will come to my office with questions about an assignment, and after we have finished our official business, will mention her concerns about the future: whether she should apply to medical school or take the less demanding physician's assistant route, or whether she should marry right away and move with her husband for his job. Often she is the one with the better opportunity, and she wonders if she can expect her fiancé to follow her as she pursues graduate education at a prestigious East Coast school. Even if she isn't in a romantic relationship, she wonders what it will mean for her goals when she is in one. Inevitably, she confesses that she is worried about the difficulty of pursuing both family and career.

The decisions are not simple. "Why," asked Taylor, a former student, "if I believe I have a professional vocation, should I not pursue it? Failing to do so would be like burying my talents in the ground." Her insight is perhaps the one unproblematic and entirely admirable legacy of feminism: Because women are human, they should be free to pursue excellence, just as men do.

Another student quoted a line to me from the post-communion prayer of the Anglican liturgy, in which the congregation beseeches God for the grace and assistance to "do all such good works as thou hast prepared for us to walk in." She confessed that she has always loved this prayer because she sees herself as blessed with multiple talents but has never been quite clear about how to pursue them all.

These sorts of conversations weren't common when I graduated from Oberlin College in the early 1990s. Nobody talked of marriage or children. The very idea of marriage was considered odd and old-fashioned, although most of my friends did marry eventually, after a period of experimentation and cohabitation. Perhaps this is still the case at Oberlin and elsewhere, but my students at Baylor worry about marriage and family.

They are no less ambitious than women in any other American college and most are as focused on success as their male peers. But many come from conservative Christian backgrounds, where the natural differences between men and women are celebrated and mothers often stay at home. They appreciate that a woman's role in the family is something unique and valuable, and they are not persuaded by radical feminist arguments that marriage and motherhood are mere oppression. How then, they wonder, can the longing to have and care for children be combined with a sincere desire to achieve something of value outside the home?

Thus, they ask a question at the forefront of popular literature about women and work: How can women "balance" professional interests and family? Like countless other women, I've had to juggle my obligations as a mother and wife with the demands first of graduate study and then of teaching and scholarship. But I've slowly come to realize that this quest for balance, the desire to reconcile radically conflicting demands, is misguided. Work and family evoke from us two distinct modes of being and of relation to others. The conflicts between these modes cannot, if we are honest with ourselves, be wished away or ignored.

I've never had much interest in academic feminism. At Oberlin, I was inundated with the most radical varieties of feminist thought and practice. Words that are now mostly laughed at—"herstory" and "womyn"—were used in earnest. The Women's Studies Department, as it was called then, brought in feminist activists as lecturers, and the library routinely featured poster presentations about the objectification of women on television and in print. There was one single-sex women's dormitory at Oberlin, intended as a haven for self-identified lesbians or for those who were "seeking." All of this was foreign to me—another world from the one I had left behind in conservative south Louisiana.

More recent feminist writers, however, have begun to say not that women should forget about being wives and mothers and start to act more like men, but that they should somehow play both roles at once. They should strive for success in the same way as men, but *also* be wives and mothers.

The most famous example of this genre is Anne-Marie Slaughter's autobiographical essay in the *Atlantic*, "Why Women Still Can't Have It All," which made the rounds several years ago, and since then, Slaughter has followed up with a book. After giving up a promising career at the State Department because she felt a duty to spend more time caring for her teenage son, Slaughter returned from Washington (with some regret) to resume her position as a tenured professor at Princeton. But she sees this as something of a failure, or at least an unsatisfying compromise. She hopes that others will not have to make such choices in the future. If only there were as many women as men on corporate boards and in the Senate and the courts, and perhaps even a woman president. This is her solution.

Debora Spar, president of Barnard College, has suggested

a more "feminine" vision of reform. This includes sharing childcare among neighborhood women and generally seeking solidarity with others in similar situations, as women in other countries have (supposedly) always done—not competing but cooperating. She diagnoses the problem as excessive individualism and competitiveness; we should foster communitarian arrangements for working women—if only women were nicer to one another and more supportive!

Sheryl Sandberg, chief operating officer at Facebook, sees the answer in empowering women. "We hold ourselves back in ways both big and small," Sandberg writes in *Lean In,* "by lacking self-confidence, by not raising our hands, and by pulling back when we should be leaning in." But men must do their part as well. "A truly equal world," she writes, "would be one where women ran half our countries and men ran half our homes. I believe that this would be a better world."

Of course these approaches have received criticism from those who say the writers don't get the difficulties of working-class women, and that these are the problems of "the one percent." These authors have also been criticized for neglecting the fact that men, too, feel deep conflicts between work and family. But many readers are grateful for a genre that seeks to confront the difficulties of having children and careers without simply saying: "work harder" or "stop working."

Yet, this is precisely where such literature fails. It presents the problem as one that admits of solution *primarily* through political or social reform. But the problem Slaughter, Spar, and Sandberg describe is not at root sociopolitical. It is rather that the personal qualities required by professional work are directly opposed to the qualities that child-rearing demands. They are fundamentally different existential orientations, and the conflict between them is permanent.

Flexible hours, parental leave, working from home, and other policy changes are necessary for women to flourish as professionals and mothers. But the core of the problem is more spiritual and psychological than political or social. A failure to recognize this is frankly to succumb to ideological blindness. To quote Spar again: "Feminism wasn't supposed to make us miserable. It was supposed to make us free." But "feminism" is not a lived life; it is a political *movement*, a set of ideas abstracted from experience and propounded as ethical imperatives. It should not surprise any thoughtful person when reality does not conform to the dreams of ambitious elites with bright ideas.

Taylor, my biblically articulate student, sees that she has a talent, and she feels called to develop it, which means giving herself to the hard work of pursuing excellence. To do so she must focus on herself, for the sake of the gifts she has been given. The problem is not that this work is time-consuming or that it reduces or eliminates a woman's ability to do other things. The problem is that the serious pursuit of excellence requires a self-culture. The excellence is *within* us and must be developed: my musical potential brought to fulfillment, my academic aptitude developed and realized through education.

Many of the women in my classes are particularly captivated by the idea that a major component of human happiness is the pursuit (if not the achievement) of moral and intellectual perfection. In working through Aristotle's *Ethics*, for instance, they find a compelling way of understanding what they do every day in their classwork. Like Aristotle, they are pursuing moral and intellectual virtues. And of course they are pushing themselves to reach concrete, worldly goals: to ace the MCATs, to write a really fine short story, to master ancient Greek, to play a Bach fugue with confidence and proficiency.

Yet in the midst of all this work, these young women are aware of the ever-present danger of pride (as are my male students, though perhaps less often). They have felt the futility of what Hobbes described so vividly as "the perpetual and restless desire of power after power." They sense that other activities and other modes of life offer a very different kind of good: Worship, poetic contemplation, and love are quintessential examples.

My students know that motherhood is more like these activities than it is like the pursuit of excellence. They sense that caring for others requires us to put aside (at least temporarily) the quest for achievement, not just to make time but also to create space for a different mode of being. Worship and love: These require no particular talent or cultivation of the sort I have been describing. They are gifts of the self, not achievements of the self.

The contrast between excellences we achieve and love we give appears in the distinction between *ratio* and *intellectus*, as Josef Pieper highlights in *Leisure: The Basis of Culture*. Pieper wanted to recover an authentic notion of leisure in a contemporary world that seems to value only work, achievement, and endless practical activity. In *ratio*, reason serves extrinsic ends and the achievement of particular goals. *Intellectus* is receptive, and even passive in the sense of "suffering" itself, to experiences that cannot be controlled. We pause from our striving toward goals to pay attention, to observe, and ultimately to love.

Parenting requires ignoring for a time the individual quest for self-perfection and excellence and focusing instead on the needs of another person. This can only be done in what Pieper calls leisure. He does not mean inactivity or the absence of responsibility, but the setting aside of goals, which is the condition of attention and activity that isn't striving. In leisure we are available, *disponible*, which is why Pieper uses this term as a synonym for contemplation.

Leisure in this fuller sense is not part of the lives of modern feminist writers. By their own admission, they are consumed with a quest for individual betterment, for greater efficiency, and for time-saving strategies in daily life, going so far as to recommend better techniques for punching the numbers on a microwave. They frankly confess that they wish to be consummate achievers in the workplace as well as in their personal lives, as they train for marathons and eat healthfully to avoid gaining weight in middle age. They reap the rewards of all this focused work: promotion, money, attractiveness, and most important of all, honor and recognition, much of it well deserved. They then expect to transfer this mentality and the same kind of pursuit of excellence directly into motherhood and child-rearing.

But, if I am right, these two endeavors require different orientations of the self, and we simply cannot approach marriage and family in the spirit of achievement at all. If we try to do so, we will find ourselves frustrated and conflicted. For well-behaved or smart children are not markers of our success; children are ends in themselves, to be loved and cared for as individuals. They need from us something other than our talents; they need us, full stop.

Most women see this difference, at least to some degree. Caring for children takes place for the most part in private. There is no payment. Most of the time there is no audience. There are no promotions and few thanks. We often talk of trying to be a good parent, and rightly so, but it's not an achievement, at least not in the same way that being a good pianist is an achievement. It is a kind of self-giving that is different from self-culture. The mode of being demanded by children isn't of the sort that allows mothers (or fathers, for that matter) to engage in the self-culture that's such an important part of any sustained pursuit of excellence.

And what do the children themselves desire? They want patience, calm, and the full attention of their mothers, which are exact opposites of what the hectic pace of professional work often requires. Children do not want a parent who is physically present but multitasking; they want that parent to look at them and listen to what they have to say. They want attention as they swim, draw, or play the piano. This requires Pieper's leisure, a categorically different kind of focused activity that is not in the service of achievement. The sorts of endeavors that allow us to use and develop our God-given talents are very different from caring for the children God has given us.

It's fashionable nowadays to call unpleasant situations "tensions" and to identify problems as "challenges," as if by denying fundamental and sometimes tragic oppositions we might wish them away. Such words are used again and again in the contemporary essays I've been describing.

The same essays imagine solutions that strike me as evasions. "The best hope for improving the lot of all women," writes Slaughter, "is to close the leadership gap: to elect a woman president and 50 women senators; to ensure that women are equally represented in the ranks of corporate executives and judicial leaders. Only when women wield power in sufficient numbers will we create a society that genuinely works for all women. That will be a society that works for everyone." This is just the kind of utopian political prescription that emerges throughout this literature. Everything is about power—gaining and keeping it. Women will remake the world!

The assumption is, as I said, that motherhood and professional work are two of the same kinds of endeavor, activities on the same continuum of achievement. A feature in the *Wall Street Journal* has made such an argument more explicitly than I would have ever dreamed possible: A movement is now afoot to conduct family life on the model of a business. We should call "family business meetings" and compose a "family mission statement." Children should be assigned tasks and receive "performance evaluations." If we could just get the family to act more like our junior colleagues all would be well. The child qua employee would happily entertain himself, helping with the laundry, while we efficiently cross out items on our to-do lists. All of life would now be one long round of tasks—but at least we'd be "getting things done."

It is worth imagining a hypothetical perfect world where women are equally represented in all political institutions and cooperate with other neighborhood women in taking care of children (on the model of a business), and formerly recalcitrant husbands at last do their fair share around the house. Women are then freed from the "burdens" of taking care of children. But are they happy?

I'm afraid the answer is still no, at least if we listen to Anne-Marie Slaughter. She confesses that even with a supportive husband who is willing to shoulder nearly all the childcare, she still does not feel comfortable being away from her son. There's no rational explanation for this, according to the theory that we just need more help and that the roles of men and women are functionally interchangeable. But there seems to be something in the nature of most women that wants not only to be sure that children are cared for but also to do the caring themselves.

If this is so, and I think it is, doesn't the "stay-at-home" argument make the most sense? Shouldn't women, and especially those who are financially stable enough to do so, focus predominantly on family and children? This idea is worth careful consideration, although the mainstream press often treats it as a strange or oppressive view.

Many women want to stay home, and even secular elites have begun to see it as a desirable option. Witness the significant number of affluent, well-educated women who have, if perhaps with a bit of shame, opted out of the workforce because they recognize the benefits to their children. They see that devoting themselves to home and family yields great goods, which include an authentic division of labor between husband and wife as well as a mother's ability to give undivided attention to her children.

It is obviously the model that feminism has often disparaged, but its appeal endures.

Nevertheless, this option does not present an easy, one-size-fits-all solution to the conflict I have been describing. Sometimes staying at home is even promoted with an ideological fervor not unlike what is found in Slaughter, Spar, and Sandberg. And while I've sometimes felt the appeal of stay-at-home motherhood, it should not be idealized, as if it presented no difficulties.

To wit: Although the rewards of caring for children are very great, motherhood can also be also tiring and frustrating, not to mention lonely. A woman must be extraordinarily self-assured to withstand the self-doubt that might cause her to wonder at times whether she has done the right thing.

A stay-at-home mother may well be just as talented as her husband, but "the world" takes little notice of the work she does. Jessica, who was an honors student at a prestigious college before she gave birth to her seven children, typically rails against her husband's colleagues after a dinner party for their obliviousness to her existence as a mind. When put in these terms, it is not altogether clear who faces the more difficult situation: the "working mother" or the "stay-at-home mom."

Moreover, the pitfalls of pride are not absent in this kind of life either. If the identities of working women tend to be bound up with achievement in their chosen fields, many stay-at-home mothers I know speak of the intense competitiveness, usually under the surface, that can spring up among women who do not work professionally outside the home. They quietly judge each other on the basis of their children's discipline habits and academic achievement, or they gossip critically about the diets, appearances, marriages, and family lives of those they know.

I've learned not to idealize the mother who stays at home as the natural and obvious corrective to the conflicted, busy, ambitious professional woman. In fact, these women sometimes pay a high price for suppressing parts of themselves that call out to be developed and rewarded.

Mary, a young, devoutly Catholic woman, told me recently that over the past few years she has watched most of her college friends marry and start families. She, however, confessed a strong desire to pursue a scholarly life, not rejecting family and children, but recognizing other goods, too. Should we discourage her? Of course not. Every time we admit a young woman into college or graduate school, we are implicitly telling her that we value her intellect and wish for her success. But she'll surely face just the kinds of difficulties I've been describing.

I've assumed throughout that women possess a desire to care for children that they feel more strongly than men. Many may balk at this, although I'm often struck by how widespread my presumption is among conservatives and liberals alike. What else could give Slaughter, Spar, and Sandberg the confidence that increased political power for women will make for a more family-friendly economy?

The observation that women, as a group, undoubtedly have more of the "nurturing" impulse than men does not yield the conclusion that sex alone should determine a woman's course of life (what I call "gender determinism"). It does imply, however, that we cannot come to terms with the difficulties women face in the present day until we consider the way that we feel about the competing inclinations in our own souls.

Modern women are right to think that both the pursuit of excellence and the desire to care for others are part of a fully flourishing life. One the one hand, excellence in a particular field requires persistence, self-confidence, drive, courage, and initiative. These are eminently admirable qualities. On the other hand, serving or loving another requires the even more admirable qualities of attention, focus, care, patience, and self-sacrifice.

The accent we place on them, and the way we put them into practice, is a matter for all of us to figure out for ourselves.

But we must not deceive ourselves. We cannot happily harmonize these two modes or pretend that they are somehow the same in kind. The disharmony is most apparent at the extremes, when we observe the two modes collapsed into one sphere of activity. We have all seen, for example, the driven mother who can talk of nothing but her own successes and those of her brilliant offspring, or the woman continually distracted by her iPhone, unable to focus on her children as she waits for the next important message to come in. Something is profoundly disordered.

At the other extreme, we probably know many women who have chosen not to pursue their own excellence. Of course there are better and worse reasons for this decision, the most admirable of which is devotion to nurturing others. Yet this also comes with costs. I've never forgotten Jessica's almost plaintive confession to me late one night, years ago, after too much wine. "My husband," she said, "has done the things that I really wanted to do, and could have, but didn't." The optimist in me wanted to tell her it wasn't too late, but it was, and we both knew it.

Both the ethical imperatives I've described—"must work" and "must stay at home"—reflect noble desires, the one for talents fully used and the other for the vocation of motherhood. But I worry that both are too often promoted ideologically, prescribed as answers to the anxieties young women naturally feel about what they should do. This problem is especially pressing for those high-achieving college students I have been describing, who cannot imagine doing anything—be it career or motherhood—halfheartedly.

It's this tacit denial of the tragedy of the human condition that I've come to resent in the contemporary literature about "balancing" career and family. This literature is full of demands for Justice and Equality, its authors motivated by ideas of social perfection: to finally place a sufficient number of women in the ranks of management and government and to effect true gender equality in the workplace as a whole. Engaged on a quest to change the world, they write with a fervor generated by a political ideal and employ the language of political advocacy, as if the divided desires of our souls can be unified by Reform and Revolution. There is a solution for everything, they imply; we just haven't found it yet.

But this simply isn't so. I know from personal experience that this conflict in the soul does not go away, no matter how pleasant and accommodating our colleagues may be, or how flexible our schedules. We are limited, embodied creatures. These limits mean that we cannot do everything to its fullest extent at once, and certain things we may not be able to do at all. The tragic aspect of this is that both excellence and nurture are real, vital goods, and the full pursuit of one often, and perhaps inevitably, forecloses fully pursuing the other.

Leaning In, Leaning Out

●　●　●　●　●　● **ALLISON BARRETT CARTER**

For some, North Carolina summers are beautiful in their laid-back, sultry, teen romance way. But for a struggling stay-at-home mom, they're hell in a diaper bag. It is sweat, sunscreen, and mosquitoes outside, or being trapped inside with a toddler climbing the walls.

When I was pregnant, I worked full time and barely noticed the seasons at all. I was consumed with my growing child, planning how I'd excel at motherhood. I'd keep the house clean, only serve organic meals, and split all the real parenting duties with my husband. Motherhood would not slow my intellectual contributions to the world at large.

Then I had the baby. Two years later, during a sweltering summer, I found myself eating microwaved green beans and suggesting to my son that we dine in front of the TV because it was just the two of us, again.

That year, the Olympics were in full swing with an impressive American swim team that had the nation in its grip. Between races I found myself continuously confronted by a commercial honoring the athletes' mothers. In a barrage of touching images, mothers were seen lifting their fallen children again and again, driving them to early morning practices, and watching nervously from the sidelines. The scenes celebrated these women as the silent, unsung force behind the amazing athletes who appeared on our television.

The commercial aired constantly, and each time it affected me. Those moms were elegantly quiet in the background, full of resolve and emotion, yet completely overshadowed. Was their legacy that they gave everything they could to someone else, so that person could swim one hundred yards? They were nameless, lumped into a group of generic "moms" in a commercial, while their children became household names and international sensations.

Was that all I was to be now: a shadowy figure who bandaged others' knees and helped them to their greatness?

I never dreamed about being a stay-at-home mom. I attended a top public university, the University of Virginia, where I graduated with distinction and loved the legacy associated with the school. As an undergraduate, I poured myself into books, forgoing a social life. I had my sights set on academic achievement, led a student-run dance company, and was a founding volunteer at the Center for Politics. I saw myself as an eventual newsmaker and powerful leader, my name in the headlines and bylines.

After I graduated, I found an amazing job at PBS outside of Washington, DC. I worked my way to senior contract negotiator, privy to inside conversations and decisions. I enjoyed it, bragging to friends that the shows they and their children watched were procured by my negotiating skills. I was about to enroll in a nighttime law program to further advance my career when I met the man who would become my husband. I followed my outdoorsy engineering beau to the hills of North Carolina while I worked remotely.

Before I knew it, I was married and pregnant. The swank

job suddenly no longer fit my life. As my belly grew and my baby kicked, I felt maternal love overwhelming all the other desires I'd had. Contracts and deadlines mattered less as my pregnancy progressed. My priority became my son before I even held him in my arms.

A couple we were very close to had their baby months before I was due to deliver mine. They both worked full-time jobs they loved, but they were beyond exhausted and fought incessantly. Every time we met to listen to live bluegrass music or watch a football game, I saw them battle over their baby's head. Their fights were varied but constant: whose job was more important, who needed to go to the grocery store bleary-eyed after work, who needed to reschedule their meetings to stay home when the child was sick, who needed to communicate with the nanny.

My anxiety skyrocketed as I listened to their arguments. One night after they left exceptionally angry at one another, my husband and I admitted that we wanted something different. He was willing to stay home if we decided it was best, but he was doubtful of his ability to be fulfilled doing so. If we both kept our jobs, we saw ourselves turning out like my poor, stressed friends. I knew that law school, the only way for me to really move ahead at work, was not a reasonable option with a newborn. Also, we had a warm house and could afford our weekly groceries without such tensions. I decided not to return to work after my maternity leave ended.

This decision, of course, drastically changed our financial situation, but I realized that my values allow for a smaller budget. If all the little things I gave up had really been valuable to me, I would have made a different choice. If I truly cared enough about better-fitting clothes, age-defying makeup, spontaneous vacations, the newest iPhone, or even to be in the best school district or private school, I would have changed my mind.

If I wanted to impact the face of public television and guide it into the next century, I would have changed my mind.

It turns out that I don't mind Target clothes and makeup from the grocery store. With research I can organize smart budget vacations—maybe not to Spain or Amsterdam, but we'll still have fun. Public television would continue on without me, but my family felt like a different story.

When my son's ongoing struggle with ear infections required multiple surgeries, I knew where I needed to be. When my son's sweaty knees snuggled into my side as we read books in the late afternoon, I didn't want anything else. I loved every single new face and lip curl he made.

But soon, even though our domestic lives seemed more balanced than those of our poor arguing friends, doubts about lost possibilities began to worm their way in. I'd wanted to write and travel, bring television into the digital age, argue points of law in superior court.

Even though I loved spending time with my growing son, I came to miss vice presidents of departments calling me for information only I knew, having Au Bon Pain while on a conference call with a brilliant legal mind in Boston, arguing details of contract language, researching digital trends in broadcasting, and proposing language to capture those rights. I missed an expendable income. A part of me—my independence and freedom—had started to disappear.

I wanted to stay relevant intellectually, but I didn't know what that meant when it came to charting my path as a stay-at-home mom. Cultural clues were unhelpful. Though our society claims to admire the hard work of women who decide to stay home, when it comes down to it, that respect isn't genuine. The same summer as the Olympics, I watched *Modern Family* after my son went to bed. Claire, the stay-at-home mom, was portrayed as a frantic, controlling killjoy. When women stay home with their kids, they're not seen as respectable intellectual equals. They're either oppressive and crazed or an untouchable martyr, the women who willingly dissolve behind the images of their children.

I happened to read Sheryl Sandberg's book *Lean In* during this time. Many stay-at-home moms I know detested that book. They seemed to feel that Sandberg's call for women to embrace their talents and get help (as men do) was a passive-aggressive attack on women who left the workplace.

I, on the other hand, loved it. I underlined, underscored, and highlighted like a dutiful student. Why couldn't I apply what she said (get a mentor, sit at the table, speak the truth, be the best, don't do it halfway) to motherhood? Here I was, privileged enough to make a decision for the life I wanted; I needed to embrace it.

Sandberg wrote, "We hold ourselves back in ways both big and small, by lacking self-confidence, by not raising our hands, and by pulling back when we should be leaning in." And later, "If I had to embrace a definition of success, it would be that success is making the best choices we can . . . and accepting them."

That stuck. So I leaned in to motherhood.

I approached my role like I did my comparative politics class back at UVA: researching who looked happiest, who seemed to be doing it right, who was turning out accomplished kids, and, from there, extrapolated what steps they took. I'd find the winning formula and follow it.

Step by painful Pinterest-fueled step I tried to mold myself into the Internet's image of the perfect mom. I prepared crafts based on the season and holiday, hosted luncheons, volunteered on every board, cut sandwiches into fun shapes, took my child to all the museums and every available adventure outside our door. I could barely keep up with myself.

One terrible day I was at home preparing for a group playdate. Overcome by my son's relentless cries from his crib, I sobbed through a shower I desperately needed. Thirty minutes later I was wearing shorts with high heels (which I felt was the required uniform) and desperately trying to get a kale and white bean stew simmering on the stove (even though I actually ate frozen French bread pizza most meals). All the while, I tripped over my stupid shoes, sprinting back and forth from the stove to my wailing child who, I learned later, had a double-ear infection. I'd spent money we didn't have on expensive candles so my house smelled like a Christmas tree farm, although it was nowhere near the holiday season.

And I was utterly exhausted. I'd stayed up too late the night before, despite knowing multiple nighttime soothing sessions were coming, preparing a craft project for all of the twelve- to eighteen-month-old children coming over the next day. I was determined to master the image, to win.

Except, I was miserable and frustrated. I didn't want to be in heels. I wanted to pull my greasy hair back into a bun, throw on sweatpants, and meet friends at the coffee shop before excusing myself early for a midday snuggle with my tired child.

Why, if I was working so hard to be the best mother, wasn't I happier, more confident, and proud of myself? Shouldn't I have been leaning *way* in to self-confidence at this point?

When I really thought about it, I realized I'd received a lot of praise and a significant pay raise from my boss every single year in every one of my jobs as a reward for hard work. In my new role for my "new company," no matter how many crafts and cookies I conjured up, no one really cared. No one valued my efforts. It deflated me to pour all of my energy into the single goal of being a spectacular stay-at-home mom and have no one notice.

After the playdate fiasco, I realized that my ambition couldn't be fulfilled by stews and crafts. By this time, my husband and I had brought another son into the world. We were now a family of four and the demands were even greater. I reentered the workforce in a part-time capacity as a content marketer and writer for an Internet company. Working didn't go well either. While the job was acceptable, trying to balance it all back home meant that my husband and I were much like that couple we didn't want to be. We fought too much, the kids were ferried from one place to the next so we could get it all done, and our time became so filled with chores and must-dos that we barely enjoyed each other.

That wasn't what I wanted, either.

Had I now inadvertently created a legacy of failure? I failed at being the world's best stay-at-home mom and then promptly turned around and failed at being a working mom.

And I was sort of missing my kids. I remembered mornings when I buried my face under my pillow, muttering I couldn't do it one more minute, then came downstairs to my sons dressed as pirates, preparing a concert on kazoos just for me. I did my best as a mom, without impact bonuses or promotions, because when I clapped at the end of their show I knew that my love and attention changed their world. I missed that feeling.

I craved happiness and a quieter life with my family, but I still wanted a legacy outside of my children. I couldn't accomplish any of this according to someone else's rule book. So I wrote my own.

I admitted that while my children will not wait to grow, I can get a job later. I am smart, creative, and useful, and those traits will not abandon me.

I had been ashamed of myself as a stay-at-home mom for a long time but for the wrong reasons. I let the Internet, television, essays, books, and blogs define how I thought motherhood should look. I spent years of my early motherhood feeling as though my ambition had to die because I made the choice to stay home with my children. The truth that finally changed my life is that ambition and being a stay-at-home mom are not mutually exclusive concepts.

Today I no longer let shame stop me from embracing things the stereotypical stay-at-home mom does. Some may think that version of motherhood is outdated and unhappy, but I actually love whipping up chocolate chip cookies while explaining detailed narrative arc to my sons, then taking a phone call about nonprofit management for an organization I volunteer for. And I do it in sweatpants with my hair pulled back in a messy bun.

Sometimes I write, join important and impactful groups, teach group fitness, train for 5km races, sporadically blog, sign up for reading challenges, and always push myself to learn something new. Even though I no longer have a full-time job I love to brag about, I always have something interesting to share at cocktail parties.

I finally allowed myself the freedom to admit that I have no regrets over being with my sons. Every success sounding out a new word, every time their eyes lit up because they read something new about hummingbirds, every tear shed at the hands of a bully, they've all been mine to witness. Not only my heart but also my physical being has been beside my kids nearly every day since their birth.

Ironically, my fierce ambition, which seemed so toxic to me in early motherhood, makes me a better mother and role model to them. My desire to achieve and be seen, to emerge from the invisible life of chores and house, makes me happy as a stay-at-home mom today.

Just because those moms in that Olympics commercial were in the shadows for the thirty-second spot doesn't mean they weren't out the next day running an executive meeting or feeding the needy. The commercial wasn't the full story. Perhaps my legacy isn't just one big thing I am leaving behind. My kids are certainly a big part of my legacy, but they're not the whole of it either. Maybe my legacy is more complicated, a rich and messy sum of all the things that have mattered to me, and that matter to me still.

The Price of Black Ambition

• • • • • • **ROXANE GAY**

You never know when or if you'll get a big break as a writer. You write and write and write and hope that someone out there will see something worthwhile in that writing and then you write and write and write some more. I think I am having my big break right now. In 2014, I published two books—a novel, *An Untamed State*, and an essay collection, *Bad Feminist*. Both books received overwhelmingly positive critical attention. The latter book was on the *New York Times* bestseller list regularly in the eighteen months after it was published. Articles about me keep telling me I am having a moment, my big break. My friends and loved ones tell me that I am having a moment. Part of me recognizes that I am having a moment, while the more relentless part of me, a part that cannot be quieted, is only hungrier, wanting more.

• • • • • •

I began to understand the shape and ferocity of my ambition when I was in kindergarten. Each student had been given a piece of paper in class bearing an illustration of two water glasses. We were instructed to color in one-half of the illustration. I suspect we were learning about fractions. I diligently shaded in one-half of one of the glasses and smugly turned my work in to the teacher. If it had been the parlance of the day, I would have thought, *nailed it.* I had not, of course, "nailed it." I was supposed to color in an entire glass. Instead of the praise I anticipated, I received an F, which, in retrospect, seems a bit harsh for kindergarten. I couldn't bring such a grade home to my parents. I had already begun demanding excellence of myself and couldn't face falling short.

On the bus ride home, I stuffed my shame between the dry, cracked leather of the seat and assumed the matter had been dealt with. The driver, a zealous sort, found my crumpled failure, and the next day, handed it to my mother when he dropped me off. She was not pleased. I was not pleased with her displeasure. I never wanted to experience that feeling again. I vowed to be better. I vowed to be the best. As a black girl in these United States—I was the daughter of Haitian immigrants—I had no choice but to work toward being the best.

Many people of color living in this country can likely relate to the onset of outsized ambition at too young an age, an ambition fueled by the sense, often confirmed by ignorance, of being a second-class citizen and needing to claw your way toward equal consideration and some semblance of respect. Many people of color, like me, remember the moment that first began to shape their ambition and what that moment felt like.

•　•　•　•　•　•

A big break often implies that once you've achieved a certain milestone, everything falls into place. Life orders itself according to your whims. There is no more struggle, there is nothing left to want. There is no more rejection. This is a lovely, lovely fantasy bearing no resemblance to reality. And yet, I have noticed that my emails to certain key people in my professional life are answered with astonishing speed whereas they were once answered at a sedate and leisurely pace. There is more money in my bank account. I enjoy that.

·　·　·　·　·　·

I am thinking about success, ambition, and blackness. I am thinking about how breaking through while black is tempered by so much burden. Nothing exemplifies black success and ambition like Black History Month, a celebratory month I've come to dread as a time when people take an uncanny interest in sharing black-history facts to show how they are *not racist*. It's the month where we segregate some of history's most significant contributors as only black history instead of also being a part of American history. Each February, we hold up civil rights heroes and the black innovators and writers and artists who have made so much possible for this generation. We say, look at what the best of us have achieved. We conjure W. E. B. Du Bois, who once wrote, "The Negro race, like all races, is going to be saved by its exceptional men."

We ask so much of our exceptional men and women. We know all too well how we must be exceptional if we are to be anything at all.

Black History Month is important and a corrective to so much of America's fraught racial history. But in the twenty-first century, this quarantining of black ambition to one month when it can be recognized feels constraining and limiting rather than inspirational.

In the *Atlantic*, writer Ta-Nehisi Coates published an essay about President Barack Obama and the tradition of black politics that reached me in a vulnerable place.

Coates writes of the president's ascension, "He becomes a champion of black imagination, of black dreams and black possibilities."

In that same essay, Coates also writes about how the narrative of personal responsibility is a false one that is, unfortunately, often parroted by our president, our brightest shining star, Barack Obama, the first black president of the United States. At the end of his essay, Coates writes, "But I think history will also remember his [Obama's] unquestioning embrace of 'twice as good' in a country that has always given black people, even under his watch, half as much."

A month after that essay was published, Obama announced the My Brother's Keeper initiative, "an interagency effort to improve measurably the expected educational and life outcomes for and address the persistent opportunity gaps faced by boys and young men of color." The initiative is certainly well intended, but it speaks to the idea that black Americans must make themselves more respectable in order to matter. In its initial incarnation, it also gave the impression that only boys and men matter. On its surface, My Brother's Keeper is a program that does nothing to address the systemic and structural issues young men of color will face, no matter how well prepared or respectable or personally responsible they are.

I have come to realize how much I have, throughout my life, bought into the narrative of this alluring myth of personal responsibility and excellence. I realize how much I believe all good things will come if I—if we—just work hard enough. This attitude leaves me always relentless, always working hard enough and then harder still. I am ashamed that sometimes a part of me believes we, as a people, will be saved by those among us who are exceptional without considering who might pay the price for such salvation, or who would be left behind.

Du Bois was a vocal proponent of "the talented tenth," this idea that out of every ten black men, one was destined for greatness, destined to become the powerful leader black people needed to rise up and overcome and advance. This 10 percent of men were to be educated and mentored so they might become leaders, the front line for much needed sociopolitical change.

We often forget, though, who first came up with the "talented tenth." The idea first began circulating in the late 1800s, propagated by wealthy white liberals. The term itself was coined by Henry Lyman Morehouse, a white man, who wrote, "In the discussion concerning Negro education we should not forget the talented tenth man. . . . The tenth man, with superior natural endowments, symmetrically trained and highly developed, may become a mightier influence, a greater inspiration to others than all the other nine, or nine times nine like them."

Morehouse offered a somewhat repulsive proposition gilded in condescending intentions; he said, essentially, that if the strongest efforts were focused on the best of black folk, a few might be saved from themselves. Here we are today, still believing this could be true.

Before, since, and during Du Bois's time, the "Negro" has been a problem demanding a solution. Historically we are, of course, quick to neglect examining how this problem began. We are, it seems, still looking for that solution even as some declare the United States is embarking upon a post-racial era. We forget that we should not only measure black progress by the most visibly successful among us, but also by those who continue to be left behind.

．　．　．　．　．　●

When my novel came out, my book tour took me to thirteen cities, beginning in Boston. There I stayed in a hotel where my room had a fireplace that kept my feet warm and toasty. I marveled at this fireplace. I still had a lot of energy for my first event at Brookline Booksmith. I had not yet realized how much energy it takes, as an introvert, to fake extroversion. I was nervous during that first event but holding my book helped. Looking down at the words I had written helped. Seeing so many supportive people in the audience helped. The booksellers were a delight.

I was next off to New York, a city that is always intimidating and exhilarating to be in. There were two readings at independent bookstores. There was standing room only at both readings and deeply engaged audiences and people buying my book and asking me to sign those books. I would encounter more of the same in every city. There were reviews, mostly glowing, even in the *New York Times. Time* magazine declared, "Let this be the year of Roxane Gay." It all felt so extravagant.

And then my essay collection came out. The crowds at my readings swelled. People stand in hot rooms and then hot lines for an hour, sometimes two, just to meet me, shake my hand, pose for a picture, have a book signed. In Los Angeles, 450 people gave me a standing ovation, and the recognition nearly brought me to my knees because it was all so unexpected and gratifying.

Another reading, in another city, standing room only. During the Q & A, an older woman recounted a story of how she once couldn't get a credit card because she didn't have a husband. I think she said the year was 1969. I thought about her story all night and kept thinking, *May I be worthy of the work you have done to make my life possible.*

At that same reading, I met a seventeen-year-old girl named Teighlor whose mom brought her to the event. She sat near the front and her eyes were shining the whole time. I threw her a *Bad Feminist* tote bag, and she held it tightly in her hands. She was first in the signing line and told me how she looked up to me, and she was wholly adorable and I felt my eyes burning at the corners because I was so moved. I kept thinking, *May I be worthy of your respect and admiration.*

At that same reading, I met a young man named Robert who also brought his mother. She began speaking to me in Creole, so I responded in kind. They were Haitian, and they were just so excited to meet another Haitian from the Midwest. The bookstore had sold out of my book by that point, but they wanted to meet me anyway. They apologized, as if they owed me something. Their presence at my reading was all I could ever ask for. I gave them my personal copy of the book and signed it. They asked if they could take a picture with me and I kept thinking, *May I be worthy of your respect. May I be worthy of our people's history.*

There were so many encounters that night and on all the nights that made me think, *May I be worthy of all of this.*

And there is a part of me that realizes how hard I have worked for this, and that I have, in part, earned this.

My novel is in its fifth printing and is going to be made into a movie at a major studio. My essay collection is in its fifteenth printing. I am having a moment, and the burden of my ambition still has me wondering if I am worthy.

• • • • • •

For most of my life, I have taken for granted how my middle-class upbringing and my loving, educated, and involved parents made it possible for me to strive for excellence. Nearly everything has worked in my favor well beyond whatever natural gifts I possess. I attended excellent schools in safe, suburban neighborhoods with healthy tax bases. I went to Exeter for high school and then I was on to an Ivy League university. Along the way, I had teachers who encouraged my talent and creativity. I had parents who supplemented what I was learning in school with additional studies. It was very easy to buy into the narrative that exceptionalism would help me, and those who looked like me, to rise above the challenges we face as people of color. All I had to do was work and want hard enough because nothing in my life contradicted this belief.

All along, though, there were insistent reminders of how even with all these advantages, certain infrastructures, so profoundly shaped by racial inequality, would never willingly accommodate me or my experiences. I would never be able to work hard enough. I didn't have to be twice as good, I had to be four times as good, or even more. This is why I am relentless. This is why I am not satisfied and likely never will be.

In high school I was but one of a handful of black students, and even among them, I was a stranger in a strange land, a Midwestern transplant in the wilds of New Hampshire. At first, my cadre of fellow black students had little in common beyond the brownness of our skin but at least we had that much needed kinship because to the white students, we were usurpers, treading upon the hallowed ground to which only they, with their white skin, were entitled.

My senior year, I received an acceptance letter to Yale. I was in the campus mail room. Everyone was buzzing as they learned of their fate. I opened my letter and smiled. I had been accepted to all but one of the schools to which I applied. I allowed myself a quiet moment of celebration. A young white man next to me, the sort who played lacrosse, had not been accepted to his top choice, a school to which I had been accepted. He was instantly bitter. He sneered and muttered, "Affirmative action," as he walked away.

I had worked hard and it didn't matter. I was exceptional and it did not matter. In that moment, I was reminded of my place. I was reminded of why my ambition would never be sated, and would, instead, continue to grow ferociously. I hoped my ambition would grow so big I would be able to crowd out those who were unwilling to have me among them without realizing their acceptance should never have been my measure.

In college the situation was much the same. I belonged there, I had earned my place, but few people would acknowledge that belonging. Not a week went by when I or other students of color weren't stopped and asked to show our student IDs. It was easier to believe we were trespassing than simply traversing campus between classes. This was a small indignity but it wasn't.

At both my master's and doctoral institutions, I was the only black student. Any success I achieved only spurred me to work harder and harder so I might outrun whispers of affirmative action and the arrogant assumptions that I could not possibly belong in those institutions of supposedly higher learning.

Like many students of color, I spent a frustrating amount of time educating white people, my professors included, about their ignorance, or gritting my teeth when I did not have the energy. When race entered class discussions, all eyes turned to me as the expert on blackness or the designated spokesperson for my people. When racist "jokes" were made, I was supposed to either grin and bear it or turn the awkward incident into a teachable moment about difference, tolerance, and humor. When a doctoral classmate, who didn't realize I was in hearing range, told a group of our peers I was clearly the affirmative-action student, I had to pretend I felt nothing when no one contradicted her. Unfortunately, these anecdotes are dreadfully common, banal even, for people of color. Lest you think this is ancient history, I graduated with my PhD in December 2010.

• • • • • •

Today, I teach at Purdue University, where this semester I have only one student in each of my classes who looks like me. I previously taught at Eastern Illinois University where I was one of two black faculty members in my department, where there were five faculty of color in all. The more things change, the more they stay the same. This is the price of exceptionalism—you will always be the only one or one of a few. There are no safe harbors. There are no reflections of your experience.

I have written three books, have a fourth under contract,

and am working on three more. I have been widely published. I am regularly invited to read and speak all over the country. I advocate, as best I can, for the issues that matter most to me. As a feminist, I try to be intersectional in word and deed. When I fail, I try to learn from that failure instead of hiding it as I did in kindergarten.

I have achieved a modicum of success, but I never stop working. I never stop. I don't even feel the flush of pleasure I once did when I achieve a new milestone. I am having a moment, but I only want more. I need more. I cannot merely be good enough because I am chased by the pernicious whispers that I might only be "good enough for a black woman." There is the shame of sometimes believing they might be right because that's how profound racism in this country can break down any woman. I know I am one of the lucky ones because unlike far too many people of color, I had far more than half as much to work with, the whole of my life. It is often unbearable to consider what half as much to work with means for those who are doing their damnedest to make do. I call this ambition, but it's something much worse because it cannot ever be satisfied.

Escape Velocity

• • • • • • **CLAIRE VAYE WATKINS**

first met my seventeen-year-old self over email. "Hello," she wrote. "My name is Jo Longley and I am interested in signing up for the creative writing workshop. My full name is Jo Brooke Ann Longley, although that may be more information than necessary."

The creative writing workshop she mentions is the Mojave School, a free program my fiancé Derek and I are putting on this week in my hometown, Pahrump, Nevada.

A bit about Pahrump: The word "Pahrump" comes from the language of the Southern Paiutes. Like many place names in the Mojave Desert it basically means, "There's water here." Specifically, "water from the rock," meaning springs flowing up from underground aquifers. But yes, we're aware the word sounds like a bodily function.

Anyway, the town of Pahrump is about thirty-five thousand people sprayed across a long, hot valley with purple-black mountains all around it. The bottommost point of the valley is a crusty, white, dry lakebed, the scene of many car commercials and music videos wishing to convey freedom and/or desolation.

Over the mountains to the east is Las Vegas, sixty miles away. On a clear night you can see the city lights over the range, our neon aurora borealis. To the west, over another mountain range, is Death Valley. Pahrump is hot and dry as hell—over one hundred degrees the whole week we're here for the Mojave School. At one point, a guy at the laundromat says, "It reminds me of the Persian Gulf." It's a place where the boys become construction workers and the girls become cocktail waitresses. The sunsets are sublime.

A population of thirty-five thousand sounds like a lot. But those thirty-five thousand are scattered over more than three hundred and fifty square miles, so Pahrump still feels pretty small. Plenty of residents would disagree with that, remembering 1980, when only two thousand people lived here. Now, there are two stoplights, one public high school, but a lot of the roads are still dirt or gravel. Most of the houses are prefab mobile homes or straight-up trailers. In this town, there is a difference. The distinction between a mobile home and a trailer has to do with whether the home is on wheels *and* an apron of cinderblocks, or just wheels. (It's a subtle distinction, but an important one when you grow up here, like the difference between free and reduced-fee lunch: Free lunch means you're a scrounge, but reduced lunch means you're regular. No one here says "poor," and they certainly do not say "working class," "underserved," "economic inequality," or any of the other names for this place I learned in college.) There's a third type of house, which we call "stick-built," even though they're mostly stucco.

Most homes are set on big, unlandscaped patches of desert. The house I grew up in, 1600 Lola Lane, was a mobile home, three and a half acres shaped like Nevada with a beautiful, big cottonwood tree shuddering at the tip. I was on reduced lunch. The lots seem empty but they rarely are. Most yards are clustered with cars, both running and not, or horse corrals, or a cache of building materials, or mounds of unspread gravel, or other trailers, or a pen of peacocks or ostriches or wolf dogs. Pahrump has no mayor, no sewer system, no alleys, hardly any sidewalks. Until the 1960s, there were no telephones. The main drag is strewn with billboards featuring blondes beckoning men to strip clubs and brothels.

After Lola Lane, my family moved to a house on the south side, near the two brothels, the Chicken Ranch and Sheri's Ranch. I learned to parallel park at Sheri's. But before I could drive, my school bus passed the brothels every morning. It was a moment I waited for, a moment I loved, because of the Chicken Ranch. The Chicken Ranch is stick-built and painted pink and baby blue, with dormer windows and a white picket fence. As a girl, I'd never seen a house so beautiful. I wanted to live there.

· · · · · ·

Coming back to Pahrump as a visitor is weird. I don't have any family here anymore, so Derek and I stay at a motel that used to be an army barracks. It later became an hourly love motel in Las Vegas. Then the buildings were towed to Pahrump, and the love motel barracks became a Best Western. This narrative is proudly displayed in framed photos hanging in the lobby. Every morning before the workshop Derek and I eat our free continental breakfast in a NASCAR-themed casino that reeks of smoke from the night before. We eat surrounded by confounded European tourists on their way to Death Valley or Zion. We eat as fast as we can, in silence. It's the one truly depressing part of every day.

· · · · · ·

A lot of people think of Pahrump as a trap. More than a trap. They talk about it as if it has this mythic power to hold people here and drain them like a succubus. My old friend Jessica married an out-of-towner, which doesn't happen that much. He's from Oregon and his name is William. One night we smoked cigarettes and played video poker together at the casino where they met when Jessica was a cocktail waitress. Jessica told me how she wore two padded bras when she was waitressing, to make her look bustier, how it was worth it, even though it hurt like a mother. My grandmother used the same trick forty years earlier, working as a change girl at Caesar's Palace. You get better tips that way—the Pahrump version of "leaning in."

"What brought you to Pahrump?" I ask William.

"I hit a deer in Arizona," he said, "and my car finally broke down here."

Mr. Carlin, a math teacher, was the speaker at my high school graduation ceremony in 2002. He was a fantastic teacher and has since left Pahrump, as everyone expected he would. I remember his speech being very funny, which would have been characteristic of him. But the only specific line I can recall was the last one, which he delivered with sudden severity: "You don't have to go to college, but you can't stay here."

All to say, I think some of the students at the Mojave School are a little confused about why I'm back. Honestly, I'm a little confused, too. But perhaps no one is more confused than Jo Brooke Ann Longley.

"Pahrump's a black hole," Jo says. "Right now, I'm just so tired of it I don't understand why anyone would come back."

Jo Brooke Ann Longley says she's getting out and I believe her. A chronic overachiever, Jo's staggering ambition is exhausting even to relay: Jo skipped two grades. She started taking classes at the local community college when she was thirteen years old. She is now a seventeen-year-old college senior, and stalking a Fulbright.

She's always been like this. At five she wrote book reports for her kindergarten teacher. At six she was doing sixth-grade math at her brother's middle school. She's volunteered at the library and participates in about half a dozen church groups. She's worked as a barista and interned at the local electric company. She sometimes works nine or ten hours a day, four or five days a week. The other two days a week her mother drives her one and a half hours east, over the Spring Mountains to the University of Nevada, Las Vegas (UNLV) and back again. She's a full-time student at UNLV. She usually overloads, taking five classes a term. When I ask her why she takes so many classes, Jo says, "So I can graduate on time."

By "on time" she means by age eighteen. She has the crystal clear vision of what can happen to women that don't get out early. She has, I know without asking, her own Jessica, her own change-girl grandma. She was raised under those same billboards.

When we meet, she's enrolled in the Mojave School, taking summer classes, and working in the two jobs typical of girls not yet twenty-one: childcare and food service. At the day care where she works, she's typically responsible for about a dozen toddlers. "Every teenager should have to work in a day care," she says. "It's great birth control." She also holds down the fort at Seemore's, the two-story frozen yogurt stand shaped like a castle with a huge plaster dollop of cream on top, in a wide patch of desert astride one of Pahrump's two highways.

One day, Derek, my stepdad Ron, and I went to visit her at Seemore's. It was 102 degrees. We met her friend Anthony, who fed toffee soft-serve to the bold and probably diabetic ground squirrels skittering between the benches. We all pretended not to notice two drunk bikers making out nearby. This was not easy. You might think there's nothing grodier than two bikers sloppily making out, but that's only until those drunk bikers have been eating ice cream, and whenever the wind dies down you are reminded of this fact, aurally.

Earlier that day, I'd asked Jo if she was bored at the Mojave

School, which we set up for teenagers who'd never taken a creative writing class before, not college seniors majoring in it. "I feel like I do know a lot of what you guys are teaching," she said. "But my goal was to come here and try to get a recommendation letter from you and Derek."

This type of resume fluffing is expected from wide swaths of American teenagers, particularly affluent ones. But it doesn't really happen in Pahrump. When I asked one class at the Mojave School whether they wanted to go to college, every single one of them said, wholeheartedly and without hesitation,. "Yes!" But when I asked them *where*, their certainty crumbled. They said things like, "What's that one in Arizona, the Christian one?" Or, "Somewhere with a good ROTC." Two said the University of Washington, and when I asked them why they said that, they told me, "Because it's green up there." One girl told me, "I don't even know any names of any colleges, except Princeton, and I think there's one called Yale. . . . And isn't there an 'H' one?"

And then there's Jo, applying for a Fulbright for graduate school at Kingston University in London. She says it's okay that she's bored at the Mojave School because she just wanted to meet me "and make contacts in the creative writing world." That Jo is engaging in the kind of savvy careerism you'd expect to find at a prep school is anomalous and, to me, beguiling. There's something else alluring about Jo: certain hallmarks of Nevada femininity are conspicuously absent from her envisioned future—no padded bras digging into her, no children. I guess that's why I came to Seemore's.

Though I know it's corny and probably self-aggrandizing, I start to think Jo and I are versions of each other. I left Pahrump eleven years ago, to go to one of the two universities in Nevada. Jo goes to the other. We got the same scholarship, from a fund created when the state of Nevada sued the tobacco companies on behalf of Nevada children like me and Jo, who'd been sucking in casino smoke all our lives. Jo's an English major, like I was, and like me she has an emphasis in creative writing. We even look similar: short brunettes with heart-shaped faces, women you might call "cute" until we actually speak, a pair of dead-pan cherubs. I am Jo plus ten years and some cooling of my hyper-achievement engine. Jo is me, minus the fooling around up on Wheeler Pass Road.

Only a few kids get to college from Pahrump, and fewer graduate. Of everyone I went to school with, I only know of four of us who have gone on to graduate school. I'm the only girl. I have a theory that only two types of kids make it out: kids gunning for something and kids running away. I find myself transfixed by Jo's ambition. I want to know: Is she a gunner or a runner?

One day after class, on the NyECC campus where opportunity may or may not be, I ask Jo why she works so much. She has a full-ride scholarship, after all. "I've just always been obsessed with making my résumé top notch," she says. "Just the more things I can do to be impressive—it just helps me feel better. I also just like staying busy. If I'm bored, I find myself slowly eking into depression."

Why London, I wonder. Jo's never been, but she knows it's basically the exact cultural opposite of Pahrump: lots of people on a little bit of land, rainy and artsy. She says, "Growing up in Pahrump, I feel like I've sort of been denied access to a culture where if I wanted to I could just go out and see a play on the weekend. . . . In London, I know that there is not a weekend that I *couldn't* do that."

Another draw to London is YouTube. Jo's a YouTuber. Username, TheLittleStar89. "There're a lot of YouTubers based out of London," she says. "And they actually have a YouTube headquarters in London where YouTubers can go and make videos and stuff like that, which is really interesting and cool."

Another appealing thing about London, aside from YouTube

and being the exact opposite of Pahrump: It's fast. In the UK most master's programs only take a year or two.

What's the rush? I ask.

"It might just be a pride thing," she says. "I want to say, 'Yeah, I'm nineteen and I have my master's and I'm going into my doctorate program. Ha.'"

In my notebook I write, "gunner."

* * * * * *

After the last day of the workshop, Jo, Derek, and I go to a sandwich shop in a strip mall. I tell her my volleyball team used to come here for lunch on game days, that it still smells like volleyball in here. She looks a little disappointed to learn I used to be something of a jock.

Jo knows the people who keep coming in and out. The sun is blazing. In this cheery bread- and volleyball-smelling place, I meet my seventeen-year-old self's fear.

Between bites of a vegan avocado wrap, Jo says she feels like when we're young, we're fluid. We can change, try on new lives for ourselves. But at a certain point, we ossify, harden into adults and stay there. Like a game of musical chairs, except the music stops when you turn thirty and that's where you sit for the rest of your life. If you're not happy with that chair, too bad.

Intellectually, she knows that's probably not how it really works, right?

"Nah," I say, as though I didn't have that exact same fear at seventeen. As though I don't have it now, at twenty-nine. Still, she says, "It's hard to convince what's in my rib cage to believe what my head is telling it."

So sprinting through her education is Jo's way of buying herself time. This way she can spend ten years trying to be a writer, getting a PhD in literature, looking for a job in publishing. And if that falls through, she'll still only be twenty-four. She'll still have time to start over in psychology, maybe become a counselor.

She says, "My ultimate goal isn't to get so many doctorates. It's to find what makes me happy and to cling to it, cling to it with all my might." There's no hint of warm fuzzy self-discovery in her voice when she says this. There's urgency, and that fear.

So fear is driving Jo to London, and poetry, too.

She says, "Ever since Harry Potter, it's represented a kind of freedom to me. Because that's where he goes when he gets his letter: Diagon Alley. So it's just been built up in my mind. I just see a community where I have a part and will be able to express myself."

She can't do that in Pahrump, she says.

"For a few years now, London has sort of been my utopian destination where when I go there everything will be complete and beautiful and life will make sense.

"I've seen everybody who's left Pahrump and then they come back and they never quite get away again. And I'm so petrified that that's gonna be me, and I'm gonna be stuck in this place where I know I don't belong."

In Jo's family, a recurring joke goes, "We care about our children's education, so we moved to Pahrump!" Her dad tells stories about his own boyhood high jinks in another small town. He tells her, "That's why we moved here." But Jo says, "That's not what I have." In her dad's version, growing up in rural America was the time of his life. Jo says, "If this is the time of my life, shoot me."

Jo has no patience for nostalgia, her dad's or mine.

"Before graduation, everyone knows it. . . . If you don't leave at once or if you come back, you're never getting out." And then, she says, "You slowly lose your teeth and your sense of manners."

I remember that feeling, the town a succubus threatening to

sap you bone dry by nineteen. Perhaps hearing the monster in her voice, Jo says, "It's not bad or evil. It's just not a place that I've ever felt welcome."

"Me neither," I say. In my mind I cross out *gunner* and replace it with *runner.*

•   •   •   •   •   •

We all want to be gunners. Gunners are admirable, driven, heroic. But runners make shit happen. I know, because I'm a runner, too.

And this is when I admit to Jo that I've started to think of us as versions of each other. It's like I'm like you in twelve years, I say. Or you're like me twelve years ago. I'm embarrassed, suddenly. I feel cheesy, like a stage mom, or a character in an after-school special.

But Jo nods. "I've seen it too."

So I ask her what I've really been meaning to ask her all week: "Do you think that us leaving is a betrayal?"

She laughs. "To Pahrump? No."

"Do you think it's stupid that I feel that way?"

She says, politely, that she can see how I might look at it that way. But soon she says what she really thinks. "It's a town. It's not a person. It doesn't have feelings." She nods to the shop. "It's not a team."

I ask her if she thinks I'm just indulging in sentimental hand-wringing.

She says, without hesitation, "Yeah." This is what happens when you get to ask your seventeen-year-old self questions: she gets real with you.

I don't know why, but I confess to Jo that I feel like an outsider here, that I have all week. "Totally like I don't belong here."

She says, "Didn't you feel that way when you were living here?"

I admit that yes, I did.

"But before, I at least felt like I belonged in little tiny parts of it," I say. "Like my friend Ryan's swimming pool. Or in the living room with my mom, watching *Star Trek*. And now those places are gone."

She asks, "Why do you want to feel like you belong here?"

I tell her I don't want to be someone who doesn't belong here. "That would mean I've betrayed or turned my back on the people here, become aloof or selfish, struck out on my own, And all that's probably true."

She shakes her head no. "You're just not as good at pretending you belong here as you used to be."

      •   •   •   •   •   •

That night, the Mojave School students give a reading at a local coffee shop to celebrate the end of the workshop. My two oldest friends drive out from Vegas to listen. Ryan and Jason are twin brothers. Ryan is, as far as I know, the only person from our class to get a PhD. He's also the only person from Pahrump I'm still really genuinely close with. After the reading, I propose we go buy some beer from the grocery store. Jason doesn't want to go because he works as a checker at another store in the same chain in Vegas, and he hates it. But we go anyway. We have trouble finding our way around inside, even though it's the same store we walked countless times, the same store where we used to go fishing for booze, hanging around the parking lot with cash we'd earned at minimum wage, waiting for an adult shady enough to buy six bottles of Boone's Farm for three teenagers. We never waited long.

We do find beers and drink them beside the motel pool. The lights of the NASCAR-themed casino are bright as a full moon, and we pretend there is one. We talk about the swimming pool at Ryan and Jason's old house, the place I told Jo about. We talk about the juniper trees around the pool, which the new owners have cut down. We do not mention our mothers who both died here within a few months of each other, and in their dying left us with no reason to come back and every reason to keep running. We do not mention all the work we did to get out, all the distance we have traveled and want to travel still, except when Jason looks up at the would-be moon and says, "It's hard to reach escape velocity."

⬦ ⬦ ⬦ ⬦ ⬦ ⬦

Today, on the treadmill at the gym at the expensive university where I teach, I saw a T-shirt that could have been a poster on the wall at the NyECC. It said, "Effort Equals Success." I'm home now, back east, and Jo is probably at Seemore's with Anthony and the bikers and the ground squirrels. Seeing that T-shirt I thought, *What's it all for? UNLV. Kingston University. London. A job as an editor, or a counselor.*

It occurs to me that Jo is working really, really hard for a life most of my female students would consider Plan B.

⬦ ⬦ ⬦ ⬦ ⬦ ⬦

When Jo imagines herself in London, she's not at the Royal Shakespeare Theatre or YouTube headquarters, or in Diagon Alley. She's at home, alone, in a tiny apartment. "It's snug and bright and open," she says. "It's just me by myself in *my* apartment! . . . It's almost a studio, but the bedroom area and the kitchen are separated by a back room, and the wall in the back is an all-glass sliding door leading into a cute, little backyard. And it's just all bright and open, and my own color palette that I get to choose."

Jo's mom's a painter and so far she's been picking the colors.

"There's a cute little folding table," she says, "that comes down and up. And the kitchen is stocked with weird vegan ingredients that I won't feel weird having because it's my apartment, gosh darn it, and I can have whatever I want."

What color is it? I ask.

"It's a tealish blue, a coralish pink, a very light yellow, a light lavender, white. White is the main color with the other colors as accents. And silver."

A tealish blue, a coralish pink. They're the same colors as the Chicken Ranch. The colors I used to hold my breath for as the school bus passed. "Sounds pretty," I say.

Jo says, "It's gorgeous in my head."

• • • • • •

Is Jo hungry for London or running away from Pahrump?

Is there really a difference?

"Effort Equals Success." It's a fantastic idea. But it takes so much damn effort for someone like Jo to scrape and claw her way within the grasp of even a modest version of success. Meanwhile someone else, from another town, another class, can just reach out and take it.

Jason was right. It's hard to reach escape velocity. You need fuel. Dreams are fuel, sure. YouTube headquarters and Diagon Alley and Shakespeare. But if you've got a really long way to go, the best fuel is anger. If Jo had asked me how to get out, I might have said, "Learn to hate the place you're from." Get disgusted by the people who stay. Call them toothless. Call them speed freaks. Call them dirt farmers. Call them scrounge or townie or white trash. Learn how real college students talk, how they walk, what they read, and what they eat. Learn what they do for a living and where they go on vacation. Learn to care about what they care about. Learn to laugh at what they laugh at. When they ask, say you're from the middle of nowhere, or buttfuck Egypt, or Podunk, or Over the Hump in Pahrump the Dump.

Or don't say anything at all. Spend all the energy you have and more trying not to look like you come from here and then, one day, you won't.

Tap the bricks on the back wall of the Leaky Cauldron and one day you'll come back for a visit, and your stepdad will tell you over toffee ice cream how hurt he was to be the only white cab driver who didn't cross the picket line last month, how sad it made him that the guys he thought were his friends were scabs, and you'll struggle not to mention the matrix of domination or identity politics. You'll *genuinely struggle* just to say, "That sucks. I'm sorry."

One day you'll come back, pass out stories to a group of kids who are and are not just like you, and when you stretch across one you'll say, "Pardon my reach." And they will look at you like you are from another planet because, congratulations, you are.

But Jo didn't ask me how to get out. She had a different question for her future self: "What was the hardest part of leaving?"

I told her what no one told me, though I'm not sure that was a good idea. I told her, "I didn't know how hard it would be to get back." I told her that all those people behind you saying, go, go, go, well, if you listen, if you go, one day you turn around and they're gone. I tell her that when they're pushing you, they're pushing you away, too. I say she might spend the rest of her life trying to get back across the chasm she's leaping now. I don't know if she listened. I hope she didn't.

Single Lead*

● ● ● ● ● ● **BLAIR BRAVERMAN**

T he day after I first won a dogsled race, my kennel partner dumped me. At that point we had been teammates
for three years, ever since I showed up on his doorstep
one January night and introduced myself as another dogsledder.
Scott was thrilled, and welcoming. He was a big guy, heavy, and
had spent the past decade getting passed on the trail by young,
light women—"jockeys"—who had been picked by other mushers to run their dog teams. And now, here he was with a jockey
of his own. I was happy to play the part, taking over training for
the B-team dogs he didn't have time to run from his kennel of
twenty-three huskies. He was getting older, and had been hoping for a teammate; I was twenty-four and a student, not ready
for the responsibility of owning my own dogs. The arrangement
seemed perfect for both of us.

I had first learned to dogsled six years earlier, when I spent
a gap year at a boarding school in the Norwegian Arctic. Then,
like many mushers, I fell deeper into the sport by working for

---

* When a dog runs in front of the team alone, rather than with a partner.

other people—for men, mostly. I'd been a handler, an assistant who does everything from training dogs to scooping poop, chopping meat, repairing equipment, and helping out at races. I worked my way through different kennels in northern Norway and Alaska. Since most mushers are self-taught, every kennel has its own wildly different philosophies and techniques, and for a while I'd been happy to start over each time, relearning each musher's commands and strategies. I had worked for a second-place Iditarod finisher and a ten-time champion of the longest dogsled race in Europe, who gave me his bib: number thirty-seven, smeared with dirt and meat. But before meeting Scott, I'd never been given my own team to train. I'd never been given a chance to race.

That year Scott and I worked together nearly every day, running dogs and caring for them, cleaning the kennel, fund-raising, and eating his homemade tomato soup in the dark evenings after our training runs. With Scott's encouragement, I trained the B-team for short-distance races of twenty to forty miles. I would debut at a six-dog race in Wisconsin, forty miles split over two days. I told myself that I just wanted to try it. Dogsledding—in which nearly everything can and does go wrong, and problems have to be solved alone—had always scared me nearly as much as it captivated me, and the kindest goal I could make for myself was to cross the finish line with happy dogs, and myself and the sled in one piece.

Dogsled races start in total chaos and pass into silence, and this first race was no exception. My sweet, manic dogs skidded to the starting chute, held back by a half-dozen volunteers; the crowd cheered and lights flashed and the huskies leapt and screamed, throwing all their weight against the lines, desperate to start running. The sled shuddered with the force of the dogs, and the referee mouthed a countdown that could hardly be heard through the commotion. And then the moment came, and the volunteers let go, and we swept through the crowd and straight into the woods. Within a minute, the only sound was the whisper of sled runners on snow. My dogs' legs punched up and down like pistons as they charged down the trail.

It took a few minutes for my heart to stop pounding—for my adrenaline to calm as I settled into the cold and quiet of the run. I told myself I didn't care about the final score, that I'd take my time and focus on a clean run. But as my mind centered on the trail, I was gripped by another desire, one that honestly surprised me: I wanted to win. I wanted to tear around every corner, sprint up every hill, pass every single team that I could. I called up my dogs and leaned hard into the turns. Pretty soon we had passed three other teams. We were doing great.

Ten miles into the twenty-two-mile race, I was running behind the sled when my leg punched through the snow. The dogs didn't stop; I fell forward onto my stomach, the air knocked from my lungs, dragging behind the sled as it surged forward. For a while I tried to haul myself back up onto the runners, but my arms weren't strong enough, and I kept slipping. And since I'd spent plenty of time getting dragged behind a sled before, and the dogs were about to crest a long downhill that would break them into a sprint, I tried a technique that had worked for me in the past: I flipped the sled into a snowbank, hoping the resistance would slow the team long enough for me to climb back on.

Sure enough, the dogs stopped. I stood and was just flipping the sled upright again, trying to ignore the sting of snow down the front of my pants, when another team passed me. In that moment, my dogs took off after them—and I, unprepared and already shaky, lost grip of the sled and watched it disappear down the trail without me.

Letting go of the sled is one of the worst things a musher can do; in all my years of dogsledding, I had never lost a team before.

But I knew well what would happen. The dogs, who wanted only to run, would keep going—and I would wait here alone, knee-deep in the soft snow, without even the snowshoes I'd packed in the sled for emergencies, until somebody in town noticed I was missing and sent a snowmobile to pick me up. My first race, and my dogs would cross the finish line without me.

I started trudging down the trail, trying not to cry. Every few steps, the snow gave way beneath me, and I fell to my knees. But standing still was even more depressing than moving, no matter how slowly. So I staggered forward, trying not to think of my dogs, all the hours we'd trained, my friends waiting at the finish line. The sky was a crystal blue, light sparkling off the trees around me. A perfect day to drive dogs, if only I'd had them.

And then, up ahead, I heard barking. I started running through the snow and came around a corner—and there was my team.

Another musher—all I could see of him was his bib number, thirty-two—had stopped his dogs and mine as well, and was waiting on the trail for me. I was so grateful I could hardly speak, but he waved off my thanks. My team followed his for a while, and then his dogs kicked up a gear and we fell back, and I had never been happier to stand solidly on a sled, with my beautiful dogs, passing through the woods. We finished close to last, but that day it didn't matter.

After that first race, I became more determined to prove myself. I studied strategy, canine psychology, nutrition. I trained out of Scott's kennel every afternoon, and over the rest of the winter, I finished two more races in the middle of the pack: nothing too great, but not embarrassing either. And when Scott took me aside at the end of the season and asked me to be his kennel partner—an equal in the operation—I accepted the position with honor.

Scott still had his first pick of dogs; I built my B-team from his rejects. But the dogs were strong. As soon as the first snows fell, I ran them on twelve-, twenty-, or thirty-mile runs almost every day, seeking out the hilliest terrain, tucking weights in the sled to build up their stamina. I worked with the dogs one-on-one, too, teaching them to lead the team and to respond to increasingly subtle commands. By the time the next season of races started up, in January, we'd be more than prepared.

I knew my B-team was fast, but it never occurred to me that they were faster than Scott's A-team. I never felt that he and I were competing against each other. We were partners, and he'd been in it longer, and I felt that my job was to help him win—and to do as well as I could for myself, too. Number thirty-two had taught me that I never wanted to win at the expense of helping out other mushers—it felt like we were all on the same side, pushing through the wilderness together. I'd also started dreaming about longer races, more demanding tests of skill, but Scott told me I wasn't ready for them. I wasn't sure if I believed him—I suspected that *he* wasn't interested in longer races and didn't want me to progress without him—but it wasn't worth arguing.

That year, in the first race of the season, I finished ahead of him. I didn't even mean to. I came around the bend toward the finish line and spotted his team there at the side of the trail, and though I slowed to wait, he waved me past him. That night, for the first time ever after a race, he didn't congratulate me.

Two weeks later, at the next race, we flew—I could feel the energy of the dogs, fit and joyful, running a steady gallop mile after mile. The wind burned my nose and cheeks. I knew before finishing that we were on fire; and sure enough, we finished in first place of out twenty-two teams, finishing the forty-mile course in three hours, fifteen minutes and fifty-seven seconds. The next day Scott called me on the phone and told me we were over. "It's not because you beat me," he kept saying, though I hadn't said anything. Anyway, it made him look good: a first-ever first place from his kennel. But something irrevocable had changed. Maybe he sensed that I won for myself and not for him. "This is a disaster," he told me, before forbidding me from ever his visiting his dogs again—the B-team dogs I'd been working with daily for two and a half years, who I loved as I had never loved dogs before. There was only one more race in the season, a one-stage forty-miler that I'd already registered and paid for, and that my parents had bought plane tickets to come watch. Scott smirked: "That's not my problem."

His sudden anger shocked me. But when I talked to a few friends, other female mushers, none of them were the least bit surprised: every single one of them had a similar story involving male mushers they had worked for. It seemed like my situation was actually pretty typical.

Dogsledding is one of the only sports—along with sailing and equestrian—where men and women compete against each other. As such, it's been lauded as one of the friendliest sports for women. And that's true, to a degree. With the dogs pulling the weight, it could seem that physical differences among the mushers are less important than in other sports; what matters are endurance, connection with the dogs, tolerance of extreme cold, the ability to keep a cool head while alone in the wilderness. A team sport where only one member of the team is human. It seems like an equal playing field, or at least about as equal as a sport can get.

And yet the higher one goes in the sport, the fewer women there are. Women make up around half of the participants in entry-level races, but by the 1,000-mile Iditarod, 75 percent of the finishers are men. The pure sexism is predictable: I've had friends get offered knee pads to give blow jobs in the snow, or encounter male mushers who refuse to let them pass on the trail. World champion Sigrid Ekran tells stories of men saying her voice was too high for the dogs to listen to, or that she'd never be able to handle herself in the cold. I suspect most female mushers have heard those things; I certainly have. Dogsledding is a microcosm of sexism in an old-school, underdog culture, but it's also an opportunity—for the wild, for the hardworking, for animal lovers who would challenge themselves and rather be out in nature with a pack of dogs than deal with other people. It's a hell of a sport for ambitious women.

But many of them don't get a chance to prove their naysayers wrong. It seems that most women remain handlers; or they get dogs but don't race; or they race, but they don't rise through the levels. I suspect this has to do with the fact that it's a very hard sport to do without assistance. Straight male mushers typically have a built-in handler in their female partner; at a public marriage proposal before one race start, as the musher kneeled before his girlfriend, a friend paraphrased the proposal: "Be my handler for life, wife." A wife's support is assumed. But I have female friends, serious mushers, whose husbands don't even come to their races.

I'm lucky. My boyfriend—now my fiancé—is my handler, and his support is uncomplicated: he loves being part of my team. But still, people tend to assume that he's the musher of the two of us. Race volunteers report to him, and hide their surprise when he points them in my direction. And when he says he's my handler, the amount of praise he receives is unsettling to both of us. Together we built a small kennel of six dogs on farmland in northern Wisconsin, along a network of forest service trails that stretch for hundreds of miles. When an Iditarod musher who was getting out of the sport offered me his kennel—fifteen more brilliant dogs, all his equipment, and a shitload of both responsibility and opportunities—I weighed my options, swallowed hard, and said yes.

I've been thinking about what it means to be "good" at this

sport, and what I am and have been working toward. For a long time, as I trained, my idea of good was never measured against anyone else. The truth is that dogsledding, even competitive dogsledding, has little to do with opponents. It's about hours or days alone on the trail, collaborating with—never controlling—six or ten or sixteen huskies, dealing with factors like thin ice and blizzards and errant moose. Making judgments in extreme situations, when your body is so numb that it's hard to think. It's about dogs that love nothing more than running, and the chance to come along for the ride.

I used to dream, when I started mushing, of a single clean run. That was all I wanted. If I could have had just one clean run—without a tangle, or a dogfight, or crashing into a tree, or getting stuck in deep snow, or encountering wildlife—then I could finally prove myself. However much I loved it, dogsledding seemed fraught with problems, thick with adrenaline; it was terrifying to have to rely on myself in an emergency.

Last year, I looked back on that dream. It seemed then that most of my runs were clean; I couldn't remember the last time I'd encountered any problem that really stuck with me. But I realized that I still had all of the difficulties I'd been afraid of when I first started out. Dogs got tangled, or they tried to chase deer in the forest, or I went the wrong way. Sled handles broke off in my hands. The change, I realized, wasn't that I had learned to avoid problems. It was that the things that used to seem like problems no longer did. Now, I just dealt with them and moved on.

I thought that my goal was to trust my experience, and to be able to run dogs simply and without fear. And now I can do those things, and rather than relax in that comfort, I'm preparing for longer races, more difficult journeys—challenges that terrify me anew. I'm moving back toward the kind of fear that

I was finally beginning to outgrow. Stepping past my comfort zone, even as that comfort zone grows.

And I'm immensely proud of that. Proud of all I've learned, and all the places that my dogs and I are going. I want to race because I want to keep learning, and to build my connection with my team, and to keep pushing into that fear, and to experience all the joy and power and grace that comes with it. This winter I'm training for a ten-day, 350-mile race, working toward it as hard as I can. And if I win, I'll be nobody's jockey.

The Chang Girls

● ● ● ● ● ● **LAN SAMANTHA CHANG**

My mother's father died the year she finished high school; she arrived in Cedar Rapids, Iowa, from China later that year with two suitcases and a dictionary. My father left his family at eighteen, escaping the Japanese occupation on foot. He never returned to his home. In the turbulence of postwar China, his mother and father vanished behind the Communists' "bamboo curtain," and he never saw them again. My parents met and married during the 1950s, in New York.

My sisters and I were launched into our American lives on the rocket fuel of my parents' hope and desperation. If they had given birth to a boy! Ah, but they had not; instead, they had four daughters. It is impossible to know what our lives would have been like if we had had a brother. Possibly the brother would have been singled out as a focus for my parents' dreams. Perhaps we girls would have been encouraged to stay close to home, taught in a thousand little ways to understand that we were secondary, and that any worldly goals of ours were not important. But there was no boy; we were "the Chang girls." The four of us were brought up with the understanding that we would someday leave our small Midwestern town. We were to plant ourselves far away in larger, more bustling places, saplings from the family tree, and to grow the Changs into an American dynasty.

Our parents expected us to be strong, accomplished, and capable. Their word for capable, *nenggan*, translates as "can-do." To make certain that we would never feel as helpless as she had as a newborn immigrant, our mother taught us practical skills. We learned to sew, beginning by threading a needle and continuing on the machine to seams, darts, hems, and facings. We spent many hours in the kitchen learning how to use a knife and the specific ways to cut each vegetable. Our mother believed that confidence in the basics would empower us and make us independent. At dinner, our father held forth on his somewhat skeptical views of office politics and the American economy in an attempt, I think, to plant our feet on the ground and dispel any idealistic notions we might have. Our parents' *nenggan* was a kind of smarts unrelated to school, a savviness. But of course, we were all expected to excel in school too. For the most part, we did. We became honor roll girls, all four of us earning scholarships to Ivy League colleges, all four of us finishing an Ivy League professional and graduate degree. Meanwhile, our parents became feminists. "In this country, every woman must be able to earn a good living," our father told us.

There were no complicated feelings, and no double messages, about ambition. Hesitation and ambivalence, it seems, are of concern only to people who hold the hope of meeting some ideal of American womanhood or possess the approval of authority, privilege. In other words, people who have something to lose. We could no more achieve the ideal of American womanhood through our choices about careers and families than we could the ideal of American beauty. In the seventies, the ideal American woman was the frost-maned Farrah Fawcett. One look in the mirror at our black hair, brown skin, and slanted eyes freed us from the necessity, and the possibility, of striving in her direction. Our ambition was unencumbered by reluctance.

The Chang girls were the only Asian girls in Appleton, Wisconsin. We looked through a plate-glass window at our small-town society with the studious curiosity of newcomers, outsiders. We observed the doctors' daughters, who every holiday helped their mothers decorate hundreds of elaborate Christmas cookies. The working-class girls, who went bowling and whose parents worked in the mill. The rich girls. The loose girls. The deliberately eccentric girls. On Wednesday afternoons, everyone went to catechism. Our parents were Buddhists. There was no model for us, no parental encouragement that we should buy into what my father called "small-town potato thinking." Moreover, we had no choice but to hold fast to our ambition: Without the impulse to strive, to bring ourselves up, we would have had no other options. We were sustained by the knowledge that we had nothing to fall back on.

Every morning, our father rose shortly after six o'clock and made each of us a fried egg, served with soy sauce. He claimed that eggs were the best food for fueling our brains. He drove my oldest sister to high school on his way to work. The rest of us finished breakfast before turning to homework or musical instruments. My mother practiced the violin with my sister and me every day: forty-five minutes before school and more in the evening. She had been trained on the piano and she coached us, sounding out the notes. Over time, she was able to earn a degree in piano pedagogy and work from home as an instructor of children.

The development of her career as a teacher, beginning with one student and building to a weekly workload of more than sixty students before her health eventually failed her, was a success story we all watched unfold over the years. She believed that no child was unteachable: She coached a mentally disabled girl from "Twinkle, Twinkle, Little Star" to a Beethoven sonatina. She brought flocks of students each year to the state piano competitions, and many earned first place. Every few years, she was able to afford a better piano, and in 1985, she purchased a Steinway grand piano for our living room. But she was not entirely satisfied with these accomplishments. In her darker moments, she thought of her own life as a cautionary tale. "My problem is that I didn't have a plan," she sometimes said to me when we were alone, sewing or ironing (our preferred household tasks). "I could have had a different career." She was proud of her domestic skills but never idealized her years at home with us when we were babies and toddlers. "I was so bored with small kids, at home, alone," she told me.

Our mother's teaching money made it possible for our parents to pay for our own music lessons, clothing, and small allowances when we left home for college. Our parents had a plan for each of us: good grades, a good college most likely far from home, then medical school. But perhaps they'd trained us too much toward independence. As it turned out, we all invented our own narratives. My sister, Tai, the oldest, was in the basement of our house in the late 1960s, watching television, when she saw the woman she wanted to be.

"It was the *GE College Bowl*," she explained recently to me, "one of my favorite shows." Our father approved of this program, a quiz show that pitted students from different colleges against one another. He believed it valorized education, intelligence, hard work. "This was one of few things that Dad let me watch because he thought it would be inspiration to do well," my sister said. "And it was—but not in the way he thought." On the *GE College Bowl*, the contestants sat behind rows of high podiums, visible only from the shoulders up. Most of the contestants, my sister said, were men, many wearing glasses. On the night my sister found her ambition, there was only one female contestant, and she caught Tai's attention.

"There was something about her," my sister said. "All of the men wore suits with skinny ties and white shirts. I'm sure she had on a twin set. I'm sure she was wearing a string of pearls. She was very pretty; she was very feminine, but it had nothing to do with a man. She was extremely well spoken and she was more put together than many of the people I'd seen on *College Bowl*. I thought: I want to be that person. I didn't want to be on the *College Bowl*. I just wanted to be that person. I think I largely did become that person."

A few years later, my sister found her way out of Appleton. Her chance came in the form of a homemaker test, sponsored by Betty Crocker. My sister, a crafty seamstress who made most of her own clothes, decided to take the test, she says, to avoid a pop quiz in advanced biology. She became the Wisconsin state winner and traveled to Washington, DC, where her eyes were opened to the possibilities of American life. "I don't think the trip changed me, per se, but I did get a preview of the future: fifty super-smart, geographically diverse, interesting people and not a single home ec major amongst us."

At Yale she met and mingled with just exactly the kind of women she had seen on the *College Bowl*—immaculate, poised, feminine, brainy—and she did become one of them. Forty-five years later, my sister has just retired after a long and successful career as an attorney. She brought up her family in Manhattan, and her three children are attending good colleges.

My second sister, Tina, was a high achiever since grade school. In one of my most vivid early memories of Tina, she is bent over a ruled notebook, carefully writing each cursive letter of the alphabet (lower and uppercase) dozens of times. She had been told she had messy handwriting and was determined to correct it. She is now a physician—as my parents had hoped—a rheumatologist with perfect penmanship.

My younger sister, Ling, attained the highest level of education of our group. She earned multiple graduate degrees. She made up her mind not to become a medical doctor, earning instead a doctorate in psychology. She is highly *nenggan,* and she has also taken on the values of the girls we observed back at home: She's an expert cookie baker, a devoted wife and friend, and a former beauty pageant contestant.

The significance of leaving home, the value of a good education, the study of a profession: all of these are part of a traditional American immigrant story. Although it respects the past, this narrative is forward-looking. Ambition is a given. Tai says, "I don't think there's anything complicated about ambition. It's only about desire." I asked her why she thought the issue might be a complex thing for some people. She replied that perhaps there is so much ambivalence about ambition because "maybe some people don't have desire, and they want to have desire. That's when it gets complicated. If you don't want anything, then you won't have ambition because ambition is about wanting something."

My sister's definition of desire seems to cancel out any possibility of ambivalence. In her mind, it seems, desire means wanting something so much that one is willing to pursue it utterly and disregard potential obstacles.

This was true in my own experience. My clearest ambitions stemmed directly from a childhood deprived of space and privacy. The seven of us—my maternal grandmother, my mother and father, my three sisters, and I—lived in a three-bedroom house. The six females shared the full bathroom and my father, the sole male, commandeered the half bath. Held securely in the middle of this group of very passionate, verbal people, surrounded at all times, with no privacy except sometimes during the midday when I was able to lock myself in the bathroom to think or read, I wanted to become a writer. What luxury!—to sit alone, in the pleasure of solitude, and think for a living. Since early childhood, I felt a powerful desire to make things and an equally powerful desire to be unanswerable to any person or rule. I was drawn to words and stories because they created a private space for me, however imaginary; I sought an inner life because there were limited resources for having an outer one.

Throughout my formative years, my dream was precious to me. It helped me to distinguish what I truly wanted from what I was told—even by my parents—that I should want. It helped me to define what happiness might mean. It was, always, the purest form of desire.

Many books I read and loved as a child and adolescent—written by Laura Ingalls Wilder, Louisa May Alcott, Willa Cather—were about young American women who sought education and accomplishment of some kind and went on to achieve it. I was inspired that Laura Ingalls and Jo March, also from families of four sisters, grew up to become novelists. As I myself turned to writing, one of my favorite novels was Cather's *Song of the Lark*—an entirely unapologetic Künstlerroman about the oldest daughter from a large family in a Colorado mining town who grows up to become a world-class opera singer. Thea Kronborg aims for greatness—and so focused is the novel on her development as a singer that Cather later added the ending of the romantic subplot as an afterthought.

Ultimately, my parents' focus on our education, determination, and development as human beings made it possible for me to rebel, to stand up to them when I realized that they would never approve of my desire to become a writer. Inspired, perhaps, by my parents' break with China, their focus on independence, even their isolation, I abandoned their plan for me even in the face of their disapproval and dismay. It would be years before I saw their quandary: that by wishing achievement in a foreign country for their children, they were in some ways pushing their children away from themselves and their own dreams. But I had to make my own way. I had nothing else. The writer and editor William Maxwell once said that deprivation is the key: "It's deprivation that makes people writers, if they have it in them to be a writer." Perhaps growing up in a life that was so bare and clean made ambition one of the few pleasures I could afford.

Over five decades, my sisters and I assembled an armory of *nenggan*, wit, advanced degrees, ruthlessness, and volition. My parents' initial hopes and fears for us evolved from anxiety (when we left school and made our ways into the world) to relief (when we began to marry and have children) and, finally, to pride. We fulfilled our parents' wishes for us, perhaps in ways they had not expected.

A few years ago, the four of us returned to Appleton for my mother's memorial service. Tina, who had been a ferociously devoted medical advocate for my mother until she died, planned a beautiful event, which was attended by hundreds, including a formidable family contingent—poised and well turned out, visual evidence of our American success. My sisters and I each delivered a eulogy. Tai was witty and incisive; Tina was heartfelt; Ling was eloquent and moving. As each of my sisters spoke, I felt her invincibility fill the room. The loss of our mother was a terrible blow, but she had ensured that we would survive.

My father, now ninety-four years old, keeps a careful eye on his six grandchildren. He's particularly aware of his three granddaughters. He doesn't hang the same desperate hopes on them as he did on his own children. He doesn't need to.

Sometimes I wonder what this will mean for them: Will the next generation of women in our family forget the Chang girls' pure faith in ambition? Will growing up with so much to lose quell our daughters' desires, make them unsure of what they want or timid about getting it?

Not if we have anything to say about it.

Goal Your Own Way

●　●　●　●　●　●　**EVANY THOMAS**

When I was growing up, my mom's big goal in life was to get me to figure out my big goal in life. She checked self-help books out of the library for me, supplied me with fresh journals for recording my hopes for the future, and signed me up for weird goal-setting classes at the local community college. But no matter how much I tried to visualize Future Evany raising a "First Place at Life" trophy triumphantly into the air, I could not for the life of me imagine what I could ever do to earn it.

I would have loved to be one of those people who grow up knowing exactly where they wanted life to take them. The Olympic gymnast who started cartwheeling before she could walk. The little girl who tells everyone who'll listen that she wants to be an astronaut when she grows up, and look: fifteen years later she's in orbit, her hair floating weightless behind her.

But the closest I ever got to setting a life goal was "Have goals someday." (My mom's response: epic motherly sighhhhhh. . . .) But I meant it. My inability to set goals always felt like a freaky deficiency in me, and I was uncomfortably sure it meant I wouldn't be able to succeed at anything. As I learned in weird goal-setting class, people who write down their goals are ten times more likely to achieve them. And oh how I wished I could take advantage of that ten-times-goal payoff promise!

Strain as I might, the clear life vision I so hoped for never materialized. I'm not sure if this ambition constipation was some kind of innate intellectual shortcoming, or whether it was pure youthful rebellion. Maybe if my mother hadn't been quite so keen to have her daughter dream big, I wouldn't have resisted it quite so much? Or maybe there was some sort of gross growing-up-female thing going on, where I subconsciously suppressed any budding ambitions because ambitious women are frowned upon.

Whatever the cause, my shortcomings in the goal-setting department stuck with me my whole life. It's become one of the ways I define myself—as the many bosses I've had over the years can corroborate. I always assumed that at some point in my career, I'd find a solid groove and the path forward would finally be clear. But it hasn't happened yet. And as I slide into legit middle age, I am pretty sure it never will. But now I've finally accumulated enough past to be able to look back and see that I've done okay even without the goals.

I had a baby late in life at age thirty-nine—nine pounds four ounces and twenty-nine hours of labor and no painkillers—which I must say is very ambitious. Then I managed, as an ancient, sleep-deprived new mother, to land a widely coveted, competitive job at male- and youth-dominated Facebook. Three years later, I parlayed my work at Facebook into a job at Pinterest, another we-only-hire-the-best tech giant. I've spoken at conferences attended by paying professionals and written industry think pieces that received multiple likes from people who aren't my mother. All things I achieved without ever setting out to do so.

Looking back on my successes, I see patterns emerge. The things I'm proudest of are the outcomes of my own set of personal rules, which I've evolved over the years as my own special brand of ersatz ambition. Shine a flashlight into the cobwebby space behind my face, and these are the eight guiding truths you'll see crawling around in the darkness.

Evany axiom #1—Listen to your rat brain

If you imagine the path of the typical goal-driven person's success story as one steady diagonal line rising ever upward, then my career path would look more like a random series of lines bouncing off the sides (Waitressing! No wait, advertising! No wait, advice columning! No wait, tech!), criss-crossing each other as if drawn by a child learning how to make a star. By not having a long-term game plan, I have the flexibility to jump on any interesting opportunities that come my way.

I know an opportunity is "interesting" when my rat brain, the part of me that sees and smells something tasty and runs through the maze to get it, starts squeaking: *What if I don't do this thing? What if someone else comes along and does it instead and it turns out awesome, and I'm left feeling all jealous and riddled with regret?* My rat brain has an almost superstitious dread of missing out.

When I first got wind of a job opening at Facebook (from a friend's post *on Facebook*, fittingly enough), my rat brain hummed. It was 2010, and the already-epic social network was the most promising pre-IPO place to work in all of Silicon Valley, and pretty much everyone in tech was trying to friend their way into a job. Also: free tampons.

I pounced. I spent three hours updating my résumé and two more writing the perfect cover letter. One phone screen with the recruiter led to a phone call from the head of the team, which led to an invitation to come in and deliver an on-site presentation, for which I spent a good twenty hours preparing and practicing. After my presentation, I had five one-on-one interviews, followed by an invitation to do some freelance work, followed by one final one-on-one with a very important VP and . . . pow! Six months later, they offered me the job. So *easy!* But by that point, I wasn't even sure if I should take it.

Evany axiom #2—Do the terrifying thing

The champagne bubbles were still bubbling over my hard-won Facebook job offer when the yays suddenly curdled to terror. Gahhhh, what was I thinking?! I had a sleep-depriving new baby on my hands. I'd done the startup thing in my twenties, and then again in my thirties, and I had the pink slips to show for it. The job I already had (working on the website for Wells Fargo bank) was safe and reliable, with a sane 9 AM to 5 PM schedule. Facebook, it was already clear, was more of a clock-rounding 9 AM to 9 AM kind of deal. Then there was the commute, which was an epic two and a half hours *each way.*

During one of my many, many interviews at Facebook, a bright-faced twenty-nothing designer asked me, "You work at Wells Fargo, right? I bet you can't wait to get out of there!" I just laughed. Like pretty much everyone I met at Facebook, he was young enough that I could have been his mother, like with years to spare. No, none of these kids were parents. They had no context as to why, after a lifetime of leaping, I'd suddenly pause now.

But then one of the dodo-rare parents of Facebook reached out. She was my would-be grand boss (boss of my boss), and she was older than almost everyone at Facebook (though still younger than me). In the soothing tones of a rescuer trying to talk someone off a ledge, she explained how she would leave every day at 5:30 PM, and that the time between when she got home and her kid went to bed was sacred—no one at work could reach her. It was only after bedtime that she would plug back in. She was reassuring proof that it could be done. I didn't know it then, but this was the trickle-down influence of Sheryl Sandberg, Facebook's chief operating officer and future author of the best-selling, how-to success book for women, *Lean In*.

What decided it was my looming fortieth birthday. As the clock ticked down on my thirties, it dawned on me that the chances of an opportunity like this coming around again were slim. Like the vanishing "pops" in a pot of popcorn on the stove, tech opportunities for people in middle age are observably few and far between. Like it or not, this could be my last chance to leap. Yes, I was a parent now, but did that mean my life of pinballing from one interesting opportunity to the next was truly over? Were my rat brain years behind me, or was there still juice left in this orange? This was my ultimate lean-in moment, before I'd even heard of leaning in.

I took the job.

Evany axiom #3—Always ask

Before I signed on the dotted line with Facebook, I negotiated for more stock and more salary, citing my bouncing new baby and new grown-up familial obligations as my rationale.

Far too few women do this, but after having it beaten into my brain during my four years at the women's college Mills, I know that one of the main reasons women don't get paid as well as men is that they simply fail to ask for more. So I've made it a lifelong practice to always ask—even if they say no, you've already cracked the door open to future discussions: "Let's revisit it again at my three-month review."

When I later went to work at Pinterest, I did the same thing. Only this time, I told them I'd just finished reading *Lean In*, and for the good and fairness of womankind, I simply had to ask for more. The recruiter laughed. And then she came back with a better offer.

A word of warning: If you're thinking of negotiating your next salary (and you should), make sure you head into battle armored with a firm number (based on well-researched competitive salary information), convincing arguments about the value you bring, and an unshakable confidence (imagine the most self-assured man you've ever known). Infuriating though it may be, studies show that when women ask for more, they risk being perceived as *too* ambitious. Much like the line between sexy and sexist in *This Is Spinal Tap,* the line between too much ambition and not enough can be mighty wobbly. Self-advocacy within a rigged system is a tricky proposition for sure.

Evany axiom #4—Use your fear

Many women suffer from wanting to be liked, and I'm right there at the front of the line. I'm like a tightly folded paper note with "Do you like me?" written inside, followed by checkboxes next to Y and N (please check Y!).

But while this fear of disappointing people—my parents, my boss, my friends, the editor of this piece, even myself—is the thing that wakes me up at night, it's also one of the most powerfully motivating forces I know. I've accomplished a lot of great things out of this fear of letting people down.

During my first six months at Facebook, I was in pure fight or flight. I worried that by negotiating for more money I'd inflated people's expectations so much that there was no way I could avoid letting them down.

I worried that I'd disappoint my husband, who had quit his job to be a stay-at-home dad so we could make my new crazy job with its crazy schedule work for our little family.

I worried that I wouldn't have an impact. Facebook is the kind of place where until you prove your worth, people don't even listen to you. So I said yes to every project, threw elbows to get into every meeting, publicized every win. When I discovered one of my teams had been meeting without me, I walked over to the impossibly young product manager's desk, leaned down, and said, "Dude! Why don't you like me back!?" Startled, he just sort of half smiled in confusion. "Bad decisions are being made," I said ominously. "You need to start including me!" I was in that next meeting.

I combated the crushing fear-of-disappointment insomnia with unimaginable amounts of coffee and drew upon every ounce of high school drama class to passably appear calm and in control. Slllllllllowly I got a feel for the work, and my confidence started to build.

It was the hardest job I've ever had, and also one of the best. It was like being enrolled in a crazily demanding PhD program, with the world's oddest assortment of lecturers. President Obama came and spoke during my tenure at Facebook. George W. Bush and Al Gore. Oprah. Gloria Steinem, too.

Gloria came for the annual women's leadership day, and I ran into her in the bathroom talking to COO Sheryl about breast pumps. Sheryl was saying how she used to pump during conference calls back at Google, and every once in a while someone would ask about the noise, and she'd tell them it was a fire truck outside. "My breast pump actually used to talk to me," I said. "The rhythmic shuffling would tell me to 'go home, go home.'" Gloria laughed. Sheryl laughed. This feminist daughter of a feminist mother glowed.

I worked hard. I helped build new features, and rebuild old ones. I was on the team that launched the Messenger app, the Groups feature, and the Facebook timeline profile. I worked to simplify Facebook's privacy settings (hoo boy). And that was all in the first few months. When I was at Wells Fargo, my team didn't complete anything the entire first year I was there. At Facebook, my desk was fifty feet from Mark Zuckerberg's digs, a window-to-window terrarium space where he held his reviews. I learned firsthand that one single "that sounds reasonable" from Zuck was the highest, most golden blessing, worthy of a full round of team high fives. The sheer force of my insistence that people like me back gave me what I needed to succeed at the job.

Evany axiom #5—Talk about the feelings

When something feels weird or wrong or unfair, my need to speak up has always bordered on the compulsive. Luckily the tech industry's love affair with "transparency" and "authenticity" and "saying the hard thing" has given me a natural podium for all my truth talking. And sometimes this need to speak up leads to good things.

Every woman I know who works in tech has a story about what it's like to be the only woman in a room full of young, hyper-driven men. They interrupt you. They repeat the thing you said that everyone ignored, and suddenly everyone thinks it's genius. But I don't just roll my eyes in silence, like so many women do. I roll my eyes and yell, "It sounded way better when I said it!"

Or like the time I was hunkered down in a war room at Facebook (war rooms being where a whole team clumps together in a room and works around the clock until their project ships), and someone had lined the walls with a dozen or so of Facebook's famous Russian constructivist motivational propaganda posters. All the posters had "PUSH" written in big red letters.

There were about ten of us there in the room, and everyone else but me was a dude, all of them under the age of twenty-five.

"Have any of you," I said to the room at large, looking around at the walls, "given birth to a baby before?"

A couple of the guys looked up from their screens, and I heard someone mutter an uncertain "Noooo . . . ?"

"Because if you'd ever spent twenty-nine hours in labor like I did, these PUSH posters . . . they sure do bring something else to mind."

An uncomfortable silence settled over the room.

"You know," I mused, "we should stop calling these 'war rooms' altogether and call them 'womb rooms' instead. It's a better metaphor, seeing as wombs actually produce something good. War is just about destruction and death and waste . . ."

One by one, they turned back to their keyboards, and the room returned to its quiet concert of clicking. I didn't get the feeling they were with me in my crusade to shoot down our warring words and breath new life into our company's go-to mctaphors.

But you never could tell. I haven't worked at Facebook in more than three years now, but a friend who's still there recently sent me a photo of a sign on the door of a war room. Someone had crossed out the war and changed it to *womb*.

Evany axiom #6—Be your own imaginary friend

Every six months during my last ten years working at three different companies, I've been forced to come up with a new set of career goals for myself and then assess my progress against them. It's part of the job. Any promotion or raise I get depends on checking off these boxes. Of course with my goal-setting hang-ups, each time goal season comes around, it fills me with the kind of dread usually reserved for confronting unresolved childhood issues. (*Huh!*)

The only way I get through it is by treating the whole process like a creative writing exercise, using the prompt, "Imagine a woman like me, at this advanced stage of her career, working as she does in the high-pressure world of tech: What kind of goals might such an accomplished person set for herself? How has she triumphed in the past? What evidence can you produce of how her wisdom and experience have paid off? If you were to shout this fine woman's story from the mountaintops, what would you say?" And then I proceed to type together a rousing tale of the many ambitious plans and accomplishments of this amazing woman named Evany Thomas. And the feedback from all my many bosses has been closer to the yay end of the spectrum than the nay, so I guess my imaginary version of myself does indeed get the job done!

Evany axiom #7—Follow the good people

The first job I ever had was when I was sixteen, and I worked at the tiny one-screen town movie theater in Sausalito, California. Any kid who has worked in a movie theater will tell you, it's the best job in the world. Free movies, all the popcorn you could cram into your popcorn hole, and endless hours of downtime to sit and chat with other people who love to sit and chat.

My high school friends and I all worked at the theater together. For three dollars and fifteen cents an hour, we sat around in our flammable orange-and-brown polyester uniforms, quoting our favorite movies, playing drinking straws like flutes, and dreaming up elaborate ways to get a fake ID. ("First we find the county records office, then we request a copy of the birth certificate for some dead baby born before 1965, *then* we take it to the DMV and use it to take the driver's test!") I loved that job so much. I'd even go in on nights I wasn't working.

For me, it's always been about the people I work with. When I went to college, I asked around until I found the school's best teachers, then I signed up for every class they taught. It didn't really matter much what they were teaching because a great teacher can make any topic interesting. And in the years since, I've tried to use that same tactic to find jobs. I seek out funny people, smart people, people I admire and who can teach me things and who bring out the best in me. And once I find good people, I follow them wherever they go. It's like finding a good vein of cookie dough in a pint of ice cream: You just keep mining it until it runs out.

That's how I got my job at Pinterest: Some of the people I loved working with at Facebook peeled off to start up Pinterest, and I followed closely behind to see where this new lesson could take us.

Evany axiom #8—Steer your story

As a wise Facebook boss once told me, it helps if you think about yourself as the protagonist in your own life. The narratives we tell about ourselves are powerful things. We get to decide what stories we tell, and whether we're starring in a comedy or a drama.

And I decided: I want mine to be a comedy. No matter how many stresses and sadnesses circumstance serves up, there's always something absurd to be found mixed in with the shittiness. And that ability to see the other side—the funny in the sadness—gives everything added dimension, and makes each experience feel more worthwhile.

Even if I'm crying in the bathroom at the office, an ultimate work low, there's still something certifiably comedic to be found in it.

Sometimes when the conflicting lava-hot passions of the people I work with boil to the surface, or the frustrations of last-second course corrections mount, or the *long* hours start to add up, the urge to rage-fatigue cry sweeps over me. So I scuttle off to the bathroom to weep in peace without freaking out my coworkers, or confusing them into thinking I'm unstable. It always leaves me feeling calmer and ready to head back into the fray and be productive again.

The moment itself—quietly boohooing in the tableau of free tampons, toothbrushes, and mouthwash, the automatic flusher blasting off beneath me every time I reach for more tissue—is its own little slice of sadlariousness to add to my story.

The story took on more meaning when my coworkers and I went to a "team-building offsite" at a bar. And because it was Facebook, home to some of the most competitive people on earth, the day was set up as a battle—who can mix the best drink and name it the best name? When my team mixed up a ruinously sweet vodka-citrus-syrup thing, I suggested we call it "Crying in the Bathroom." All the dudes on our team just turned and looked at me, confused, all "I don't get it" and "What does that even mean?" They had no idea. And there was something sad about that, all those men missing out on such a great way to siphon stress.

Months later, I shared the story with Sheryl, also a self-confessed work crier. I told her about mixing drinks, and how my "Crying in the Bathroom" suggestion boggled all the men on the team, so completely unaware were they of the phenomenon, or the need for it. "What can we do to get more of these poor guys crying in the bathroom?" I asked her. "I think they could really benefit from blowing off the steam."

This is how I've gotten to where I am today: seeking out humor, truth, and good people in the daily act of working. I still can't say with absolute clarity that I want to be an Olympic astronaut gymnast, or even a COO, but what I want—interesting problems, inspiring people, chances to steer old conversations in new directions—is happening all around me, all the time.

Sheryl laughed. "I'm going to use that story," she said. And I thought, *And I'm going to use this story about how you used MY story in this here comedy of life I'm starring in.*

Let the credits roll.

Astronauts

• • • • • • **NADIA P. MANZOOR**

I was five years old when I revealed my biggest aspiration to my father, Abbu. I wanted to become an astronaut. I remember his forehead creasing, him slowly folding his newspaper to look at me. "Women can't be astronauts," he said with a thick Pakistani accent. "Beta, who will cook? Who will clean? Who will feed your husband if you are floating about in space?"

I looked at my mother, Ammi, for support. She stood in front of the stove, blue-checkered apron tied around her slim waist, laughing as she stirred one of her famous pots of *biryani*. "Parvez, your *roti* has gotten cold! Uff, now you will be late for office! Take *my* hot *roti,* I will eat cold one." With one hand she cooked; with the other she served, and if she'd had a third hand, it would have sat supportively on Abbu's shoulder at all times.

Ammi was the embodiment of female sacrifice. Someone who had left her education at nineteen, walked away from her love of painting, put aside her athletic aspirations, and put on an apron. She cooked and she cleaned, and she found joy in the accomplishments of her family. I was meant to walk in the footsteps of my mother. Space travel aside, my only worthy ambition was in becoming a bride.

When I was seven, we flew to Pakistan to attend my uncle's wedding. Abbu felt it was important for me to see my destiny in the flesh, for me to experience what a woman who maintained beauty could look forward to. I remember seeing the bride for the first time, seated on a golden throne, surrounded by draped, white silk. She was decked out like a Christmas tree on crack, a goddess. Long red fingernails, and lips that shimmered like a fish, but her eyes remained glued to the floor. "Abbu, why won't she look at us?"

Abbu explained that she was a modest bride, her eyes meant only for her husband. "Nadia, one day this will be you. On a stage, everybody looking at you!" I stared at her, feeling a mixture of awe and boredom, for reasons that I didn't yet understand. Here she was, the most desired object in the room, hundreds of guests leering at my uncle's prized possession, and throughout it all she had nothing to say. I wanted her to speak to me and tell me what it was like to be a real-life "princess," but she remained silent, her long eyelashes fluttering. Like my mother, her voice had been stifled for that of a larger cultural purpose, to maintain the traditional notion of "woman."

Since the only goal I was supposed to realize was marriage, the skill set encouraged by my father was maintaining the size of my ass. He was often snatching pieces of fried *pakoras* away from me, and plopping them into his own mouth. "No one wants to marry a potato!" he would say. Even though by the age of ten, I could entertain my family for hours with dramatized storytelling and impersonations of most of my relatives, Abbu never focused on any of my actual abilities.

My twin brother Khurram, however, was being raised for world domination. While he memorized all the capitals of the world, reciting his multiplication tables backward, and shouting out political terms in Mandarin, I was learning how to ration my daily food allowance. If I became too round and too fat, I would be sucked into the black hole where oversized female fruit went to rot. All I had to do was stay thin and trim like a carrot, tamed and predictable like a parrot, and I too could occupy that bridal throne, be on that most coveted stage.

Although I understood my traditional future as inevitable, it made me want to eat my own tongue. I hated helping Ammi in the kitchen, dicing tomatoes and cucumbers for the *raita*. I didn't know how to cook a delicately seasoned curry; I just knew how to scoff one down, and burp silently afterward. I didn't want to spend the rest of my life preparing food for men. I wanted to play the "guess the capitals" game with Abbu, learn foreign gibberish, and run wildly outside on the football pitch with my friends, possibly topless. I wanted to live.

> *Dear Diary,*
>
> *I want to fly into the sky and taste the clouds and dive into the sea, and meet God, if he still lives there, although sometimes I think he's a she and she actually lives in the mountains, but that's not what the Koran says so I must be wrong.*
>
> *I wish Ammi and Abbu would just let me have a proper paper round, that way I could bike around and give people their news, then they would read about the world because I had been at their doorstep, and it would be a real job.*

My father recoiled at the idea that I, his fifteen-year-old daughter, the good Pakistani girl, would ever want a job. When my white friends got jobs in cafés and doctors' offices, I pretended to work, acting out scenes of being a retail clerk in my bedroom. I spent hours putting on different personas, imagining myself as different women, all free to make their own choices, all living out their own dreams. The more my parents prevented me from experiencing seemingly normal activities, the more I found escape through my imagination.

When my high school offered me a summer expedition to Ecuador, I thought my time for independence had arrived. We were promised adventurous trekking up dormant volcanoes, digging a water drainage system for the locals, and immersive Spanish lessons. It was guaranteed to be the best trip of my life. I wanted to fund-raise alongside my peers and demonstrate my own physical aptitude in the fitness tests, but Abbu had different ideas.

"It's not healthy for a girl to know too much about being alone. Independence is a Western concept!" I looked at Ammi, expecting her support. I knew she shared my own adventurous spirit. "Jaanu, but what will I do without you? I will miss you too much. In our culture girls don't do such risks."

In our culture, girls didn't seem to do much of anything. Everything I wanted was always seen through the lens of how it would impact my husband. I hated being seen as a conduit for making a man's life better. I wanted the freedom to do whatever I liked, the way my brother was permitted. He was being pushed into exciting school trips and extracurricular activities; he was being pushed into becoming a fully experienced, confident human being. He was taught adventure, and I was taught to venture home, always home.

I didn't have the words then to articulate the clear injustice of how my brother and I were raised; I just knew I didn't like it. But the repeated roadblocks put up by my father began to wear on me, and I started to accept our apparent gender-based differences. I genuinely believed that I was not as physically or intellectually capable as my brother.

I accepted the constant refusal from my parents for independence because I understood that in my community there was no space for such a girl. Pakistani girls didn't go against their families. Pakistani girls that did usually ended up alone or dead. Although I was never in fear for my life, honor killings in the West are a very real thing. That women can be killed by their own families for having ambition, for wanting something more from their lives, speaks directly to the amount of silenced dreams among us.

My parents wouldn't have killed me, but they would have abandoned me, and that was a burden I didn't understand how to handle. There were no examples of women from within my community who had done it differently, chosen to live for something other than family. My aunties and older female cousins hadn't begun to reorient themselves economically or socially, and so for me the lack of role models was terrifying. I had no one to impersonate. The only options outside of "wifedom" always came from the Western outsiders, the ones I was constantly warned about. "Beta, these white women all have babies out of wedlock, and then their husbands all leave them because they are selfish. Just look at the divorce rate in the West, huh? All because women want to work!"

As my parents' hold on me tightened, my dreams and aspirations for a different life continued to boil inside me. I couldn't stop thinking about all the possibilities for my future; of all things I could accomplish, of all the potential people I could impact. If I was only given the chance.

At eighteen, I thought I had finally figured out who I was meant to be. "Doctor!?" Abbu exclaimed. "But that is seven years of your life. No one will marry you when you are twenty-five!"

I wanted to be a doctor. It felt like a noble profession. I'd walk through a hospital in a white coat, saving people from life-threatening diseases, giving renewed hope to families. "If you are floating about in Africa, trying to heal the world, your children will go hungry and die!" Abbu insisted that I study psychology, so I could better understand the needs of the pious Muslim husband he would select for me once I graduated. Apparently, studying human behavior would improve my marriageability. Yet again, I was taught that learning how to support men was more important than learning how to support myself. I walked away from my dream to study medicine and signed up for a degree in psychology. The subject of my studies became less interesting to me because I had no power over choosing it. The only thing I cared about was the opportunity to leave. I convinced myself that I needed just three years of freedom—meeting new people, learning about the world, partying—and I would then return home and marry whomever my parents had selected.

Being a good Muslim woman at an English university took effort. One night, in an attempt to fit in with my new cool friends, I found myself in an Irish bar, knocking back vodbulls, dancing awkwardly to Oasis, and eventually throwing up all over my Converse sneakers. It was the bartender who saved me. He carried my limp body back to my all-female dorm, put me to bed, and left a handwritten sonnet under my pillow.

In the following months, I felt like I was living in a water-color painting. The bartender, Brendan, visited me every night with freshly picked roses and foil-wrapped mints. He told me he missed his family and wanted to earn enough money to buy his parents a house. I told him I wasn't allowed to talk to boys, and that I dreamt of doing something meaningful with my life. It was the first time I let a man touch me without feeling afraid or aware of my need for modesty.

My father had so feared this—that I would become loose, drunk, and English; that I would lose my way. He wanted me safe, tucked away under his guidance. I was becoming the west-ernized girl Abbu had always feared, and I loved it. Everything about this new experience of love was alive, and I felt like I was finally spinning in the direction I wanted to go in, one in which I could make my own choices. It was liberating. What became scary to me was the future. Now that I had witnessed what living independently could mean for me, I didn't know how I would reconcile my family with my freedom. How was I supposed to navigate the rest of my life?

In the midst of my mind-blowing love affair with Brendan and with the uncovering of my new self, Ammi was diagnosed with breast cancer.

. . . . . .

I sat with Ammi, night after night in her hospital room, feeding her mashed sweet potato and listening to her breathe. I could feel her changing. More and more her gaze would wander out of the window, staring for hours into the distance.

"Ammi, what are you looking at?" I wanted to see what she saw. "Ammi!" I almost shouted at her. "Look at me! I'm right here!" I shook violently at the realization that my mother was leaving. She turned to me slowly, a soft smile appearing on her face. "Nado, my sweet Nado, maybe . . . maybe we can all be astronauts?"

When Ammi took her last breath, my twin brother and I sat beside her. It's hard to describe how that immediate burst of grief flows over you, where half your body is no longer in the room, transcended to another realm it seems, like a hovering translucent balloon. The other half of you, stuck to the walls, like mud. I couldn't tell if I was floating or falling.

After Ammi died, the fabric of my family, of everything I knew and understood fell apart, and I didn't know how to repair the fractured fragments of myself, let alone of anybody else, and so I left. I was barely twenty. The good Pakistani daughter would have stayed with her family and supported them in their grief. She would have understood her obligation. But I wasn't a good Pakistani girl—I didn't know who I was.

For the next ten years, I was lost. My ambition had always

been denied, and in my solitary struggle to find it, I couldn't. I didn't have the tools to manage the new freedom I had. I worked different jobs and studied various subjects but nothing seemed to ever take shape. I was taught to always live in the shadows of someone more powerful, and I struggled to find power in my own life. I lied about the shitty relationships to my family, lied to my friends about why my body had started to look like that of a skeleton, and lied to myself about why I had stopped dreaming. It wasn't until I could barely look at my reflection in the mirror that I had to reach deeply inside and pull out the lost seed of desire.

I started writing in my diary again. I filled journal after journal with what could have been, working through the guilt of my mother's death and the shame of leaving my family.

Those diary pages allowed me to see myself, and the more I wrote, the more I wanted to share it with others, and when my writing group urged me to tell my story of a traditional woman who struggled to find her own freedom, I listened.

The first time I performed, my acclaimed one-woman show, *Burq Off!*, the Black Box Theatre in the East Village was sold out. Jewel-toned fabrics hung behind me, like the insides of a Bollywood circus tent. Draped elegantly, falling into pleats, like my mother's saris used to. My hair was tightly pulled back into a French braid, with black high-tops on my feet and a red scarf wrapped around my neck. For ninety minutes, I transformed into the twenty-one characters of my past, taking the audience on a journey about a little Pakistani girl who dreamt of becoming an astronaut.

Not once did my eyes look to the floor like a modest Pakistani bride. They were wide open and staring into the eyes of my audience, taking them all in. It was the first time I had been on a stage performing something I had written, something I had spent months rehearsing, and although every cell in my body was jumping with fear, it also felt perfect. There were moments where I left my body and watched myself perform, but throughout it all, as I told my story to hundreds of people, I knew that that stage was exactly where I was meant to be. I couldn't believe it. I was a performer. Everything just made sense.

During the standing ovation, Abbu, who was sitting in the front row walked up to me on stage, a bouquet of flowers in his hands. "Nadia, I am so proud of you. Look what you have done."

• • • • • •

Recently, while I was on the phone with my twin brother, he said something that shook me: "Nadia, as soon as people don't feel that they're needed anymore, they die. That's what happened to Ammi. Don't let that happen to you." It sounded severe, but it also vibrated with truth. Our ambition, our desire for definition and recognition is essentially us creating our own need in the world, our own space, and our own truth. I always wanted something big to need me. It wasn't enough for me to only be needed by my husband and children, and because my community didn't support that, I had to create a new space for my existence. I had to create a new need. My ambition wasn't to become *something* necessarily, like a doctor or an astronaut or even a performer; those ideas were goalposts in my attempt to self-define. My biggest desire was to become myself.

After the first run of *Burq Off!*, I told my team that we must take the show to as many places as possible, that it needs to become recognizable in its own right. I wanted to go on a world tour. They thought I was delusional. How could a brand-new performer with no industry support take her one-woman show on a world tour? After fifty shows and two continents later, I've made a believer out of my team and more importantly out of myself. Turns out Abbu was right: I was meant to be on stage, just not the one he had in mind.

The Snarling Girl:
Notes on Ambition

● ● ● ● ● ● **ELISA ALBERT**

A funny thing happened when I published my first book, more again when I published the second, and still more yet again with the third: People began to treat me differently. The typical exchange opens with a disinterested "What do you do?"

"I'm a writer," I say.

Here a very subtle sneer: "That's nice. Have you published anything?"

"Yup." I offer up my abridged CV.

Suddenly they stand up a little straighter. A light goes on in their eyes.

A moment earlier they were talking to nobody, a *nothing*, but *now* they're speaking with *somebody*, a person who *matters*.

"Wow," they say. "That's amazing." And sometimes: "I always wanted to write a book." And sometimes: "I have a great idea for a book." And sometimes: "Maybe you could help me write my book."

This dynamic awakens a ferocious dormant animal, a snarling girl with a big mouth, too smart for her own good, nothing to lose, suffering privately. She's me at fifteen, more or less. When she is ready to stop suffering privately, she'll become a writer.

Oh *really*, she says. *Now* I matter? Wrong, motherfucker: I mattered *before*. (Also: Nope, can't help you write your book, best of luck.)

She's a little trigger-happy, this snarling girl. She is often accused of "not living up to her potential." She is neither inspired by nor impressed with prep school. The college admissions race leaves her cold. Her overbearing mother berates her about crappy grades and lack of ambition. (O-ho, the snarling girl says, you want to see lack of ambition? I'll show you lack of ambition!) Where she is expected to go right, she makes a habit of veering left. She is not popular, not likely to succeed. Her salvation arrives (maybe you saw this coming) in the form of books, movies, music. She obsessively follows the trail of breadcrumbs they leave behind. Here is a neat kind of power: She can be her own curator. She can find her way from one sustaining voice to another, sniffing out what's true, what's real. In her notebooks she copies out passages from novels, essays, poems, and songs. She Sharpies the especially resonant bits on her bedroom walls. This is how she learns to trust herself. No easy feat. These are epigraphs to the as yet unwritten book of her life, rehearsals for the senior page she is keen to assemble. These stories and lines and lyrics are companionship, proof that the universe is much, much bigger than her radioactive family and rich bitch west LA and Hebrew school and Zionist summer camp. Behold: She is not crazy! She is not alone! She is not a freak! Or, rather: She *is* crazy, she *is* alone, she *is* a freak, in the glorious company of all these *other* crazy, lonely, amazing freaks.

Here are her notebooks, all in a row.

They live in my little study now, above shelves full of my

books, galleys, audiobooks, foreign editions, literary journals, anthologies, Literary Death Match Champion medal, a plethora of newspapers and magazines in which I'm celebrated as this amazing thing: a writer. A novelist. Legit. But witness, please, no coincidence, the notebooks occupy top shelf, *above* that stuff. Spiral-bound, leather-bound, fabric-bound, black, pink, green, floral. *This Notebook Belongs to*: **Elisa Albert**, neatly printed in the earliest, **1992.** Fake it till you make it, girl! The notebooks have seniority. Here is how she began to forge a system of belief and belonging, to say nothing of a career. Am I aggrandizing her? Probably. I am just so goddamn proud of her.

· · · · · •

Ambition. The word itself makes me want to run and hide. It's got some inexorable pejorative stench to it, why is that? I've been avoiding this essay like the plague. I'd so much rather be writing my novel, my silly secret sacred new novel, which will take a while, during which time I will not garner new followers nor see my name in the paper nor seek an advance from the publisher nor revel in the hearts and likes and dings and dongs that are supposed to keep my carnivorous cancerous ego afloat. I will simply do my work. Hole up with family and friends, live in the world as best I can, and do my work.

The work: This is what I would like to talk about—the work, *not* the hearts and likes and dings and dongs. And maybe I can float the possibility that the work is best done nowhere near the hearts and likes and dings and dongs. Maybe I can suggest that there is plenty of time for the hearts and likes and dings and dongs once the work is done, and done well. Maybe I can ever so gently point out that a lot of people seem addicted to the hearts and likes and dings and dongs, and seem to talk about and around writing a hell of a lot more than they actually do it.

Maybe we can even talk about how some self-promote so extensively and shamelessly and heedlessly and artlessly that their very names become shorthand for *how not to be*.

I mean: ambition *to what?* Toward what? For what? In the service of what? Endless schmoozing and worrying and self-promotion and maniac flattery and status anxiety and name-dropping are available to all of us in any artistic endeavor. But the competitive edge is depressing. That thinly (or not at all) disguised desire to *win*. To best her or him or her or him, sell more, publish more, own the Internet, occupy more front tables, get tagged, have the most followers, be loudest, assume some throne. Is it because we want to believe that we are in charge of our destiny, and that if "things" aren't "happening" for us, we are failing to, like, "manifest"? Or is it because we are misguided enough to think that external validation is what counts? Or is it because of some core narcissistic injury, some failure of love we carry around like a latent virus?

Perhaps it's because knocking on doors like we're running for office is a lot easier and simpler than sitting alone with our thoughts and knowledge and experience and expertise and perspective, and struggling to shape all that into exactly the right form, during which process we take the terrible chance that we might get it right and still *no one will care*. Maybe we are misguided enough to believe that what's most important *is* that people care, *regardless* of whether or not we get it exactly right. Maybe getting it right doesn't even *matter* if no one cares. Maybe *not* getting it right doesn't matter if *everyone* cares. If I write an excellent book and it's not a bestseller, did I write the excellent book? If I write a middling book and it *is* a bestseller, does that make it an excellent book? If I wander around looking for it on bookstore shelves so I can photograph it and post it online, have I done good? If I publish a book and don't heavily promote it, did I really publish a book at all!?

Here is what we know for sure: There is no end to want. Want is a vast universe within other vast universes. There is always more, and more again. There are prizes and grants and fellowships and lists and reviews and recognitions that elude us, mysterious invitations to take up residence at a castle in Italy. One can make a life out of focusing on what one does not have, but that's no way to live. A seat at the table is plenty. (But is it a *good* seat? At which end of the table? Alongside whom!?) A seat at the table means we are free to do our work. What a fantastic privilege.

Feeling like one does not have "enough" of something (money, status, power, fame, recognition, shoes, name it): that's where every kind of terrible shit starts. And the benchmarks of success constantly shift. Ambition is a fool's game, and its rewards fool's gold. Who is happy, asks the Talmud? She who is happy with what she has.

Fine, okay, but I've been publishing for a decade now. When my first book came out, I was a wreck. I smoothed my dress and crossed my legs and waited smugly for my whole life to change. I looked obsessively at rankings, reviews. Social media wasn't yet a thing, but I made it my business to pay very close attention to reception. I was hyperaware of everything said, everything not said. The positive stuff puffed me right up, and I lay awake at night in a grip of fury about the negative. You see this a lot with first timers. It's kind of cute, from afar. *Do I matter? Do I matter? Do I matter?* Rookie mistakes. What's sad is when you see it with second, third, fourth timers. Because that hunger for validation, for hearts and likes and blings and blongs, is supposed to be shed like skin.

· · · · · ·

Ambition: *an earnest desire for some type of achievement or distinction, as power, honor, fame, or wealth, and the willingness to strive for its attainment.* Note: We are not speaking here about trying to pay our bills, have a decent place to live, buy decent food, access decent health care, get a decent education. For the purposes of this particular discussion, those fundamentals are assumed. And there's nothing in there about spiritual betterment, social service, love, or happiness. The entire concept can therefore be seen as anti-feminist. I believe an ideal matriarchy would concern itself exclusively with the *quality* of our days. Wither the collective desire to make life better for *everyone*? Ambition is egotistical, because it is by definition about being in service of the self, which has never, not once in the history of humanity (can you tell I've not bothered to read Ayn Rand?), made anyone anywhere "happy."

Anyway, haven't we collectively imbibed sufficient narrative about the perils of success and fame, already? Haven't we seen how fame can destroy and corrupt, how ambition and greed are twins? How recognition can pervert and compromise? We're all struggling with our own unique little demon conglomerate, and we all have some good luck and some bad luck. Nobody can tell you how to be happy because being happy is one of those things you figure out *by figuring it out*, no shortcuts. Or maybe you don't figure it out, maybe you never figure it out, but that's on you. Everything worthwhile is a sort of secret, anyway, not to be bought or sold, just rooted out painstakingly, one little life at a time.

● ● ● ● ● ●

I'm searching the old notebooks for one quote in particular, though. It came flooding back soon after I accepted this hellacious assignment. (I mean, women and ambition!? Too vast and complex. What the hell can possibly be said? Women: Be more like men! Lean this way! Lean that way! Lean sideways! Pick a direction and contort yourselves heroically toward it at any cost! Never give in, never surrender! You are entitled to dominate! You owe it to all women! Don't tell us what to do! Hear us roar! I dunno, you guys. I do not know.)

It's a line from an essay by Christine Doza in an anthology called *Listen Up: Voices from the Next Feminist Generation*: "When I was little I wanted to be the president, a firewoman, a teacher, a cheerleader, and a writer. Now all I want is to be happy. And left alone. And I want to know who I am in the context of a world full of hate and domination."

I find Doza online and message her: "Are you the same Christine Doza who wrote 'Bloodlines' in *Listen Up: Voices from the Next Feminist Generation*?"

I want to include her in this narrative. I want to let her know how much her essay continues to mean to me, twenty years later. She's not a "famous writer." I can find nothing she's published since that essay. But I want to tell her how forcefully she (still!) resonates when I am asked to formally consider the topic of women and ambition. She managed to articulate something difficult, profound, and specific (which is hard and rare), and in so doing, she gave me a gift. A jumping-off point. Affirmation. Recognition. A clear-eyed dispatch from further on up the road. Fate brought my eyeballs and her words together, the end.

She never responds. I wonder what her deal is. Whatever.

Maybe my great ambition, such as it is, is to refrain from engagement with systems that purport to tell me what I'm worth compared to anyone else. Maybe my great ambition is to steer clear of systems. Any systems. All systems. (Please like and share this essay if you agree!) What I would like to say is *Lean In* my hairy Jewish ass.

•　•　•　•　•　•

My mother was one of eight women in the UCLA Law School class of 1965. A lot of professors and students treated them horribly, those eight women, because they were "taking up a space a man could have had." Appalling, right? Except, uh, it's true: My mother did not actually want to be a lawyer. Her parents wanted her to be a lawyer. It was fairly radical of her to become a lawyer. She is badass by nature. But she didn't really want to be a lawyer.

Upon graduation, those eight got together and decided to just ask interviewing firms outright: *Do you hire women?* Legend has it one honcho stroked his chin thoughtfully and replied, with no apparent maliciousness, "Well, we hired a cripple last year."

She practiced law for a total of about one year before she got married and had kids and settled into the kind of furious soul-eating misery that is the hallmark of thwarted women everywhere, from kitchens and gardens to boardrooms and private jets and absolutely everywhere in between. To this day, if a stranger at a party asks her what she does, she'll lift her chin in a gesture I intimately recognize as *Don't Fuck With Me*, and say, with cement grit and dirt and bone shard in her voice: "I'm an attorney."

And isn't everything we do, everything we reach for, everything we grab at, each of us in turn, a way of struggling onto that ledge, that mythical resting place on which no one can fuck with us? *Don't Fuck With Me* seems as good a feminist anthem for the twenty-first century as any.

But the mythical resting place is . . . mythical. And trying to generalize about ambition is like comparing apples and oranges and bananas and flowers and weeds and dirt and compost and kiwi and kumquat and squash blossoms and tomatoes and annuals and perennials and sunshine and worms. Wanting to be first in your class is and is not like wanting a Ferrari is and is not like being the first in your family to go to college is and is not like wanting to get into Harvard/Iowa/Yaddo is and is not like wanting to summer on Martha's Vineyard is and is not like wanting to rub elbows with fancy folk is and is not like wanting to shatter a glass ceiling is and is not like wanting to write a lasting work of genius with which no one can quibble. Our contexts are not the same, our struggles are not the same, and so our rebellions and complacencies and conformities and compromises cannot be compared. But the fact remains: Whatever impresses you illuminates your ambition.

* * * * * *

Some ambition is banal: Rich spouse. Thigh gap. Gold-buckle shoes. Quilted Chanel. Penthouse. Windowed office. Address. Notoriety. Ten thousand followers. One hundred thousand followers. Bestseller list. Editor in chief. Face on billboard. One million dollars. One million followers. There are ways of working toward these things, clear examples of how it can be done. Programs, degrees, seminars, diets, schemes, connections, conferences. Hands to shake, ladders to climb. If you are smart, if you are savvy, who's to stop you? Godspeed and good luck. I hope you get what you want, and when you do, I hope you aren't disappointed. Remember the famous curse? May you get absolutely everything you want.

Here's what impresses me: Sangfroid. Good health. The ability to float softly with an iron core through Ashtanga primary series. Eye contact. Self-possession. Loyalty. Boundaries. Good posture. Moderation. Restraint. Laugh lines. Gardening. Activism. Originality. Kindness. Self-awareness. Simple food, prepared with love. Style. Hope. Grace. Aging. Humility. Nurturance. Learning from mistakes. Moving on. Letting go. Forms of practice, in other words. Constant, ongoing work. No end point to be found. Not goal-oriented, not gendered. Idiosyncratic and pretty much impossible to monetize.

I mean: What kind of *person* are you? What kind of craft have you honed? What is my experience of looking into your eyes, of being around you? Are you at home in your body? Can you sit still? Do you make me laugh? Can you give and receive affection? Do you know yourself? How sophisticated is your sense of humor, how finely tuned your understanding of life's absurdities? How thoughtfully do you interact with others? How honest are you with yourself? How do you deal with your various addictive tendencies? How do you face your darkness? How broad and deep is your perspective? How willing are you to be quiet? How do you care for yourself? How do you treat people you deem *unimportant*?

So you're a CEO. So you made a million dollars. So your name is in the paper. So your face is in a magazine. So your song is on the radio. So your book is number one. So you got what you wanted and now you want something else. You probably worked really hard; I salute you. I mean, good, good, good, great, great, great. But if you have ever spent any time around seriously ambitious people, you know that they are very often some of the unhappiest crazies alive, forever rooting around for more, having a hard time with basics like breathing and eating and sleeping, forever trying to cover some hysterical imagined nakedness.

I get that my foremothers and sisters fought long and hard so that my relationship to ambition could be so . . . careless. I get that some foremothers and sisters might read me as ungrateful because I don't want to fight their battles, because I don't want to claw my way anywhere. My apologies, foremothers: I don't want to fight. Oh, is there still sexism in the world? Sigh. Huh. Well. Knock me over with a feather. Now: How do I transplant the peonies to a sunnier spot so they yield more flowers next year or the year after? How do I conquer chapter three of this new novel? I've rewritten it and rewritten it for months. I need to do my asana practice, and then I need to sit in silence for a while. Then some laundry. And the vacuum cleaner needs a new filter. Then respond to some emails from an expectant woman for whom I'm serving as doula. And it's actually my anniversary, so I'm gonna write my spouse a love letter. Then pick up the young'un from school. And I need to figure out what I'm making for dinner. Something with lentils, probably, and butter. Then text my friends a stupid photo and talk smack with them for a while. Taking care of myself and my loved ones feels like meaningful work to me, see? I care about *care*. And I don't care if I'm socialized to feel this way, because in fact *I do feel this way*. So! I am unavailable for striving today. I'm suuuuuper busy.

Yes, oppression is systemic, I get it, I feel it, I live it, I struggle, I do. Women are not equal, we're not fairly represented, the pie charts are clear as day, thank you gender police, thank you privilege police, thank you, we know, truly we do: nothing's fair, nothing at all, it's maddening, it's saddening, it's not at all gladdening. We all suffer private and public indignities big and small. Tell the gatekeepers to shove it, don't play by their rules, and get back to work on whatever it is you hold dear. Nothing's ever been fair. Nothing will ever be fair. But there is ever so much to be done. Pretty please can I go back to my silly sweet secret sacred novel now? Take care.

• • • • • •

My little boy is beside me. He is designing cars on BMW's website. (Cars are a fleeting obsession.) He'd like a BMW someday. His dad and I hide our smirks. Sure, kid, whatever floats your boat. Yesterday it was a Porsche. Tomorrow a Maserati. Apparently he's in an id phase.

"Why don't you guys like fancy cars?" he wonders.

"They're a little show-off-y," I say.

"I like fancy cars," he says. "When I grow up I'm going to get a Tesla and a Bentley and a Cadillac and a Rolls-Royce."

I smile. "Can I have a ride?"

"Of course!"

Wait, though, there are plenty of material goods I covet. I have a shameful thing for clothes. There's this pair of Rachel Comey high-waisted pants, oh my god. I own like six pairs of clogs. I fill my walls with art by friends. I live beautifully. Nice textiles, what have you. There's a Kenzo sweater I might be saving up for. I so enjoy the darkest of chocolate and juice extracted in the most exceptionally newfangled way, I really do.

What I would *like* to say (so that I might be forced to align myself) is that there is nothing material or finite that I will allow myself to *rest* on wanting. Okay, so dresses and clogs and art and peonies float my boat. But fool myself into thinking that these things constitute an end point, or that their acquisition will make me whole, or that people who are impressed by these things are my *friends*? Nope. No way. Not for a minute. (Well, FINE, maybe for a minute. But *certainly* not for two.)

When asked for writing advice, Grace Paley once offered this: "Keep a low overhead."

●　●　●　●　●　●

So becoming a lawyer was more or less an exercise in *Don't Fuck With Me,* but what *did* my mother want? In her seventies now, she's studying Joyce and Dickens. She spends her summers at Oxford, studying Shakespeare. She is delighted and enlivened and occupied, and I wonder why she doesn't go ahead and get herself a graduate degree in literature. She would make a formidable English professor.

"I'm too old," she says.

"Bullshit," I say.

"I'm stupid," she says. I squint at her.

"I'm lazy," she amends, and my heart breaks for both of us.

She used to tell me *I* was lazy, back when I was refusing to care about my GPA, refusing to run the college admissions race, refusing to duly starve myself like all the good lil' girls, refusing to wax my asshole or get manicures or chemically straighten my hair, refusing to do much of anything other than consume books and music and movies and books, then scrawl my favorite bits all over the damn place. She was talking to herself all along. She was talking to herself! Remember: Our most haunting, manipulative ghosts always, always, always are.

• • • • • •

I wrote a magazine piece a while back, and it's been shared online some sixty thousand times. It's a fine piece, but is it the *best* thing I've ever written? I don't think so. Is it the most *original* thing I've ever written? Nah. Is it the most challenging, bold thing I've ever written? Nope. Sixty thousand shares is not a *win*, see; it's a random, synchronistic event. The number of eyeballs on a given piece of writing does not confer nobility or excellence upon said piece of writing. If the number of eyeballs on a piece of writing excites and impresses people *around* me, that's cool, in that it makes possible more of the work I want to do. But it doesn't make said work any easier! And I'm going to do said work regardless, so . . . what?

So *What?* Let's add it to our list of proposed feminist anthems: *So the Fuck What?*

• • • • • •

You should write for a larger audience, my friend Josh told me a year before he died. He had read my first novel and written to congratulate me. I was on the road, touring, short-tempered. *I am not writing for an audience at all*, I snapped. *I have no control over audience and zero interest in thinking about it.* I could look up our exchange, but I don't want to because I'm sad he's dead and I'm sorry I snapped at him, and I want to transcend physics to tell him I love him, and he may have been right, and I'm sorry, I'm so sorry, Josh, and here's a dumb cameo in this dumb essay about dumb ambition.

But I don't *want* to write for a large audience, silly! The masses are by definition kind of mindless as a matter of course, are they not? I mean, no offense, masses, but Donald Trump's memoir sold better than all my past and future work combined. (He didn't *write* it, but still.) The media star of the moment could take a dump on a square of Astroturf and there'd be a line around the block to sniff it. What makes a work of art special and meaningful is your private relationship with it, the magic of finding it amidst the noise and distraction, the magic of letting it speak to you directly. You *found* it, it's *yours*. (This, however, requires the awesome skill of being able to think for yourself in the first place; hardly a given.) Art can change you; it can move and validate and shift and bait and wreck and kindle you in the best way. And others who feel similarly about said work can be your kin. It is not a more-is-better equation.

(I repeat: more is not better.)

Josh, darling, I don't write because I "want to be a writer." I don't want to be famous, and I don't need my ego inflated. I write to make sense of things, to make order from chaos, to make something from nothing. Because what I have found in the writing of others sustains me. Because while I am struggling to live, the writing—a kind of parallel life—helps me along. Because language is my jam. Because I never learned to play the guitar and no one ever asked me to sing in a band.

I mean, writing is liberation! Or so I tell my students, over and over and over again. Flex your muscles, I say. Feel the sun on your face, the wind in your hair! Struggle with your short-comings. Leave everything out on the field! Do it again tomorrow! What rigor. What joy. What privilege. Say whatever the hell you want to say, however you most accurately can! Complete and utter freedom.

"The notes for the poem are the only poem," wrote Adrienne Rich. There's my ambition: Notes.

•   •   •   •   •   •

Oh, but get off your high horse, lady. Fucking relax. You Google yourself on the regular. Whenever you deign to log on to Twitter it's to roll your eyes, sure, but *also*—BE HONEST—to type your name into the search box and see if anyone's talking about you. You don't *even have to* type your name in, BE HONEST: it's already there, in the app's fucking memory! Hypocrite. A nice notification or something can float you for about three minutes; a shit mention somewhere can feel like a slap in the face, even if it's barely literate, even if it's ignorant and hateful and so muddled it's obviously not about *you*. And even as you're skimming it, telling yourself you don't look at this shit, telling yourself you don't root around in this shit, you don't play these games, you don't care, you don't care . . . you *are* looking at it, you *are* rooting around in it, you are you are you are you *so are*. Be honest.

· · · · · ·

The Latin root, by the way, is *ambitio*, which literally means *to go walking*, as in canvassing, as with a political candidate. A friend who's running for city council tells me this, giggling. "I am the definition of ambitious," she says, incredulous, because she happens to be one of the most unassuming people I've ever met. She's been going door to door for months on end leading up to the election. I hope she wins. She would do a magnificent job, and her corner of the world would be better for it. But she's not who I have in mind, here. The root bears little resemblance to the plant that shoots up from it. (Reader, she won!)

· · · · · ·

Last week a younger writer emailed me to ask for advice. How could she get more attention for her book? Where should she send it? The subtext: She wants what (she imagines) I have. It was funny, given that, in truth, I had right at that moment been pouting about my own status (Not Good Enough). I barely know this girl, haven't read her, she's a bore on social media, but hell, what does it cost me to be generous? I wrote back right away.

Send it to writers whose work you admire, I told her. Keep your head down. Do your work. Focus on the work at hand, not the work that's done. Do the work you're called upon to do. Engage with what moves you. Eventually you'll get recognition. And if you *don't* get recognition? Well then, all the more badass to continue working your butt off in the service of your calling. Recognition has nothing to do with the work, get it? The work is the endeavor. The work is the process. Recognition comes, if/when it does, for work that is already done, work that is over. Recognition can really fuck you up. Remember the famous koan? The day before enlightenment, chop wood and carry water; the day after enlightenment, chop wood and carry water. Substitute recognition for enlightenment, putting aside how ironic that is, and there you have it.

It wasn't the advice she was hoping for, obviously. She never even wrote back to say thanks (tsk tsk, ambitious girl!). I thought of her a few days ago, when Ani DiFranco sang "Egos Like Hairdos," a formative favorite: "Everyone loves an underdog / But no one wants to be him . . ."

●　●　●　●　●　●

Here's what bothers me about conventional ambition, the assumption that we all aspire to the top, the blah blah blah, the winner's circle, the biggest brightest bestest, and that we will run around and around and around in our little hamster wheels to get there: Most of these goals are standardized. Cartoonish. Cliché. Beware anything standardized, that's what I would teach my daughter. Health care, ambition, education, diet, culture: Name it, and you will suffer endlessly from any attempt to go about it the same way as some projected Everyone Else. You cannot be standardized. You are a unique flower, daughter. Maybe the Ivy

League will be wonderful for you; maybe it will crush your soul. If the former, I will mortgage the house to pay your way; if the latter, give that shit the finger and help me move these peonies, will you? You are not defined by such things, either way. Anyway, let us discuss what we want to whip up for dinner and take turns playing DJ while doing so.

"She can, though every face should scowl / And every windy quarter howl / Or every bellows burst, be happy still." That was Yeats.

I mean, fuck ambition, that's where this is going, okay? I don't buy the idea that acting like the oppressor is a liberation, personal ambition being, in essence, see above, patriarchal. And yeah, *about* recognition. What about when genius and/or hard work isn't recognized? Because often it isn't, and what do we make of that? And what happens when the striving becomes its own end? What's been accomplished in such cases? You can get pretty far on striving alone, god knows. The *striving* might get recognized, but what relationship does striving have to mastery? And what's the *cost* of the striving? And what if we confuse striving or incidental recognition *with* mastery? What then!? Then, Jesus, we are so very lost. And we'll have to acknowledge, yes of course, sure, that we were born at the right time in the right place and we've never felt bad about working toward what we want, but want is tricky, so beware *that* particular sand trap. Right, and okay, be ambitious, whatever that looks like for you, but don't confuse your own worth with anyone else's definition of success. And don't think that if you happen to impress people you must be very impressive indeed. And don't imagine that if you play by someone else's rules you can win. Anyway, there is no winning. Anyway, the game is suspect. Anyway, write your own rules! Anyway, WHO HAS TIME FOR GAMES!?

"The highway is full of big cars / going nowhere fast." Maya Angelou.

• • • • • •

There is a way to spin it so that I am a winner, a big success. Six-figure book deals. Media attention galore. Professorships. Invitations to read and lecture and teach and reside. Fan letters. Hate mail. Hollywood knock-knock-knockin' at the door. Some fossilized nutcase trying to take me down in an op-ed. There is an equally factual way to spin it so that I am a middling mediocre failure, a nonstarter. I've been rejected by plenty of highbrow writer shit. I'm no household name. I barely tweet. I get ignored. You can't buy my books in the airport. It just depends on the story you want to tell, the parts to which you are privy. Be assured, my website lists the hits alone.

"The quality I most abhor in women is humility, which seems like a chickenshit response to the demands of the world, or the marketplace, not that I can tell them apart." That's Emily Carter Roiphe, who I really wish would publish her second book already.

It hasn't helped that I rarely deign to *apply* for the highbrow writer stuff. Or that when I do, it's in vaguely mocking tones, as sort of an elaborate joke. I'm pretty terrible at applying for things. I should work on that. The snarling girl resents the expectation that she bow down before some purported authority so they might consider throwing her a bone. If they don't want her outright, she doesn't want their farty old bone, anyway. Maybe she's not so dormant as I like to think. Or maybe my mother was right: Maybe she *is* just goddamned lazy.

• • • • • •

Last thought. I met a celebrated young writer at a party. The finest MFA, flashy blurbage, what have you. I'd heard good things about her first book, and I introduced myself with my first name, told her I was looking forward to reading it.

"Thanks," she said, looking right through me.

Our mutual friend said, "Oh my god, have you read Elisa's book? It's so good."

The writer could not have been less interested. "What's it called?" she wondered in monotone. "You'll have to forgive me, but I really don't keep up with much contemporary writing."

The condescension was burlesque. Our friend told her the name of my recent book. The light went on in the writer's eyes. Ding. "Oh!" she said. "Oh, yes!" Then she looked at me eagerly, hungrily. I excused myself immediately.

It's creepy that I "matter" to these kinds of people now, that's all I want to say. I "matter" *not* because of the books themselves, *not* because of the work therein, *not* because of what prompted the work, *not* because of my *actual humanity,* but because various and sundry radio programs and magazines and newspapers and podcasts and shares and mentions and likes and dings and dongs and film agents and foreign translations and lists *say* I matter. Some supposed authorities have deemed me worthwhile, and so now I "matter." That is, until *these* authorities fade away, to be replaced by *new* authorities. Gawd, I hope *they* like me. Just kidding. Fuck authority.

○ ○ ○ ○ ● ●

Last-last thought. I wish I had gotten some other lessons from my mother. More about what to make for dinner and how to move the peonies and just how tender and trustworthy love can be, for starters. But we get what we get, so I suppose I appreciate her gift (such as it is) of *Don't Fuck With Me.* Especially because, have I mentioned? I'm busy channeling it, hard at work. How freaking fortunate is that? (Hashtag blessed. Hashtag grateful. Like? LIKE??)

•   •   •   •   •   •

Last-last-last thought: I showed a draft of this essay to a trusted advisor. He didn't like it at all. "You sound arrogant," he said. "You're not arrogant, so why are you putting on this front?"

"Uhhmmm," I said. "Fake it till you make it?"

"You sound like you think you're above all the bullshit, and that's a real turnoff."

I was stunned and frustrated. I had expected a nice pat on the head for striking out boldly, taking a stand, engaging the crucial shadow self, whatever.

"I'm trying to articulate something difficult about art and commerce and popularity," I protested.

"Try and be more vulnerable," he said. "You'll come across better."

Come *across*? I don't have *time* to orchestrate how I *come across*, dude. My job is to write shit *down*.

More *vulnerable*? I feel like I'm walking around without *skin* most of the time, *hello*? Anyway, my vulnerability is not for god-damn sale. I'd rather suck a thousand dicks.

I was overcome with weariness, and I thought: *Fuck it, I give up*. But of course that's not true either. Nope! Not at all. Onward.

Ambitchin'

● ● ● ● ● ● JULIE HOLLAND

I was born in 1965 and grew up in the long-haired, bell-bottomed "Let It Be" seventies. But fifties-era gender roles die hard, and I received plenty of messages, overt and covert, instructing me to rein in my delight with, and my drive for, achievement. It simply wasn't ladylike.

My father would occasionally pull me aside, asking me to "tone it down a little." I gleaned, painfully, that my youthful confidence was off-putting to others and was particularly intimidating to my sensitive sister. And so I learned early to pepper my speech with "maybe" and "I think," to begin my sentences as if I were just musing, even when I was sure. I tried to camouflage my ambition, at least sometimes.

Some places felt more free, though, and I'd forget the camouflage. At summer camp color wars, captaining my team like a drill sergeant, I let no laggard lose us the championship. I shouted at the slower girls to keep up as they lasered me with lethal glares. The long footrace culminated in the final contest, a single arrow shot by each captain of the remaining two teams:

my boyfriend, the counselor for the oldest boys, and me, the counselor for the oldest girls.

It had grown dark as we gathered at the archery range, the target barely visible, but I was sure, when I heard the *fwapp*, that I'd bested his shot. He wouldn't speak to me after the event, appalled at how competitive I'd been.

But we won.

I walked off the field, the mown grass clinging to my sweaty calves, attempting to savor the sweet taste of victory while swallowing the bitter bile of rejection from the sexiest man I'd yet known. I felt powerful. And utterly rejected.

Ambition is a difficult word for women because it forces them to try and square messages—often very subtle—from the outside, patriarchal world with natural, internal drives. But it's further complicated by the natural flux of women's cycles and the fact that, at different stages of life, different drives reign supreme. It's not only nurture, but it's also nature. In my twenty-plus-year career as a psychiatrist and my lifetime as either a daughter or a mother of a daughter myself, I've seen women react to their own natural, biologically based complexities with shame and embarrassment. I encourage the women I work with to let the science of their own bodies help them accept and embrace all the parts of who they are.

Our interior lives are complex and ever changing, and the many phases of our lives echo the natural fluctuations of the hormones underlying many of our basic behaviors. Our estrogen levels rise and fall cyclically for decades, and these shifts and spurts often inform our changing moods. Learning to surf their waves can be challenging, but potentially exhilarating.

Estrogen, testosterone, and oxytocin weave a tapestry of

quintessentially female and male behaviors. Estrogen peaks mid-cycle, when we are most alluring, accommodating, and fertile. Testosterone surges in adolescence and early perimenopause, when we are most horny and driven. Oxytocin accompanies orgasm, nursing, and female bonding, encouraging us to mate, nurture, and get by with a little help from our friends.

Estrogen levels rise and fall monthly, if you are not on the pill (I like to call this "free range") and you are not postmenopausal (the calm after the decade-long storm). In the first half of the cycle, as the egg matures and becomes ready for ovulation, estrogen levels rise. Designed to attract a mate, and then nurture a family, estrogen is all about giving to others: keeping our kids happy and our mates satisfied. In the mating years, it seems as though we live for our family and accommodate them by default. Most of us who choose this life learn to love it, for the most part. We thrive by cultivating relationships and nurturing those around us. Estrogen creates a veil of accommodation.

It also enhances resilience, reacting to stressors by surging when things get tough, so little difficulties slip away like water off a duck's back. When we have high estrogen levels, we are usually more adaptable—breezy, even. We allow for others' needs better and can remain more convincingly detached. Estrogen not only helps women feel sexy and nurturing, but it also allows them to be more forgiving and quicker to calm their temper. Evolutionarily, these are all qualities that may help seduce a mate, and they've been singled out, praised, and encouraged by patriarchal cultures for obvious reasons.

I had a patient who referred to herself as a "pathological accommodator" when we first met. We were both fascinated as this behavior ebbed away once her periods stopped. Over several years, her responses morphed from cooing, "Sure, I'll take care of it, honey," into snapping, "Why don't you do it yourself?!"

When estrogen levels drop, as happens in PMS, postpartum, or perimenopause, it's common for moods to plummet as well. Waning levels of estrogen help us to be more emotional, allow us to cry more easily and even to break down when we're overwhelmed. During these low estrogen states, that veil of accommodation is lifted. We are no longer alluring and fertile; we are no longer so invested in the potential daddy sticking around, because there's no baby to consider. And so, PMS is the time to clean house. During the rest of the month you put up with all kinds of bull that you wouldn't tolerate the week before your period. To women who feel sheepish about their behavior during this phase: You are getting upset over real things; it's just that you usually hide your sadness and anger better. Be authentic, and yes, be a bitch, if that's what you need to call it to get the job done. You can't clean if you don't see where the dirt is.

Perimenopause is PMS for the big girls. It is the ultimate time for pruning. It is our version of the midlife crisis, when we weed out those who are toxic, prioritizing and further honing our mission, whatever it may be. The majority of divorces in America, 60 percent, are initiated by women in their forties, fifties, and sixties. When estrogen levels fall, we start to slowly transition from maternal self-sacrifice to a more assertive "You're on your own, pal." Less capitulation isn't just better for us; it's probably good for our kids, too. A mother's perimenopause may occur around the time when children—adolescents, in particular—are ready to take on more responsibility, so perhaps there is a benefit for everyone in changing that family dynamic.

My own mother was a great role model, taking her menopausal symptoms in stride and referring to her hot flashes as "power surges." She made this time of life one of professional ambition; she got another degree and switched careers, which appealed to me as a teenage girl. I saw her rise in power, putting her energy to good use, making changes that were long overdue. In the workplace, perimenopause often coincides with having gathered enough experience to transform yourself into a take-no-prisoners leader. Screw everyone. It's my turn.

For all of us, there are times when clear-eyed assessment, confrontation, and speaking up for oneself are called for. In other situations, capitulation and accommodation would be wisest. Naturally dipping and rising estrogen levels can actually help balance these behaviors. A major part of my maturation was learning to strike this delicate balance, again and again, to regain harmony with my surroundings and within myself, month after month.

⸰ ⸰ • • • ⚫

Growing up a girl in America, balance was a fantasy. I was conditioned to assimilate my brassy, bossy stance into something more estrogen-tinged, and subordinate and dithering, in an effort to be better liked. But what about all the other parts of me? And what about authenticity?

Now that I can see this indoctrination more clearly, I can promise you one thing: I will not subject future pledges to this hazing ritual. I will not teach my daughter to tone down her self-confidence or pull back on her ambition. It's more important for her to trust her gut, to speak firmly and bravely, and know that she deserves to devour the world, her oyster.

Little girls need every ounce of self-esteem they can get. To paraphrase Frederick Douglass, it's easier to build strong children than repair broken adults. I've spent my entire professional life seeing firsthand how true that is. Girls who hold on to their assertiveness and self-esteem are less likely to grow up to be depressed women. Speaking your mind is part of a healthy lifestyle. Suppressing your feelings is not only going to make you miserable; it may well make you physically ill. Women are more prone to emotionally induced heart attacks than men are, and we die of heart disease in staggering numbers in America. Clinical studies demonstrate a correlation between self-abnegating women and medical illness. We're acquiescing ourselves to death.

●　●　●　●　●　●

I've been involved in clinical research of schizophrenia when I designed a protocol as a psychiatric resident, and for the past several years, I've been involved in research of two treatments for Post Traumatic Stress Disorder, one using MDMA (Ecstasy) assisted psychotherapy, and the other testing various strains of cannabis. If I had stopped trying every time a man told me something was impossible, I'd be nowhere. I like what Michele Roberts, the first woman leader of the NBA union, said, that her past was littered with the bones of the men who underestimated her. My past includes men who told me it'd been done before, when it hadn't. Or that it just wouldn't work, making me doubt myself when it turned out I was right and should have stood my ground. Or men in power who tried to dissuade me from my ideas and goals as an underling, only to later take credit for formulating and implementing them.

Sometimes men were simply dismissive or belittling. There was the program director, a man twenty years my senior, who, on the heels of a great conversation about all things neuro-chemical during a fellowship interview, ended it by saying as I rose from my chair, "You're cute. How old are you?" I rode the elevator to the lobby, mentally scratching off his program from my list of possible placements after residency. I felt small, invalidated, and wholly pissed off. I don't know what the feminine equivalent of emasculating is, but that comment took away my power. Then again, hell hath no fury and all that. Enter testosterone.

In women, testosterone is made in the adrenal glands and

ovaries, spurring our competitive drive, our assertiveness, and our lust. In adolescence, a girl's level of testosterone rises five times above normal, but it is in the context of her estrogen increasing ten to twenty times above normal. Estrogen may make us more receptive to sex, taking the brakes off and helping us to be uninhibited, but testosterone is the gas pedal.

We know testosterone fuels the alpha male behavior; is it simplistic to think that it can act similarly in women? It is, because we also have estrogen spurring us on. When researchers measured estrogen in women engaged in competitions of physical prowess, they found that levels were higher in women who had a stronger desire for power, and those levels rose further when they won their competitions, creating a positive loop. In women with less drive, their estrogen levels were more stable. We have two hormones swirling and surging when we are driven, not just one.

That combination doesn't always make success and victory in women palatable for the men around her. *Bitchy, bossy, strident, shrew . . .* these are words solely applied to women. If you look at women's employment reviews (see Kieran Snyder's "The Abrasiveness Trap" in *Fortune*), certain words show up repeatedly, like *bossy, abrasive, strident,* and *aggressive.* This is when women *lead*; words like *emotional* and *irrational* are used when they *object.* In reviews, men are exhorted to be more aggressive in the workplace, but not so with women. In the workplace, women are expected to get ahead by some mysterious combination of femininity and intelligence while simultaneously getting things done and disguising drive.

Perhaps part of the problem is with effort. It's poor form, somehow, if they see you sweat. Thus, our slacker culture. Women, while not encouraged to grow scruffy beards and ride skateboards, are held to a different standard: effortless perfection. My astrological sign is Sagittarius, the archer, and I felt at home on the archery range. I loved the feel of a taut bow, the twang of a full release. It was never lost on me that the male symbol I wrote in my science notebooks was a circle with an arrow. Man is in his element when he is reaching, striving, when he has a vector and is following a trajectory. But I wasn't a man. I was a tomboy. I resented the female symbol, the reflecting hand mirror. (Especially given recent research suggesting that men preen in a mirror even more than women do.) My ambition, my drive, my tenacious embrace of anything I pursued, was one of my defining traits. I'm a striver.

The Zen monks have a word for striving to *not* strive, called *mushotoku*, the goal of having no goals. In this state of mind, there is no attachment to outcomes; there is no obtaining anything, nor giving while expecting something in return. To strike a target, a Zen master must become one with the bow, aim without aiming, and let the arrow release itself. There is no doing, only being.

Easier said than done, and perhaps not my style anyway. Amy, my favorite Bikram yoga teacher, often reminds us to "find the ease in the effort." I prefer that. It's a blending, a balance, yin and yang. As with most things in nature, it is not either, but both.

In my own life I was mostly yang until my biological clock kicked in. Over time, I became less interested in hooking up and more invested in mating. My reaction to those Upper East Side stroller-pushing moms morphed from dismissive eye rolls to a yearning in my pelvis. It was when I went off the pill, actually, that this shift fully took hold. Normalized estrogen levels that cycled monthly were a big part of it, but also, I was in love.

Oxytocin is the hormone of bonding, whether between lovers (oxytocin levels rise during hugging and skyrocket after orgasm) or between mother and child (ditto for cuddling and nursing). The drug MDMA (better known as Ecstasy or Molly) is being investigated as a catalyst to psychotherapy because it reliably raises oxytocin levels, helping people to feel closer with others, more open and trusting, and, importantly, less fearful. Oxytocin is a key component in maternal aggression; it tamps down our fear response, allowing us to do whatever's necessary, fighting like a mama lion to protect our young.

When men are stressed, their bodies go into "flight or fight" mode, with adrenaline as the key ingredient. For women, stress can bring about a different response, which is sometimes called "tend and befriend." Here, oxytocin acts as a stress hormone, surging in response to a stressor and underlying the behavior of women bonding with each other, which is key for our survival. But this is not indiscriminate bonding. Oxytocin helps discern who is with you and who is against you; it's about excluding those not in your tribe. In some experiments, with extra oxy on board, people are more harsh against those they feel aren't a part of their group. Because it is more potent in an estrogen-rich environment, oxytocin's release affects women more powerfully than men (though it can certainly engender a "bromance" or two).

All of these fluctuations are natural, and though they can be difficult to navigate, chemically altering them can have a bad result. Your brain is full of estrogen receptors, ditto for serotonin, which is often yoked to estrogen. When one is up, the other is likely to be as well. This is part of the reason for PMS mood symptoms; diving estrogen levels tank serotonin levels. So here's what I worry about: Record numbers of women are taking antidepressants, especially SSRIs (selective serotonin reuptake inhibitors), the most common treatment for depression and anxiety. But those steady serotonin levels unlink the natural ebb and flow of mood with fluctuating estrogen. Estrogen fluctuations help to keep us sensitive. SSRIs deaden our sensitivities, making us more rational and less emotional. At higher doses, feelings are neither fully felt nor processed, and the capacity for elation, empathy, or sorrow becomes muted. It not only becomes difficult to get horny or climax, but also to cry.

Adding birth control pills to the mix, a popular medication combination for millions of women, drives estrogen levels upward and flattens them out, modeling the more static sex hormone levels that men experience. You potentially get more accommodating behavior all month long, as well as losing that natural monthly enhanced sensitivity. (And FYI, the pill saps your testosterone levels over time, so your libido wanes.)

SSRIs can reduce aggression, poor impulse control, and irritability while increasing cooperation and affiliative behaviors. This emotional blunting encourages women to take on behaviors that are typically approved and modeled by men: appearing to be invulnerable, for instance, a posture that might help women move up in male-dominated businesses. Primate studies show that giving an SSRI can augment social dominance behaviors, elevating an animal's status in the hierarchy. So antidepressants that increase serotonin may well help women get along, and even get ahead, in the workplace, but at what cost? I understand that many women will require antidepressants at some point in their lifetimes due to severe depression or anxiety, but many more women in America are being offered a medicine that isn't appropriate for them, that has real behavioral consequences that aren't being fully explained in their doctor's office.

I had a patient who called me from her office in tears, saying she needed to increase her antidepressant dosage because she couldn't be seen crying at work. After dissecting why she was upset—her boss had betrayed and humiliated her in front of her staff—we decided that what was needed was calm confrontation, not more medication. Was it ambition that made her feel she should erase every emotion to conform to the hostile environment in her workplace?

In *mushotoku,* there is no profit agenda. Unrestricted growth, the type seen in many corporations, has a different name in medicine. It's called cancer. Checking corporate malignance is perhaps the most important reason to rely on emotional authenticity. If I give in to my patient's request to ratchet up her happy pill dosage, her boss's emotionally incorrect behavior remains unchecked, and the unrestricted growth of corporate greed and malfeasance continues unfettered. It's not easy. I, like my patient, have teared up in a meeting with my boss, or worse, my boss's boss, and crying is the last thing anyone wants in the office. But that part of ourselves that gets us misty-eyed when something is amiss is a vital feedback system that the corporate world needs. Cut it off, and the center will not hold.

For centuries, men have been taught to silence their feminine side, their yin energy. Boys are told not to "cry like a girl," or they're encouraged to "man up." Now, these same messages are being carried to girls and women, and we're buying into it. This is not only mentally unhealthy for each of us, but it's also a disaster for our culture. The world needs more emotional sensitivity, not less.

Your tears underlie an important lesson that people around you need. They teach emotional correctness. Do not modify your emotional expression for the comfort of others. Do not fear being called hysterical to the point where you say nothing. And don't buy into Big Pharma's story that every behavior and feeling is a symptom begging for a pill. Obviously there are people who need psychiatric medications, but 80 percent of those prescriptions are written by nonpsychiatrists.

This is such a natural, easy way to temper our drive: with sensitivity to its effects. Women are particularly well positioned to lead by example, balancing our yin and yang energies, as we navigate the waters of our ever-changing hormonal tides. Our sensitivity and capacity for empathy are gifts we need to share with the world. There is a surplus of aggressive energy evident in our culture these days. You can see it in our wars, our gun violence, our rape culture, and our capitalist greed. Women don't have to feel just one way about ambition. We don't have to hide from it or enlist it without restraint. Our ability to embrace complexity is not only a sublime quality, it's deeply engrained in our biology. It's the rest of the world that is out of balance, and it's going to be up to us, ambitious women, to turn this ship around.

Original Sin

●　●　●　●　●　● **FRANCINE PROSE**

There are few things more necessary than ambition, more essential to the progress of what we have agreed to call civilization. Without ambition, we might still be living in caves, dependent on the nomadic vagaries of the bison and antelope population, without even the consolation of the paintings done by the artists who—without ambition—might have lacked the will and the desire to decorate the walls. Without ambition (and its important but not always reliable sidekicks and enablers: curiosity, skill, talent, and energy) we would have no bridges, no skyscrapers, no airplane travel, no automobiles, no books, no paintings, no music, no theater, no modern health care. Without the sort of ambition that inspired the earliest tribes to migrate in search of better conditions and that drove the explorers and the pioneers to set out for unknown territory, we might all be living somewhere else. And those who imagine a simpler, more relaxed or forgiving world—an Eden before the destructive onset of the cutthroat, dog-eat-dog, Darwinian scramble to the top that we associate with ambition—might pause to consider the miseries, and the average life expectancy and living conditions of our ancestors.

So given the ways in which we depend on ambition, the extent to which our world would be poorer, more dangerous, less pleasurable, and indeed unrecognizable without ambition, it does seem odd that half our population (the female half, to be specific) is not supposed to or encouraged to be ambitious. Or if, by some chance, women are born with the desire to actually do something—to invent or compose or design something, to become powerful, to run a company or a country—they must rather rapidly (certainly by adolescence) learn to hide those desires, to conceal the hopes and dreams and plans that cannot be realized without ambition.

My mother was a doctor. She was the first in her family to go to college, let alone to medical school. She'd grown up on the Lower East Side of Manhattan; her parents ran a small restaurant for dockworkers and stevedores who worked at the harbor in Lower Manhattan. She was fifteen when she graduated from NYU; her age and that she was a Jewish woman made it impossible for her to get into a medical school in the United States. She traveled first to Glasgow, where she attended medical school for two years. Then, when the war broke out and American students were discouraged from returning to the active or endangered zones, she completed her degree in neutral Switzerland at the University of Lausanne.

By then she had met my father, a fellow student and later a fellow doctor, to whom she always deferred. Over the years, I often asked her how a girl from her sheltered background got the courage, the ambition, the *idea* to do what she did—when she was just a teenager. She always said she didn't know, and I believed her. And over the years, I noticed habits of reflection and introspection were not highly valued by my mother and her friends, several of whom she'd grown up with, all of whom came from large families, as she did, in Lower Manhattan.

Perhaps, men are expected to have and freely display ambition: The aspect of character that (at best) combines at least two of the cardinal virtues (wisdom, courage) and (at worst) can involve twice as many deadly sins: anger, greed, pride, and envy. Men are raised to want to rule the world, or (worst case) to destroy it.

The factors that have discouraged and discredited female ambition go back to the roots of our history and culture. The names of a few (a very few) heroines and artists have come down to us (Antigone and Sappho) from Greek antiquity, but we can assume that these remarkable women were vastly outnumbered by those women who (most egregiously in Athens) were forbidden to make decisions concerning marriage, to inherit or control property, to pursue activities unrelated to the domestic sphere, or to be considered full citizens. (Their sisters in Sparta and elsewhere fared somewhat better.)

The first ambitious woman about whom most of us know is, of course, Eve—the mother of sin, the source of Primal Sin, forever guilty of an unfortunate, if admirable, confluence of disobedience and the desire for knowledge. Indeed, much of Genesis and the Old Testament provide a kind of object lesson about the perils and consequences of women stepping outside the boundaries drawn by God—or by their husbands or societies: Eve exiled (along with the rest of us) from the Garden of Eden; Jezebel ripped apart by dogs; Delilah presumably killed in the destruction of the temple that Samson (hair regrown, restored to strength) pulled down. There is one judge who is a woman (Deborah) and a few heroines (Esther, in a book that had some trouble making it into the canon), but ambitious or heroic women are few and far between. Mostly they exist to bear male children, to tempt men, to cause discord and war—a form of negative ambition, I suppose you could say, but not necessarily aimed to achieve an effect that any of us might reasonably desire.

Nor did things improve much with the advent of Christianity. The Apostolic Constitution, a fourth-century compilation from older writings on the church liturgy and canon law, tells us that if Jesus wanted women to hold ecclesiastical office, he would have chosen a female disciple from among the many women who followed him. And, according to the same document, there would be other barriers to a female achieving any sort of ecclesiastical office: If the man was the head of the household, the existence of a female priest in the house would mean that the body was ruling the head, and how unnatural would that be? Women in church were expected to be so quiet that, in prayer, they could only move their lips without making a sound.

As modern literature grew out of the Renaissance, and as the eighteenth-century novel began to reflect something resembling daily life, we begin to find ambitious women in plays and on the page, and we can't help but notice that by and large they are monstrous.

A woman in Shakespeare's audience would of course have had the example of Queen Elizabeth, a career possibility if one inherited the throne and was willing to behead her rivals to secure her power. But it would have been hard to watch Lady Macbeth without being frightened and duly warned by the scene in which she laments the impossibility of washing the blood from her hands. Lady Macbeth gives us one way to channel our ambition: that is, we can encourage our ambitious husbands to betray their friends and to commit multiple murders.

The nineteenth century saw a (somewhat cramped and limited) flowering of female ambition. The Industrial Revolution and the breakdown of the family increased the number of women who, like everyone else, had to scramble to survive. Jane Eyre was one of those women, and in Charlotte Brontë's novel, one can't help noticing that survival itself requires considerable drive.

Marriage as a career goal is another, parallel narrative of female ambition, an older, more durable though possibly waning goal, incrementally giving way to the goals of selfhood and work, and to a wider concern of how we see the world and how the world sees us.

George Eliot was a phenomenon of ambition, producing magisterial novels, concerned with her reputation and her career. It was no accident that she chose to use a man's name, as of course the Brontës did as well. Virginia Woolf and Katherine Mansfield loved and admired one another and were deeply in competition. Woolf's driving ambition, energy, and productivity are often shadowed by the image of her as Bloomsbury aesthete, neurotic and suicidal.

As I write this, the ways in which gender and ambition are playing out in the U.S. political arena are at once obvious and appalling. Regardless of what we may think, or whether we agree with either of them, there are different styles of power, entitlement, and degrees of latitude that Donald Trump and Hillary Clinton take, and are given.

• • • • • •

No matter how far we believe we have come, no matter how many successes we feel we have achieved, it's still hard to get away from that disparity, that essential inequality.

In a film such as *The Wolf of Wall Street*, one may note that its hero sees what he wants and goes after it: a great house, lots of money, a nice office, fancy suits, cocaine snorted off a hooker's ass. It's hard to imagine a woman playing Leonardo DiCaprio's role, and make any of it look like a good idea—not even at the beginning, before all the drugs and orgies. Ambitious women in film either ultimately fall in love or show their tender sides, or else they remain ambitious and single: human nightmares taking out their disappointments and frustrations on the people and world around them.

* * * * * *

To be fair, there are occasions on which both men and women feel compelled to hide or at least mask their ambition. Some years ago, I had the pleasure of spending a year in the company of writers and scholars who had been given a fellowship to spend time at a research foundation. None of the fellows had reached the point of being invited to such a place without having been ambitious. But one of our colleagues—a young man—appeared to have missed the lesson about hiding it, about clothing our naked hopes and desires. He asked for the names of our literary agents; he wrote an article about the rest of us for a national magazine. I had the sense that he made the fewest lasting friendships that year. In a sense, the institution had turned us into children in a schoolyard, looking for someone to exclude: And that person was the openly (the too openly) ambitious one.

In any case, mannerly ambitious people who pretend not to be ambitious represent only a very small fraction of how people feel and behave in regard to ambition. More reliably, it breaks down by gender. An ambitious man is admirable, a hero or sinner or both. At worst, we may think he's an asshole, but where would we be without them?

Whereas, an ambitious woman is a witch out of hell. That fabulous harpy fashion editor that Meryl Streep plays in *The Devil Wears Prada*; the private school principal fascist that Anjelica Huston plays in *Daddy Day Care*; the stop-at-nothing, cold-blooded striver that Reese Witherspoon plays in *Election*; the gangster matriarch Brianna Barksdale that Michael Hyatt plays in *The Wire*.

What should also be clear is that the performances I have mentioned are interesting and memorable, fun to watch. This leads us to another thing about women and ambition. Ambitious women are interesting. Hundreds of years after Thackeray's *Vanity Fair* was written, the sheer outrageousness and the wacky charm of what Becky Sharp is willing to do to get ahead propels us through the novel; we would never get through the novel if it were entirely about the disillusionment and awakening of the good girl, Amelia Sedley.

I'm glad for the existence of a book such as Sheryl Sandberg's *Lean In*, if only for the reassurance it provides: its suggestion that the additional obstacles women face are neither self-created nor part of their imaginations. It is so clearly a catch-22: A woman must be doubly ambitious to withstand the low opinions of men who automatically assume that women are less intelligent and capable because they are women, while at the same time monitor themselves for any signs of that demon ambition that might cause these same men to see them as she-devils of competitive aggression. For women in that situation, the glass ceiling begins on the ground floor.

The only thing we can hope for is that little girls notice how much more interesting and attractive ambitious women are than the modest, self-effacing, big-eyed, semi-helpless princesses so in need of rescue as seen in the Disney films. And we can only hope that girls somehow hear this sage advice, instead of learning that women are not allowed to work and strive and achieve, that women should feel embarrassed and try to hide their ambition.

Not long ago, I asked my eight-year-old granddaughter what she wanted to be when she grew up. I felt free to ask because she'd been surprisingly early to get the idea that adults do something: they work. Her father is a musician, her mom an anthropologist. In the past, she'd said she wanted to be a scientist or a

her own mother, for reasons that I didn't quite understand at that age. To me, my grandmother seemed funny and friendly and talked with what I considered a peculiar accent. Whenever she visited every few years, she wore muumuus and brought canned macadamia nuts and odd pieces of costume jewelry that dazzled in their impracticality for a child.

This time she happened to be walking through the living room and overheard my declaration.

"Molly," she said. "You can't say that about yourself."

I felt embarrassed because her tone suggested that I ought to be, but more than that I was confused.

"Why?" I asked.

"Because it's bad manners to talk about yourself like that. Other people can say that about you, but you can't say that about yourself."

I didn't have time to consider the validity of this statement because the moments that followed were a blur. My mother, who was in the kitchen with my aunt, overheard what my grandmother said and flew into the living room in a rage. My sister, brother, and I were ordered out to the car. Our things were gathered hastily. Even outside I could hear the voice of my normally shy mother yelling obscenities at her. We drove home without talking, and there was no further explanation.

Later, I pieced together puzzling complexities of my mother's relationship to her own mother and realized that, in a sense, in that moment I had been an avatar for her. She had never received even the slightest parental encouragement of any kind. Hearing her mother criticize me had enabled her to stand up and roar at her in a way that she never could have as a child. My grandmother may have done her best to squash her ambition, but my mother would be damned if she would stand by and listen to her do it to me.

To be fair, I will never know my grandmother's true motivation in attempting to shame me for being boastful. I suspect it was a generational thing. Back when she was raised, women weren't supposed to talk about themselves in such a way. In fact, women weren't really encouraged to talk much at all, and if they had ambition of any kind, it was to be a wife and a mother. Not that there is anything wrong with these pursuits. I am both a wife and a mother, but it isn't all that I am, and it's never all that I wanted to be. At the same age that I was playing with dolls in kindergarten, I was also performing in front of an audience, singing with my father's jazz band, and acting in local community theater. As soon as I was old enough to write, I began writing stories. Then, sometime in my teen years, it was as if a wall came down, and I stopped doing everything except for the one artistic pursuit for which I was the most known: acting.

I'm not sure why I made this decision. And although I'm not one to blame outside forces for my decisions, I can't help but feel like I let other people's voices (voices like my grandmother's) into my head. The world has always been full of these kinds of voices—the naysayers, critics, and underminers. The Internet age has given us even more arbitrary and vitriolic versions of the same voices—haters and trolls, whatever you want to call them. They attack your physical appearance, your life choices, artistic choices, even your will to live. Underneath it all seems to be the underlying message of "How dare you?"

How dare you try? How dare you take more than what you deserve? How dare you have a political opinion? Get back in that box labeled "actress." It's where you belong.

It isn't hard to be influenced by those voices. Most of us (myself included) have them built into our own brains. Freud named this critical voice the superego, though I think everyone should feel free to give it their own name. I call mine "Brenda." "Brenda" is helpful when she tells you not to text while driving, or maybe you shouldn't go to that after-party when you have to wake up in the morning and drive your kids to school. But when her voice becomes dominant, she is deafening. The voice overpowers everything, halting creativity. Even worse, she gets in there before you have the chance to become creative because she entirely consumes ambition. Her voice is so loud and screeching that you'll do anything to shut her up. Go back to bed. Binge-watch television. Buy things you don't need on eBay. Feel bad.

"Brenda" is like a devious super villain because she takes on so many different disguises. She has the ability to leave your brain at times and rematerialize in other forms. Once, in my twenties, I auditioned for a small part in a prestigious film. I didn't get the part, which surprised me since I thought I did a pretty good job. I knew the material very well, as the film was adapted from the work of one of my favorite authors. I was able to speak knowledgeably about the book, and I enthusiastically shared my passion for the writing. I was also arguably a better actress than the one who ended up getting hired, so I was flummoxed as to why I was passed over. Years later, when I ended up in a film with the same man who directed the movie, I couldn't resist asking him what had made him choose the other actress over me. He passed on these nuggets of advice: "Men don't want to know what you think of the material. Don't be so 'smart.' Listen to what *they* have to say and repeat it back to them." I'm paraphrasing the conversation, of course, but these choice lines are the ones that have knocked around in my head for twenty years. *Know your place.*

• • • • • •

Maybe I would have landed more parts had I implemented the advice of "Brenda" housed in that small actor/director's body.

After all, being an actress does involve inhabiting the creation of the writers and directors and capturing the fantasy of the spectator. But I couldn't see why there wasn't room for both. Why couldn't I act and still show these other interesting parts of myself? The mythology that pervaded Hollywood when I was growing up was that part of your job as a young actress was to assume the role of an object of desire. This was the false narrative that I struggled with as I evolved into womanhood. Everywhere I turned the many envoys of "Brenda" made me understand that choosing to puncture a hole in that illusion through any kind of overt ambition, whether educational, political, literary, or otherwise, was also accompanied by a warning to proceed at my own peril. *Know your place.*

And the worst offense of all? Age.

Everyone knows that Hollywood isn't exactly known for its "best practices" when it comes to ageism. Women are discarded just as they cease to resemble girls. Even a very talented Academy Award–winning young actress was recently told by the "Brendas" in her life that she was losing out on parts to younger women. How long, I wonder, can this business get away with denying ageism on the singular back of Meryl Streep?

· · · · · ·

The only silver lining of this overt ageism is that it has freed me up to fulfill my creative ambition in any way I see fit. Turning forty was as scary and traumatic for me as it is for most women. I felt certain doors definitively slamming shut behind me, but at the same time, I looked around this new place and it intrigued me. It almost seemed like "Brenda" got locked on the other side (no doubt lurking around, sniffing for new blood). With this newfound freedom, I thought, why not publish the writing? Why not sing jazz? Why not do anything and everything I can do? For me, the issue of time became my imperative, rather than someone else's idea of my success. In my twenties, I used to worry about what people would think if I expressed an opinion too vociferously; now I feel proud that I can converse with anyone on any given subject. When I go home at the end of the night, I find myself considering not so much what was thought of me but whether I learned something new—if I spent my time wisely.

*   *   *   *   *   *

Of course, "Brenda" pops back in from time to time. When I hear her voice, most often in the middle of the night, it's when I'm thinking of the post–Gen X generation/millennial generation and marveling at how they feel the freedom to take what is theirs with ease and confidence. It seems as though they have managed to establish themselves successfully as true multi-hyphenate actresses-directors-creators from the beginning, and no one looked at them askance. I battle "Brenda" in my head when she tells me that it's my fault—that I cared too much what people thought, that I was too fearful, unfocused, or lazy. That I wasn't a good enough writer, or that I made the wrong choices. Sometimes she even tells me that I would have been better off without the red hair.

*   *   *   *   *   *

Last week I was having dinner with a sixty-something-year-old artist I admire. I confided in her about these thoughts I have in my head, and she kindly interrupted me.

"But Molly, you couldn't have. Don't you see?"

I stopped talking and considered what she was telling me. She also happens to be the mother of one of the brightest millennials of her generation.

"None of these young women could've done what they are doing now if it hadn't been for what you have done, or what I have done. Just as the future generations will get to do more because of these young women."

I thought a lot about what she said on the train ride home. I made lists in my head about what I'd like to achieve for myself in the next ten years, and it's long. (Get ready, "Brenda"!) The list making took me all the way to my stop. And then, because I also think about how my own daughters feel about ambition, the next day I asked my eldest, who is twelve (a part of what has been dubbed the "Founders" generation), what her biggest ambition is.

She considered my question and after a moment answered definitively. "My biggest ambition is to not stress about ambition." She smiled and shrugged. "I just want to be happy."

Maybe this generation is on to something.

Ambition: The Cliffie Notes

• • • • • •   **JOAN LEEGANT**

S pring, 1971. Sanders Theatre, Harvard University. It's a
Saturday; perhaps it's raining. I've been in this lecture hall
before. I'm a student here, a *Cliffie*, as Radcliffe women
were called, a term made famous the year before, after Ali Mac-
Graw showed up at the Radcliffe dorms to impersonate one for
the filming of *Love Story*. Some of my friends tried to sign on
as extras; I was, apparently, too busy. In this giant room inside
Harvard's neo-Gothic, red-bricked Memorial Hall, Harvard
Law professor Paul Freund teaches the wildly popular Social Sciences 137: The Legal Process. Eight hundred rapt undergraduates, myself among them, squeeze into the narrow seats twice
a week to hear Freund expound on the moral underpinnings
of the law, beginning with the fictitious case of the Speluncean
Explorers, trapped travelers who cannibalize one of their number to survive. Are they guilty of a criminal offense? Is morality
relative? Is the law fungible? How do we decide what's right?

Today, though, I am not here to listen to the great professor.
Today is the LSAT, the law school admissions test. Although I
am an English major—a switch from government made earlier

this year, and one of my few smart moves during college—I am determined to stay true to my plan to become a lawyer. I don't have much of an idea of what lawyers do except become Harvard professors or Supreme Court Justices or what I see on *Perry Mason,* and also that they talk a lot, based on a verbose uncle in upstate New York. But I've been told by teachers and family members and assorted other adults all my life that I am destined to do something responsible and productive. Being responsible and productive comes naturally to me. A serious child, then a serious adolescent, morally minded and precociously tall, always taken for older—I was five-foot-six by age twelve—I seemed perfectly cut out for the part. By high school, I owned several suits. Though what probably appealed to me most about the law in particular when I first conceived of the idea in eighth or ninth grade—and what continues to appeal to me this day of the LSATs, conduct of the Speluncean Explorers aside—is its near worship of rules. I love rules. My home life was chaotic. Fixed codes of conduct would have helped.

At the LSAT, the proctors wait for us to get seated, to shed our jackets, settle our bags on the floor. The room smells of wet socks, a musty, dry heat from the radiators, the metallic breath of hundreds of twenty-one-year-olds who've forced down a fast breakfast of black coffee. A faint cigarette smell sits among us, brought in on the hair, the jeans. I have a two-pack-a-day habit and a fresh box of Marlboros. No sandwich, no candy, as I also have an eating disorder. The test will take all day, with officially scheduled food, cigarette, and bathroom breaks. The room is hushed, only the sounds of test booklets being moved to the optimal spot at the center of each desk, of regulation pencils lightly tapping. Personal computers, even the bulky desktops, haven't been invented. There are no cell phones to turn off or check at the door. Nobody speaks.

One of the proctors looks at a clock. Another gives instructions. Do only one part at a time. Do not move on to the next part until instructed. If we finish a section with time to spare, we're to read our answers over or sit quietly. If we don't finish a section when they call it, let it be—there is a cost to guesswork that makes guessing riskier than leaving the answer blank. It's a matter of odds, we've learned in the informational letter we received weeks before, giving us our identification numbers and reminding us of the time and place: You might get the question right, but you might get it wrong, and wrong is not a zero; it counts against you.

A proctor tells us to take up our booklets, open the seal. Then: Go! Five hundred pencils scratching paper. Five hundred audible mouth breathers. If I don't hear all five hundred, I certainly hear the couple dozen in my immediate vicinity. We are tightly packed. I can't see other booklets and answers—it would be difficult to cheat—but I see hands moving, pencils darkening the circles of multiple choice. I see someone's foot nervously bobbing across the aisle, hear a fingernail drumming wood, the people on either side of me shifting in their chairs.

So, when at the roughly fifteen-minute mark, I begin to sneeze and cannot stop, I know that those nearby can hear me. Soon I know everyone in the room can hear me. I'm keeping one hand over my nose, the other searching my bag for tissues, trying not to attract attention, and I'm mortified. Also mystified. I hadn't felt a cold coming on the night before, or this morning; I hadn't felt sick or strange at all. Nor do I have allergies. Soon the sneezing is constant, convulsive. It's as if a giant allergen has jumped up onto my little desk and squatted on my test booklet and sent forth its tentacles directly into my nasal passages. Sneezes are coming an average of every ten seconds. Within three minutes, I'm exhausted; within five, worried; within seven, a pariah.

It's a major disturbance. Nobody who can see me can concentrate, and though I don't know about the ones who can't see me,

I'm pretty sure they're having trouble too. Those closest to me are getting agitated. They're staring in my direction. A proctor lifts her head. Any moment, one of the students will raise a hand and ask the proctor to speak to me. I get up, gather my jacket, my bag, my rain hat—for it was raining, after all, when I arrived—my test booklet, gather it all up as unobtrusively as I can and make my way to the front before another convulsion seizes me. I turn in the booklet, cancel my score, leave the room, and step outside. The sun is shining. I put on my jacket, skip the hat.

And immediately stop sneezing.

•   •   •   •   •   •

Three years before, in September 1968, three hundred newly admitted Radcliffe freshwomen sit in the auditorium in Agassiz Hall on a crisp New England afternoon listening to greetings from Mary Bunting, a plain-looking, gray-haired woman wearing a pastel cotton shirtwaist and glasses, looking for all the world like an aging Sunday School teacher or someone's grandmother. It is somewhat startling, therefore, to consider that Bunting, Radcliffe's fifth president, was then only fifty-eight years old, a PhD microbiologist whose research had once involved studying the effects of radiation on bacteria. She had come to national attention in November 1961, two years after assuming the Radcliffe presidency, gracing the cover of *Time*, in which she identified a societal problem she called "a climate of unexpectation" for girls. Nobody cares, Bunting said in *Time*, what women do with their education. While everyone asked little boys what they wanted to be when they grew up, little girls were asked where they got their pretty dresses. The result was a "waste of highly talented, educated womenpower," a "prodigious national extravagance."[1]

1. Karen W. Arenson, "Mary Bunting-Smith, Ex-President of Radcliffe, Dies at 87," *New York Times*, January 23, 1998, accessed September 9, 2016, http://www.nytimes .com/1998/01/23/us/mary-bunting-smith-ex-president-of-radcliffe-dies-at-87.html.

Bunting set out to change that and devoted her career to raising expectations among and about women, and to helping create opportunities for them that they'd previously been denied. During her presidency, women were admitted for the first time to Harvard's graduate and business schools, Radcliffe students received Harvard diplomas—their classes had been coed with Harvard since World War II—and Radcliffe undergraduates were explicitly and vigorously exhorted to achieve, especially in the highest echelons previously reserved for men. Though Bunting herself had four children and two husbands, the implication was clear: We were to look beyond marriage and family, and beyond fields traditionally populated by women. Teaching, nursing, social work, anything carrying the stigma of a support role: not acceptable. Ditto for working in an ordinary business or service industry or at a trade. The acceptable paths for a Radcliffe student were to the professions, the arts, the life of the mind.

It was not merely a privilege but a duty to aspire to the highest ranks, Mary Bunting told us in the Agassiz auditorium that September day after reciting a litany of achievements already amassed by this roomful of eighteen-year-olds before we'd even gotten started: this many concert violinists, that many Westinghouse Science Scholars, this many championship athletes. A roomful of Most Likely to Succeeds. If there was a climate of unexpectation out there, none of us had grown up in it. We were the future of women's achievement, Mary Bunting said. We were being given the gift of a superior education coveted by many—admission to Radcliffe that year made it the most selective college in the country, far more selective than Harvard. Entry was ours to take and use wisely.

The message was unmistakable: You've been selected. Don't let us down.

• • • • • •

In the winter of 1971, a few months before the LSATs, a nagging, unwelcome thought was hovering at the periphery of my mind. I tried to ignore it, but it refused to go away, and it was this: Though I'd performed satisfactorily enough in my pre-law courses in government, I'd fully loved my English classes. I couldn't care less about literary criticism, the tediously analytical essays we had to read, the equally tedious papers we had to write, but I loved the novels and stories and poems and plays. Irish Theatre, the Harlem Renaissance, Slavic literature, a whole semester of Faulkner. When each term's catalog came out, I was a kid in a candy shop, greedily devouring the descriptions. I wanted them all. All year I read like a starving person. I got mediocre grades in English, my work decidedly undistinguished, but I didn't care. Who cared about grades when you had fourteen weeks of Chekhov?

Why, then, was I looking at law schools? If I loved literature, if I spent hours in the listening rooms at Radcliffe's Hilles Library plugged in and headphoned to old LPs of poets reading their work, the gravelly voice of Robert Frost forever engraved on my memory, why was I persisting in the notion of being a lawyer? I wasn't an activist; the student protests against the war had ripped through my undergraduate life like a tidal wave, shutting down the campus, canceling final exams, bringing out the National Guard, and I had watched it all from the sidelines, a mildly interested observer. I might be a decent advocate, could articulate a point of view, but I hated confrontation, hated arguing. I had never joined a debate club or had a taste for verbal sparring. I had no aptitude for strategy, for posturing or bluffing for the sake of a win.

But I couldn't align my future with my love of Tennessee Williams and Turgenev. In 1971, the country was burning. I was a middle-class Jewish girl from Long Island whose relatives were union organizers and wholesale dress salesmen and accountants, and, notably, Allen Ginsberg, my father's cousin. I'd met him once when he was performing Buddhist chants at an outdoor theater. Our family members weren't English professors in tweed jackets, discoursing on Spenser and *The Faerie Queene* and living in stately houses on Cambridge's Brattle Street, a neighborhood with an aura so rarefied it might as well have been its own country. A choice pressed itself on me. My teachers, my family, Gloria Steinem writing in *Ms.*, Mary Bunting, they'd all let me know what I needed to do: stand up and take my rightful place in society, claim the authority women had been unfairly denied, and run things. Reading novels and writing poems was not standing up or taking any rightful place or running anything.

My roommates were going to medical school, business school, for PhDs. Law schools were heavily recruiting that year to try to raise their numbers of women from an average of 5 percent to 20 percent. Six months after the debacle of the spring LSAT, I was back in the cavernous lecture hall of Sanders Theatre, signed up for another round. A girl I knew from my hometown who had gone to Tufts and whom I remembered as being excessively studious was seated in the aisle across from me. We'd said hello on the way in. I hadn't seen her since high school.

Once again a proctor looked at the clock. Once again a proctor told us to break the seal and open the booklet. Once again someone called: *Go!*

I worked through the first section, perhaps the next. At some point, I glanced across the aisle to see my high school acquaintance furiously coloring parts of her test booklet with a yellow highlighter. Back and forth, back and forth went the bright neon ink. I'd never heard of anyone using a highlighter for the

LSAT. She was expert, practiced. She moved the marker across the page efficiently, quickly. It was mesmerizing.

By the time I woke up, a half hour had passed. I forced my head off the desk and worked on questions until the proctor shouted, *Time!* I put my pencil down. Perhaps there was a bathroom or cigarette break then. I'd have time to consider. I could cancel the test score, which surely would be a poor showing.

Or I could finish the exam, turn in the booklet, live with the results. Because if I didn't, I'd have to wait another year to apply. And what would I do then? Not go?

　　　•　•　•　•　•　•

In 1969, a little-known experimental psychologist named Matina Horner published a report on her doctoral dissertation research. She was studying women's relationships to achievement and had identified something that was holding women back that she called, apparently after herself, the Horner Effect, or the Fear of Success Syndrome. Later, this would be called, simply, Fear of Success, or FOS, as opposed to FOF, Fear of Failure. Fear of Success was described as particularly afflicting young, often well-educated, middle-class women who were smart and likely to succeed, from families that not only encouraged high motivation but also expected their daughters to fulfill traditional roles. Unlike Fear of Failure, which means you're worried you aren't up to the task and might blow it, Fear of Success assumes you're entirely capable but fear the consequences of that capability. Maybe you think you'll be threatening to your significant male others—husbands, boyfriends, fathers, brothers—who won't like your competence. Or you fear you'll be seen as unladylike in your white doctor's coat or blue suit while running a shareholders' meeting. Or if you're married or a mother, maybe you'll feel guilty about the time you're spending on your research or job or whatever it is you're succeeding at, and not enough time with the husband and children. So Fear of Success, the theory goes, conveniently comes along to shoot you in the foot. It undermines you from pursuing your goals, thus rescuing you from anxiety and the consequences you're worried about. To the untrained eye, your behavior may look like Fear of Failure—you don't apply yourself, you're riddled with doubt and second-guessing, you procrastinate or blow off requirements or, in the case of one study, get pregnant just when your success is about to peak—but it has nothing to do with the terror of failure and all to do with the terror of succeeding.

Matina Horner, the daughter of Greek immigrants, was raised in the Roxbury neighborhood of Boston. In 1961, Horner graduated the all-women's Bryn Mawr and, eight years later, with a newly minted PhD in hand, she and her husband went to Harvard with three young children, where Horner took a position as a lecturer, moving up a year later to assistant professor. Two years after that, in 1972, Radcliffe tapped her to become its sixth president, succeeding Mary Bunting. Horner was thirty-two years old, the youngest president in the college's one-hundred-year history. It seems shocking to me now that Horner at the time was a mere ten years older than the seniors who graduated that year, myself among them.

At Radcliffe, Horner's ideas took off like wildfire. It was the perfect storm of theory and cultural shifts. In Mary Bunting's time, the focus was on removing external obstacles to women's achievement—admission to professional schools, equal access to education and careers. Now Matina Horner came along to say that obstacles might reside within the women themselves. Whereas before, we had to give ourselves pep talks to not fear failing, now we had to scour our psyches for the ostensibly real—but hidden—reasons for not forging ahead with that graduate school application, that job possibility, to see if what was causing us to doubt or think twice was something we couldn't see and sounded counterintuitive: the fear of actually doing it well.

There is something both brilliant and crazy-making about this way of scrutinizing one's motivations. If, say, you find yourself not working hard enough to produce the publications you need to qualify for tenure at a university job about which you're ambivalent, you might reasonably conclude that the low productivity is your way of making sure you don't get tenure, thus resolving the situation. In short, getting you off the hook. But with Fear of Success as the operative theory, you have to probe deeper and ask if your unproductive publishing behavior is a sign that you really *do* want the tenured position and are undermining yourself by *thinking* you don't; you then behave in ways to ensure that you don't succeed, because you're afraid of the ultimate side effects of a successful tenure award. So you plod away at the publishing, ignoring the impulse to search out another line of work.

If you're in doubt about a life choice, scrutinizing your thinking and conduct for Fear of Success means not trusting your instincts because your instincts may be your fears in disguise. If—as a twenty-one-year-old with little life experience and an outsized need to please others—you're on the path to a career you don't think you want but don't know why, Fear of Success tells you to stay the course because it's your worry about being successful talking, and women must not let that worry hinder their achievement. In a situation of doubt or ambivalence, assuming a Fear of Success keeps you *in*, when what you really want is *out*.

• • • • • •

A year before Matina Horner was appointed Radcliffe's president, I took a summer school course with her. It was called Psychology of Women. Horner was thirty-one years old and friendly and informal. She was nothing like the Harvard professors I'd had the previous three years, all of them austere, remote, and male. The class was small. We got more personal attention than we'd ever gotten. I learned all about Fear of Success and thought it could probably explain a lot of things for a lot of women. Maybe also me. Was I confused about my future because I was afraid of being good at it? Had I fallen victim to the terrible things holding women back? It was possible; it made sense.

But here's the dirty secret. I liked my class with Dr. Horner, who was warm and caring and the only female professor I had in my college career, but nothing about the Fear of Success rang true to me. I'd been succeeding my whole life, and though I wanted to be doing something different from what I was headed toward, I didn't fear success and hadn't experienced the negative consequences Horner's theory seemed to insist on. To the contrary: Success was expected of me, a given. I didn't feel guilty or embarrassed by being successful. I liked it. The recognition, the praise, the approval. I even liked the suits.

I sat in Dr. Horner's class that summer and thought there must be something wrong with me. Maybe I wasn't a true woman; maybe because I wasn't worried about *not* putting a future husband first—though who'd want a husband like that? I wondered—or being seen as unfeminine if I wore business attire meant that I was a secret man. I scoured my psyche to see if my confusion about my future had telltale signs of Fear of Success so that I could reassure myself that I was a real female. Because that's what women, real women, Dr. Horner told us, felt. I couldn't find any. This made me worry more. I didn't have, it seemed, normal women's psychology. Later, after I'd become a lawyer, the first purchase I would make would be a pair of the highest heels I could manage, so that I would be over six feet tall in the courtroom, able to stand up to, or tower over, the men. The shoes were a pointy brown number with bows.

In 1972, I went to law school. I did my course work but had little ambition beyond that. I assumed I was simply a low-key, noncompetitive person. I spent summers waitressing instead of chasing down legal experience, except one miserably hot August, the same month Richard Nixon resigned, working for a federal agency in Washington, the highlight of which was watching the resignation on TV with all the government employees a mile from where Nixon was making the announcement. Otherwise, what elicited the most enthusiasm for me during law school was feminist irritation, if not outrage, over the insensitivity of certain faculty. The torts professor relied on football analogies to explain negligence, and the man who taught Civil Procedure refused to switch to the newly mandated "Ms." when calling on female students, saying it sounded like something an illiterate Southerner would say. He insisted on asking each woman, "Is it Miss or Mrs.?" I joined a delegation charged to try to set these recalcitrants straight, which met with moderate success.

When it came time to take the bar exam, I had a little talk with myself. I told myself I didn't have to practice law, but that I couldn't fall asleep or have a sneezing attack that would drive me from the room. I convinced myself and passed. I took a job in western Massachusetts working for the only woman lawyer in the county. I'd found her by knocking on her door, résumé in hand. By chance, she too had gone to Radcliffe. Class of 1953.

Three years later, looking for a reason to break away from what had become my life, I went to Jerusalem for what turned into a three-year stay. I told my family I wanted to explore my Jewish roots. The closest friends I made there were Radcliffe graduates. Some were in their twenties, others well into their thirties. There had been no reunion or institutionalized gathering bringing us together; that's just who I met. We all had the same story. We'd been good students and successes in the world and had received praise for skills and talents that didn't really fit who we were. We'd bucked traditional female roles, lived up to our potential, and now we wanted to escape. Each of us had found an excuse to get away—one to explore the religion, another to solidify her conversion and try to save her marriage, a third to teach English and get over a divorce—but all of us were just trying to figure out who we were and what we wanted.

Decades later, after I'd begun to publish short stories, my father, then in his eighties, told me he'd always wondered why I'd become a lawyer when he knew I loved literature.

"Why didn't you tell me?" I said, surprised, even a little upset. He knew? Better than I had? *Why didn't you say anything?*

"Because," he answered, "you never asked."

Doubly Denied

CRISTINA HENRÍQUEZ

I called my mother. I said, "Am I ambitious?"

She said, "You? Yes."

"Really?"

"You don't think so?"

"What's your evidence?" I asked.

"Well, you've been successful. You're good at what you do."

"Okay."

"You've wanted things. You wanted to go to graduate school, for example, and you did it."

"But is that because I'm ambitious?"

"Isn't it?"

"I'm not sure," I said.

I emailed a friend. I wrote: "Question. Would you say I'm ambitious?"

She wrote back: "sure. i mean, you've accomplished a hell of a lot in your thirty-something years, so you're definitely something. why??"

I wrote: "I have to write an essay about ambition, and I can't figure out if I am ambitious."

Her response: "maybe you're committed. is that how you spell that? anyway. you're the real deal—you work regularly, you stay in touch with the world of literature. you clearly HAVE ambition. or ambitions."

      •   •   •   •   •

I asked my husband as we sat on the couch one night, watching television, "What's the most ambitious thing I've ever done?"

He looked at me for a few seconds, thinking. Then he said, "What's the definition of ambitious?"

Exactly.

      •   •   •   •   •

It was only a word, but I kept dancing around it. If someone had asked, I might have said I was tenacious, or that I worked hard, or that I was diligent, or determined, but I never would have said I was ambitious. My mother was right. I had wanted things out of life, but simple desire doesn't necessarily mean a person is ambitious. Ambition, it seemed, was something that other people possessed—men mostly, or Hillary Clinton—but it wasn't something that felt quite like me. But why not?

I lay in bed at night thinking about it. I conjured up memories of when I was just starting college and the thought was forming that maybe, possibly I would like to be a writer, and that maybe, possibly, I had what it would take to make that happen. What kind of writer, I didn't know (in an admissions interview I had been asked what I liked to write and my response was, "Letters"), but a fantasy was taking root in my mind about a life where writing was at the center, a vision that included things like scarves and coffee and stacks of well-worn books, and me, by candlelight, scribbling into the night.

I went to Northwestern University, halfway across the country from Delaware, where I lived, and I used to wander along the edge of Lake Michigan and through the majestic, neo-Gothic Deering Library, awed by where I had ended up. I knew by then that I loved writing, but I still didn't know exactly what I would do with it. Would I actually write books? That seemed like a wild, far-off dream.

Not long into my freshman year, though, I learned that Northwestern had an undergraduate writing program. It was highly competitive, and each year students applied with the hopes that they, and their work, would be deemed worthy. At the end of my sophomore year, I submitted a manuscript, a few very short stories, and waited to learn my fate. I don't remember how the news was delivered, but when it came, I do remember feeling that I had been punched in the gut. I didn't get in.

I could have stopped there, I guess. I could have interpreted the rejection as the universe's way of telling me that I should find something else to do. But although I was devastated (I wrote entry after tearful journal entry about it), I was stubborn, too. I applied to the program again the following year. That time, I was accepted.

A similar story played out when I was leaving college. My wild dream of writing books for a living had solidified by then, and I thought the best course would be to go to graduate school to learn how to do that. I knew almost nothing about graduate programs, so I found a copy of *U.S. News & World Report* and looked up the most recent rankings of graduate writing programs, chose five in the top ten, and applied. Every single one turned me down.

For the next two years, I worked in the publicity department at a university press. During my lunch break I wrote stories—one about people stuck in an elevator, one about cliff-jumping during the summer, one about a man who cuts off his pinky finger—and at the end of the day, I went home to my studio apartment and wrote more, banging out stories on the manual typewriter I had bought at a church sale. When the stories were finished, I put them in envelopes and mailed them to a former professor, who read them and gave me feedback that he jotted down and mailed back to me. I sent stories to magazines, ridiculous pipe dreams like the *New Yorker* and the *Atlantic* and *Zoetrope* and *BOMB*, and all of them got rejected. Incredibly, none of it put me off course. Eventually I applied to graduate programs again. Different ones this time, and I submitted different material. I hoped—God, I hoped—it would be enough.

It was. The first school I heard back from was the Iowa Writers' Workshop, the top-ranked program in the country, telling me I had gotten in.

Was it tenacity? Resilience? Just plain hardheadedness? Or could it have been ambition, churning somewhere inside of me all that time? And if so, why was it so difficult for me to simply call it what it was?

· · · · · ·

Growing up, I can't recall any discussion of ambition in my house—at least, not in an overt way. I was the oldest of three, and though expectations were high (A's were good, A-pluses were better), my parents gave all of us wide berth to explore our interests. They opened doors, as many as they could, and then left it up to us whether we would walk through. In grade school, they rented me a violin when I said I wanted to learn. They bought me the books I wanted to read from every Scholastic book fair. They went out of their way to plan trips so that my brother and sister and I would have the benefit of encountering new places. They allowed my natural enthusiasm—and from that my ambition—to flourish on its own, in its time, and then let me follow it in any direction I chose. In certain ways, this seems like one of the best gifts a parent could give a child.

And yet, when it came time for me to start thinking about college, I do remember my father telling me, "I think you should apply to Princeton."

I remember I laughed.

This was at the time when bulging envelopes filled with glossy folders and brochures touting the glories of schools all over the country arrived daily in the mailbox. I lay on my bed and pored over them, captivated by photographs of happy students walking through leaves and sitting on grassy lawns in the sun.

"I'm serious," he said. "It's a good school."

I thought he was nuts, of course, but when I look back on it now, I see that my father was trying to teach me something. He must have known how improbable it was for me to go to Princeton. (Northwestern, where I ended up going, was enough of a long shot.) *But it's important*, he seemed to be telling me, *to reach for things that might seem beyond your grasp*. The only way to *get* further is to *reach* further, after all. To be ambitious is to connect yourself to the future. It's a movement outward, forward, toward something new.

It's not surprising that it's a lesson I learned from my father. When he was eighteen, my father came from Panama to the United States to study chemical engineering at the University of Delaware. It was the first time he had been away from home, and he traveled by himself with a trunk and a suitcase and a student visa in his pocket. He came with hope and fear and what surely can only be described as ambition. To be an immigrant, after all, to uproot your life, to walk away from everything you have known with the goal of going somewhere new and with the hope of finding something better is to be, necessarily, ambitious.

But if his leaving Panama seemed the very embodiment of ambition, my father also brought with him certain attitudes that seemed to undermine it, at least where women were concerned. He was raised in a culture that operates within the structure of traditional gender roles, which meant, for example, that he expected my mother to serve him dinner every night, no matter how late he arrived home from work, and that he had to adjust when she wanted to get a job after my brother, sister, and I were grown. I saw all of that, of course. And seeing it against the backdrop of my father's personal story, I received two messages about ambition, both of which came through loud and clear: the importance of striving and the importance of staying put.

• • • • • •

A year after my first book had been published, more than a decade after my father brought up Princeton, I had my first child. I lived halfway across the country from my parents by then, so as often as I could I called my mother on the webcam. I was in the throes of new motherhood, lonely and feeling much of the time like I had been sideswiped by a truck. In those early months, I struggled, as many new parents do, to get through the days. My husband was back at work, and I shuffled around in my bathrobe, which I didn't even have the energy to tie, and nursed my daughter while I gazed down at her long eyelashes and full cheeks, and fell asleep on the couch when I could, and stared in the mirror at the deep blue circles under my eyes, and tried to make sense of what had happened to me. My mother was my savior. Over the computer, she sympathized and told me how hard it had been for her at the beginning. She recounted being home with young children, being far from family, the consuming loneliness when my father was traveling for work, as he often did. She told me in no uncertain terms how important it was to be doing what I was doing, how important it was to have this time to bond with my daughter. She believed, she said to me more than once, that when they could, when financially it was a viable option, at least one parent should stay home to be with their children. She was trying to comfort me, I know, to assure me that I was doing something good, even noble. But she was sending another message, too: It was what I was *supposed* to be doing.

I had decided by then that I was going to try to stay home with my daughter. I was in the middle of my first novel, but I could write while she napped, I reasoned. I could write at night. And later, when my daughter was in preschool, I could use that time to write, too. I wouldn't get the book finished quite as fast, but that was okay. Eventually I would complete it. Eventually I would get back on track.

Except that I never did.

Writing during naptimes was a bust. It was laughable that I thought that would work. Evenings were a bust, too. Most nights, all I could do was stuff a new breast pad into my nursing bra before collapsing in bed. And preschool, of course, was still years away. Oh, they go fast! everyone always tells you. Maybe, but I needed the time *right then*.

The longer I went without writing, the more frustrated I became. I was crazy about my daughter, utterly in love. But I missed connecting to that part of myself I had honed over so many years. And I couldn't figure out a way to get writing back into my life. Or not, I should say, a way that didn't involve leaving my daughter for periods of time. "Hire someone," my husband told me. "Your work is important." But I couldn't bring myself to do it. I kept hearing my mother's voice in my head, telling me how vital it was to be at home. If I didn't do that, would I have failed? But if I didn't continue writing, wouldn't I be failing in another way? Had I turned into a walking cliché of the woman who wants it all?

When people asked me what I did, sometimes I said that I was writer, but more and more I started answering that I was a stay-at-home mother. "I'm surprised to even hear you describe yourself that way," a friend of mine said. But wasn't it the truth? The overwhelming majority of my time was spent taking care of my child or taking care of the house. Writing was just something I was squeezing in—a quick paragraph while I sat in the car in a parking lot because my daughter had fallen asleep in her car seat, a page or two on a weekend morning when my husband was around—if I was doing it at all.

The imbalance altered my sense of identity and, along with it, my concept of my own ambition. *Ambition* is a word that most people associate with professional life, after all. Ask someone if they see themselves as ambitious, and if they answer yes, most of the time they will tell you about something related to their career. And yet, motherhood exists outside of the bounds of professionalism in our country. It's not a job, society tells mothers, at least not a real one. And because it's not viewed that way, the concept of ambition gets divorced from the concept of motherhood. Insofar as I identified as a stay-at-home mother, I didn't identify as someone who had—at least not anymore—much ambition at all.

Eventually, I did hire a sitter. I asked her to come only three mornings a week—a compromise with myself. It was enough time to slowly, slowly finish my second book. But the decision was fraught. I was happy to be writing again, even in limited doses, but I felt awful every time I walked out the door. "Why?" my husband kept asking me, genuinely confounded. It would be different, I told him, if I were going to an office and getting a regular paycheck. At least then I would have something to show for it.

"But you *will* have something to show for it one day," he argued.

"But what if it takes me ten years to finish this book?"

"So? That's like me saying what if I only got paid once every ten years? It doesn't mean I wouldn't go to work every day."

It was all so cut-and-dry for him, which I found incredible and also made me a little resentful. Why was it so easy for him to walk out the door each morning, while I felt trapped inside this dense tangle of choices and guilt and expectation and desire? But I saw his point. What if I really didn't finish a book or get paid again for another ten years? What if I never published a book and never got paid? What if I kept writing merely because I wanted to? Because I had this fire in me that wouldn't die out, and I wanted to feed it? Because every time I sat down to write I had the thought that I wanted to create something great? Wasn't that ambition? The urge to reach for something beyond what I had accomplished in the past, to strive toward new heights? Why did I feel like I needed the promise of some financial reward or public acknowledgment before I could claim my own ambition, before I could say, yes, I want to do this thing? Was I looking for permission to be ambitious, to really grab hold of it, because I didn't believe I deserved to claim it otherwise? Had I been shying away from the word all this time because I didn't feel I deserved it, not unless someone else told me I did?

·   ·   ·   ·   ●   ●

Years and years ago, when I applied to Northwestern and got in, a friend of mine who hadn't been accepted said to me, "You know the only reason they let you in is because you're Hispanic, right?" I can only assume he meant it as a joke, though it came across as anything but. Affirmative action. Quotas. Dumb luck. These are the reasons I got what I got. It could not have been that I had worked hard for years, toiling over papers in my room, staying up late to study. It could not have been that I was naturally curious, a high school student who was reading Dylan

Thomas and Samuel Beckett and the letters of Zelda Fitzgerald in her spare time. It could not have been my record of community service nor my strong GPA. It could not have been that I wrote one hell of an admissions essay. It could not have been, simply, me.

A woman is denied her ambition on the grounds of gender. Ambition is active, not passive; it's forceful, not meek; it's stubborn, not yielding. It's everything that society tells women not to be. It's unfeminine, for goodness sake! And yet to be a woman of color—even a woman of some color, like me—is to be told all of that and more. A woman of color who exhibits ambition and who makes good on that ambition to achieve something, no matter how big or how small, is often told—subtly, overtly, it doesn't matter—that she didn't actually achieve much at all, and that what she did achieve, she didn't deserve. To be a woman of color is to be doubly denied.

This is how things get taken from you. Somewhere along the way, a seed was planted, and a part of me began to believe that maybe my accomplishments—academic degrees and published books—were not much more than a matter of luck or a helping hand. In my better moments, I knew that was stupid. But at times when I was feeling low, or vulnerable, or unsure of who I was anymore, the seed bloomed like ivy, threatening to strangle. At those times, I began to believe it: that I got what I got because of forces beyond my control, not because of any particular talent or skill or ambition, and certainly not because I deserved it.

•   •   •   •   •   •

The other night I visited a book club—approximately twenty middle-age women who had read my novel and invited me to join them. We sat in the host's beautiful living room with its stone fireplace, and ate candy corn and drank wine. After we discussed my book, one of the women asked me what I was working on next. I mentioned that I was trying to finish an essay about ambition. I said, "Do you all think you're ambitious?"

Immediately, a petite woman with red hair spoke up. "I absolutely think I'm ambitious." She went on to tell the group how she had known, since she was twelve years old, that she wanted to be a lawyer, and how she let nothing stand in the way of achieving that goal. She told us about her daughter, who she described as driven, and who had just been accepted to a prestigious PhD program. "Have you had explicit conversations with her," I asked, "about her own ambition? About claiming it?" Yes, the woman told me. She paused. "But I'm of an age now where I want grandchildren," she said almost apologetically, "and I would like them before I'm too old to do anything with them." The rest of the women nodded. I could see where this was going. All along, she'd been sending her daughter one message, and now she didn't want to send a second—one about how she hoped her daughter would take time to start a family—that seemed counter to the first.

"But maybe we're too limited in our definition of ambition," another woman said. "I had a lot of ambition, but I didn't necessarily succeed in anything I did. I failed at most of it, but I still consider myself ambitious."

Can failure be part of ambition, too? All along I had been thinking that achievement was the end point. I thought of ambition, I realized, like a curve on a graph where desire was the point of origin, striving was a sweep upward in the middle, and achievement was the result. But maybe I'd been thinking about it wrong.

Another woman said, "I don't know. I wanted to stay home with my kids, so I turned my ambition toward them. My kids are older now, but I remember back then worrying that by staying home with them I was putting aside my ambition. But now the way I see it is that I just redirected it."

"I think that's true," someone else said. "And I think that's the difference between men and women. Men measure ambition by their professional achievements, whereas women measure it by how much of a difference they've made in the world."

"Exactly," another woman offered. "I don't think of it as ambition so much as passion."

"Like finding your purpose."

"Right. And going after it."

I smiled. Here we were, dancing around the word again, only now we were all doing the dance together. It was a slippery concept for everyone, apparently, one that was hard to get a handle on. And yet, as I sat there among these women, I felt a certain clarity that I hadn't before. Maybe it was something they had said, or maybe it was because I had spent so much time in the weeks leading up to that moment considering ambition and scrutinizing it, untangling all of my associations with the word. I thought about how, not long before, I had asked everybody I knew whether they saw me as ambitious. But I didn't need anyone or anything else, I realized—not a person, not a book deal, not a paycheck—to tell me what I already knew. I do want things—sometimes I want all the things—and often those things feel out of reach, but I stretch my arms out for them regardless, in my way. My ambition was there, and it had always been there, subdued at some times and thunderous at others, but never absent. I only needed to look within myself to see it.

The conversation went on for a while, but near the end of it one of the women threw the question back at me. "Do you think you're ambitious?" she asked.

I turned to her. "Yes," I answered without hesitation. "I think I am."

Becoming Meta

●　●　●　●　●　●　HAWA ALLAN

*A noun is the proper denotation for a thing. I can say that
I have things: for instance that I have a table, a house,
a book, a car. The proper denotation for an activity, a
process, is a verb: for instance I am, I love, I desire, I
hate, etc. Yet ever more frequently an activity is expressed
in terms of having; that is, a noun is used instead of a
verb. But to express an activity by to have in connection
with a noun is an erroneous use of language, because
processes and activities cannot be possessed; they can only
be experienced.*

—ERICH FROMM, *To Have or to Be?*

have been to a few Madonna concerts in my day, so I may or
may not have been straining to get a view around the pillar
planted in front of my discount seat when I beheld the super-
star kick up into a forearm stand in the middle of the stage.
For non-initiates, a "forearm stand" is a yoga pose wherein you
balance your entire body on your forearms—lain parallel to one

another on the ground, and perpendicular to your upper arms, torso, and legs, all of which are inverted skyward. Imagine turning your body into an "L." And then imagine Madonna doing the same, except spotlighted before thousands of gaping fans in a large arena.

I hadn't done any yoga at that point, so the irony of Madonna flaunting her ability in a discipline meant to induce inner awareness was totally lost on me. I just thought it was cool. Precisely, I interpreted Madonna's forearm stand as a demonstration of power—power that was quiet yet fierce. An expression of power that I immediately decided I wanted to embody. So, not too long thereafter, I went ahead and enrolled in a series of free, introductory lessons at yoga studios across Manhattan and Brooklyn. My modus operandi: take advantage of the introductory classes and skip to another studio (once I no longer had a discounted pass). I was doing this, I told myself at the time, to test out different teachers—to find "the right fit." In hindsight, I can see that this was just an excuse for being itinerant and cheap.

In any case, I had a fair amount of time to shuttle between boroughs. My schedule was relatively flexible because I was in my second year of law school. Of course, with law school being law school, my schedule was not absolutely flexible, just *relatively*—relative, that is, to the circulation-cutting constraints of my first year, which is both notoriously and actually all-consuming. I hadn't seen any of the films you are supposed to watch before your first day of law school, the ones in which some curmudgeon badgers you with cryptic questions and cleverly insults you as you strain to answer them amid the muffled chuckles of your peers. In my experience, all institutional education was rife with illegitimate authority and bullying, so I didn't see why law school should be especially different. If anything, I was up for the challenge. I was quietly determined.

My quiet determination, mind you, had very little to do with the subject at hand. Of course, I cared deeply about injustice, which, unlike the lofty concept of "justice," was down to earth and concrete—evident in the myriad of detrimental effects that structural inequality was having on actual human beings who lived in the real world—and, moreover, I thought law school would provide the practical tools to upend injustice. However, as it turned out, I just didn't care very much about the law. A "tort," as far as I'd ever known before that first year, referred to a kind of cake. And subjects like constitutional law, which were, to me, less esoteric and more pertinent to eradicating "injustice," were systematically drained of all intrigue by the sheer volume of material we were expected to retain.

My charge that first year was not to think and critique, but to memorize and regurgitate. There was no time to consider what the law *should* or *might* be, only to apprehend what it *was*, and then dutifully apply it to a hypothetical fact pattern while ignoring my moral compass. Throughout this experience, I fully grasped the meaning of that saying about the unpleasantness of sausage factories. "Justice" was no longer an abstract concept. "Justice" was sausage. "Justice sausage," moreover, was oft composed of the dismembered carcasses of injustice; but once we students arduously cranked it through this elaborate machine, we were too exhausted by the process to question the fairness of the outcome. (Burning crosses, for example, was totally constitutional, a protected form of free speech, even—as long as you burned them on your own lawn.) And so, for many, the legal process in and of itself came to justify the result, whatever it happened to be. I watched many a fellow student transform from a sentient being into an android that spouted legal precedent on demand.

My growing distaste for the law notwithstanding, I still wanted to do very well. So, I suspended disbelief and went with the program. I tagged textbook pages with fine-point pens. I dropped the holdings of cases into classroom mics. Like a dutiful subject of colonial education, I imbibed and disgorged. In the end, my results that year were mostly in the B+ range. I was told that I had done "very well," as we were all graded on a strict curve. But I was appalled. I'd studied harder than I ever had—all the while denying myself an active social life and lugging around brick-thick books and rainbow packs of highlighters in an unflattering purple Jansport—just for a bunch of B-pluses? I thought this was unacceptable. I would have to do much better the next year. I was quietly determined.

•   •   •   •   •   •

"Education is transformational. It changes lives," former U.S. Secretary of State Condoleezza Rice has said. "That is why people work so hard to become educated and why education has always been the key to the American Dream." I found this quotation in *Think and Grow Rich for Women*—a female spin on the 1937 motivational classic by Napoleon Hill, who studied successful businessmen of his day and distilled their secrets into a subset of principles anyone could presumably follow toward his dreams. (I'm not using "he," "him," and "his" loosely here, merely indicating the target audience of the time.)

The 2014 version for women features Rice's quote in a chapter titled "Specialized Knowledge"—one of Hill's promulgated steps to success. The chapter title implies that a deep knowledge of one's subject area or corner of her profession gives her a wide lead in the rat race. However, though Hill points out in the original text that all employers value specialists, he spends the rest of the chapter dismissing the intrinsic value of knowledge. Knowledge, Hill says, is only useful insofar as it translates into some tangible—i.e., monetary—value. He illustrates the insufficiency of *mere* knowledge by noting that, while university faculties possess "practically every form of general knowledge known to civilization . . . [m]ost of the professors have but little or no money."

So, knowledge, for Hill, is a means and hardly an end in itself. And specialized knowledge is not gleaned solely to deepen one's understanding of any given subject, but to capture a niche in the marketplace. Specialized knowledge, moreover, is a commodity that can be bought or sold. Hill illustrated this point with automobile magnate Henry Ford. Having filed a libel claim against a newspaper for publishing editorials that called him "ignorant," Ford—testifying in court—became frustrated when he found himself unable to answer basic questions about U.S. history. Ford eventually went on the offensive, telling his cross examiner: "I have a row of electric push-buttons on my desk, and by pushing the right button, I can summon to my aid men who can answer ANY question I desire to ask concerning the business to which I am devoting most of my efforts." Why then, Ford continued, should he "clutter up" his mind to answer "foolish" questions when he could just order the men around him to do so.

Hill referred to the consortium of men Ford had at his fingertips as a "Master Mind" group—a collective of informed peers with whom one could brainstorm and strategize, or, for Ford, who were hired to know things that he didn't want to know. Former President George W. Bush must have considered Rice to be a master mind. "One summer day in 1999, Condi, Laura and I were hiking on the ranch. As we started to climb up a steep grade, Condi launched into a discourse on the history of the Balkans," Bush wrote in his 2010 memoir *Decision Points*. "Laura and I are huffing and puffing. Condi kept going, explaining the disintegration of Yugoslavia and the rise of Milosevic . . . I decided that if I ended up in the Oval Office, I wanted Condi Rice by my side."

It's all well and good that specialized knowledge can put one in a coveted position of being an indispensable advisor—one who can supply knowledge that is in demand. However, what is missing from Hill's discussion of this knowledge is how one gets to be in the position of a George W. Bush or Henry Ford. In other words, Hill doesn't tell you how you get to be the one who does not have to know.

• • • • • •

At some point during my second year of law school, I availed myself of a discount membership to the campus gym and enrolled in an Iyengar class that counterbalanced my yoga-hopping. Iyengar is a school of yoga that emphasizes the precise alignment of one's body when doing an asana, or a pose. A stern woman with long black hair who was more like a stereotypical law professor than any of my actual law professors taught the class. She reprimanded me for whispering for help from my neighbors. She wondered aloud about whether my voluminous box braids would impede my practice. When we all stood our backs against the wall with arms raised, she pushed my own biceps in line with my ears, pooh-poohing my alarm when we both heard something in my upper back crunch. She was intense.

My law school classes, by contrast, seemed far less challenging. This was due, in part, to my ability to select course subjects, which were a welcome substitute for the mandatory curriculum of my first year. However, the load—the bulk of information that I had to stuff into my head—was comparable. If this portion of the essay were a film montage, Madonna's *Don't Tell Me to Stop* would be playing in the background, its acoustic guitar alternately lilting and stuttering as I struggled to hold an asana, then streaked textbook pages with a neon pink highlighter, then raised my hand in class to mouth an answer that was inaudible behind the music but appeared to be correct as, after a pregnant pause, I smiled to myself in response to some off-camera validation. This kind of sequence would repeat with some variation, the key difference being that I would hold the asanas with seemingly less effort. Also interspersed in this sequence would be some shots of me hanging out with college friends somewhere in downtown Manhattan, as I was also going out incessantly during this period. You would not, however, spot a purple Jansport in any of the frames, as I wisely shed it for a more fashionable tote.

Suffice it to say that, by the end of my second year, I earned almost all A's.

· · · · · ·

There was more to Rice's quote in *Think and Grow Rich for Women*. She declared that education "erases arbitrary divisions of race and class and culture and unblocks every person's God-given potential." Rice's mother and father, a schoolteacher and college administrator, respectively, instilled in their only child the importance of education. Born in Birmingham, Alabama, about six months after the *Brown v. Board of Education* decision, Rice was afforded as many advantages as her parents could afford. She started piano lessons at the age of three and moved on to take lessons in ballet, flute, violin, ice-skating, tennis, and French by her adolescence. Her parents relocated to Colorado, where Rice attended a racially integrated school for the first time and eventually enrolled into the University of Denver at age fifteen. After getting a master's degree in international relations at Notre Dame, she became a professor at Stanford and went on to become the youngest, first black, and first female provost.

During Rice's tenure as a professor, a graduate student she

was a minefield. I grew so terrified of speaking in class that, one day, instead of raising my hand to ask my third-grade teacher if I could use the bathroom, I sat there as the urine soaked through my pants, filled the plastic seat bolted to my desk, and dripped onto the floor. (My teacher, God bless her, covered for me, saying the pee was apple juice, otherwise I never would have heard the end of it.)

All emotions, I have since learned, require an outlet. Like dreams deferred, they fester and run or, perhaps, explode. In my case, my anxiety expressed itself as a near-constant stream of commentary, often humorous, that I just had to share with my neighbor in whispers and notes. I became, as my teachers often called me in report cards, "a social butterfly." I became, in other words, "a problem."

As Frankfurt school psychoanalyst Erich Fromm discussed in *To Have or to Be?*, nouns have increasingly displaced verbs to describe certain phenomena. Patients seeking help from a therapist, for example, are more likely to say that they "have" a problem than to report that they "were" troubled. "[S]ubjective experience is eliminated," Fromm explained, "the *I* of the experience is replaced by the *it* of the problem." While Fromm thought this shift in language usage indicated alienation from one's self, my being a "problem" rather than being "troubled" represented my alienation from the rest of my class. I was not perceived as a human being experiencing a feeling, but rather as a problematic object that should be removed—akin to how Western medicine beholds a tumor as a foreign, malignant entity that must be lanced from the patient, rather than, as holistic health practitioners would interpret, a symptom of a systemic issue affecting the entire body.

Moreover, knowledge was no longer transferred to me as if through osmosis, suffusing and transforming my very being;

it was, rather, something that I came to possess and stockpile, like ammunition. Knowledge became less a thing to be shared and more a weapon with which to defend myself, and let fly with spite.

• • • • • •

A funny thing happened after I took the bar exam and before I started working at a large corporate law firm in Manhattan. I kicked up into a forearm stand—granted, I did so against a wall and with the aid of a blue foam block that my trial yoga teacher of the week advised us to frame between our hands for balance. Nonetheless, I was proud; I suppose it was fitting for pride to arise from entering into an asana whose Sanskrit name, *pincha mayurasana*, means "feathered peacock pose"—as I interpret it, the kind of asana you show off in. Heading home that day, my yoga mat rolled and pinned under my arm, I felt the sort of smug elation someone might feel after she'd just purchased a very expensive pair of shoes.

This feeling, however, faded quickly and was a distant recollection by the middle of my second year at the law firm. Though a bona fide Juris Doctor, working at a law firm was still reminiscent of being in law school: We had "classes" filled with all of the other associates who joined the firm the same year; each member of the class advanced every calendar year, as one would advance to the next grade. Instead of teachers, we had "partners," whose approval every ambitious associate sought to obtain by producing good work product and promptly responding to emails at all hours of the day. Hungry associates were voracious for partner validation, disseminated in the form of positive feedback in periodic reviews and "sexy" work assignments that might eventually appear in the *Wall Street Journal* or *Financial Times*. Accordingly, some associates were known to make you look bad in front of your superiors, aka, "throw you under the bus," to appear more competent or to "cover" their collective "ass." One day, walking with a stack of documents in my hands, I imagined collapsing from exhaustion in the hallway and one of my cohorts stepping over my unconscious body without losing his stride.

The aforementioned summation of law firm life is not one I am only making in hindsight. It was not lost on me at the time that this environment was also rife with illegitimate authority and bullying. But I wanted to do very well. So I worked very hard. If this part of the essay were in a film, you would not see a montage, but rather a time-lapse shot of me sitting behind a desk in my erstwhile office as the sun rose and set and rose and set and rose and set outside the window.

I was miserable. However, as in well-plotted genre fiction, the extreme situation that I'd found myself in forced me to reconsider all that I'd thought I'd known about myself. Who knew that I had a latent affinity for the Fourth of July, a holiday that had failed to stir any feeling in me until I found myself, two years in a row, due to work, unable to attend a lame barbecue with the rest of America? I also learned that I didn't want to spend the rest of my working days immediately answering emails sent from all time zones. Most importantly, I discovered my erroneous conflation of "doing well"—a position that is inextricable from accumulating accolades on one's transcript or periodic performance evaluation form—with "being well."

I'm not proud to admit that the global financial crisis, for me, personally, was a profound relief. I didn't lose my job or housing, and the deluge of work (that had been aggravated by an apparent-in-hindsight bubble) suddenly subsided. My email stopped pinging, my BlackBerry stopped vibrating, and I could once again hear my thoughts above the droning hum of the built-in temperature-regulating apparatus in my office. I soon realized that I hadn't done any yoga in several months. It's true that I had been incredibly busy. But when I searched my memory files for the last time I'd regularly attended a yoga class—that is, not just popped in sporadically—I realized that it had not been too long after I'd kicked up into a forearm stand for the first time.

Soon thereafter, in the eerie post-apocalyptic silence of the financial crisis, I started to do yoga again.

* * * * * *

Is it needless to say that most of the associates and partners at my law firm were white? Is it needless to say that most of the students and professors at my elite law school were white? For the purpose of this essay, it is not, because—as with the whiteness of my gifted and talented class—this backdrop helped set the tenor of my ambition. You don't have to be a yogi to be enchanted by a mantra. We all have mantras. The difference is that yogis choose the words that are repeated in their heads, while the average person typically doesn't and becomes entranced by unconscious spells. I can see now that one of my mantras was *I'll show you*.

"I became an overachiever to get approval from the world," Madonna apparently said, according to one of those websites that aggregates decontextualized quotes from persons of note. Nonetheless, I can picture these words spoken by both Madonna and Condi, with a challenge in their eyes and capped with a gap-toothed Cheshire smile.

I could be projecting, of course. My own gap-toothed smile notwithstanding, I could very well be seeing something in the two of them that I recognize in myself. Whether Madonna's "Blond Ambition" or Rice's particular brand of black ambition, I am intimately familiar with that drive to prove that I can do whatever a man and/or white person can do—and more. The law firm, where white men abounded, was a psychodramatic playground in which to exercise this ambition. It was also a playing field in which—as in the coveted worlds of Henry Ford and George W. Bush—there appeared to be a marked divide between those who *had* to know, and those who *did not* have to know. The "rainmakers" were those partners who must have known something at some point, but—due to the amount of business they were capable of bringing in—no longer needed to know as much. Rainmaker business was then handled on a day-to-day and, frankly, mundane level by the "service" partners, a kind of Master Mind group for law firms. The service partners obviously had to know quite a lot about their respective niches of specialized knowledge, knowledge that was essential for completing the documentation that would "paper the deal" for the firm's client.

The path to becoming a service partner was, at least theoretically, clear: accumulate sufficient specialized knowledge and demonstrate your proficiency in it to whatever partners were paying attention. The road to being a rainmaker, by contrast, was far less straightforward, depending as it did on such dubious factors as "proximity" and "access" to said rainmakers, factors that effectively amounted to being "chosen" or "tracked." While it was unclear how to become a rainmaker, it was certainly clear to me that, in the context of the law firm, this is who I would rather be. It was also clear that I didn't see any women or people of color making it rain.

When I finally had time to contemplate all of this, during those precious slow months after the financial crisis first hit, I started to feel like a pawn in a much larger game, being slid here and there by some invisible hand. Incidentally, two white male partners—both libertarians—seemed to authentically value my efforts, giving me the illusion of agency. Nonetheless, I finally appreciated the ways in which my life was not like a clichéd, mainstream movie, in which, after a number of tightly plotted moves, I would arrive at some static scene of "success." Life was more complex than that. I also decided that I'd done enough showing off.

In her memoir *No Higher Honor*, Rice reflected on her trying relationship with Donald Rumsfeld, who appeared to be less congenial toward Rice in her role as a peer rather than as a subordinate:

> . . . [T]he two of us were walking side by side through the Rose Garden portico. I turned to Don and asked, "What's wrong between us?"
>
> "I don't know," he said. "We always got along. You're obviously bright and committed, but it just doesn't work."
>
> *Bright?* That, I thought to myself, was part of the problem.

Epistemology is the philosophical inquiry into *how* one knows what she knows. What has preoccupied me of late is, rather, *why* anyone knows what he or she knows. Becoming meta, I now understand, is a long, unending process. Perhaps I thought it was a state that I had "achieved" after having been metaphysically body-slammed into a state of alienation by my "gifted and talented" white peers. But I was not some transcendent observer, wisely watching over myself with compassion. I was merely dissociated, a hungry ghost repeating history in a futile attempt to satisfy my desire for validation.

When I kick up into a forearm stand now, at least there is no longer another version of myself by my side, playing on loop the canned applause of a studio audience. Instead, she stands there silently, watching the inflow and outflow of my breath.

REFERENCES

Bush, George W. *Decision Points.* New York: Broadway Books, 2010.

Fromm, Erich. *To Have or to Be?* New York: Continuum, 2005.

Hill, Napoleon. *Think and Grow Rich.* New York: TarcherPerigee, 2005.

Lechter, Sharon. *Think and Grow Rich for Women.* New York: Penguin, 2014.

Rice, Condoleezza. *No Higher Honor.* New York: Crown, 2011.

Letters to My Mother and Daughters on Ambition

● ● ● ● ● ● **SARAH RUHL**

Dear Mom,

Today you called me on the phone and I said, "How are you?" and you said, "Okay," and I heard a hesitation and I said, "Why only okay?" You said, "Well, I am still having trouble with a sense of what my mission is in life."

You are seventy-two. I am forty-one. What could I possibly have to say to you about mission and ambition and mothers and daughters. This is a conversation we've been having since I was ten years old.

I have always been terrified of the word *ambition*. I find it distasteful, menacing, as though it was always pursued by its invisible compound partner "blind"—blind ambition. If someone asks me, "Do you like him or her?" and I answer, "He or she is—*'ambitious,'*" I am making a polite backhanded insult. I am saying that I have met a young person who seems more interested in a career or money or power and plunder or in scaling mountains than in the thing itself, the work. I treasure people who do the work itself for the sake of the work, and I am afraid of ambition. It stinks of oiled-up leather boots and money and calculators and corpses of friends cast aside—of the specific attempt to do better than others. But perhaps there is something to scrape away at, to investigate. Why do I fear the word *ambition*? Is it because I am secretly ambitious? Is it because I am a woman? Is it because I grew up in an Irish Catholic family and you were taught to keep your head down, to be wary of strivers?

My friend Emily Morse, the artistic director of New Dramatists, talks of focusing on the idea of mission rather than ambition. What happens if we take the "amb" out of "mission"? What is an "amb"? The second foot of an iamb. "Amb," pertaining to walking. Does the "amb" in *ambition* make the mission move? Is the missing "amb" a way in which a mission feels stuck, stagnant, not moving?

But I digress. You, my mother, called me today. You spoke to me of feeling a lack of mission, not ambition. I was in a taxi on the way to an appointment to get my blood drawn and my urine collected so that I could get life insurance in case I drop dead and still need to take care of my children somehow after I am dead.

All my life you were doing something. You were grading English papers, you were in a play, you were gardening, you were driving me somewhere, you were reading, you were planning, you were directing a play. You were in motion and seemed interested in playing as it lays. You did not have a plan—an ambition—to get to x or y place before you were thirty, before you were forty. You took pleasure in the tasks before you. I thought this was good. I thought this made you who you were—warm, and in motion.

Now that you are seventy-two there are fewer tasks before you demanding your attention. When you are in a play, I find that you often have a sense of mission. Every night there is something before you. But you are in a play now and still you feel your sense of mission waning. Is it because theater is transitory and you want to leave something behind? Is it because the contemporary theater itself lacks a mission? Or is theater not enough, you want a legacy? I once asked you if it was not enough that you had two daughters, one who wrote plays and one who was a doctor, if that counted as a legacy, and you said, "Not really, that is not mine. It is yours."

What is a mission and what is an ambition, and what if we have one but not both? And does having one make us a nice little missionary and does having the other one make us a bitch?

When my sister was in medical school one of her professors told her she'd make a good surgeon. "What does that mean?" my sister asked my uncle (a doctor), and he said: "It means he thinks you're a bitch."

Mom, you grew up in the fifties. The feminist movement came along just as you were having babies. You were not part of any consciousness raising groups. You did not look at your vagina while you were standing over mirrors. You did not talk about how you would infiltrate the patriarchy. You served on the PTA. You made us lunches. On my brown-bagged lunch, you would make little drawings, and a small crossword puzzle of my name. This comforted me when I felt lonely in the cafeteria. You read us *Mrs. Piggle-Wiggle* and did funny voices. You took our temperatures. You made us chicken soup and baked potatoes. You knitted us sweaters and recited the words of absurdist playwrights. You made us laugh.

I want, before you die, for you to feel at rest, to feel you've accomplished enough. To look around at this earth and say: It was good.

And I wonder if that counts as a mission or ambition—to want fullness or satisfaction for your parents or your children. Can ambition be directed toward others, and involve satisfaction and rest? Or does ambition only count as checking things off your own list and moving ever forward? An ambulatory kind of mission. Scaling heights. Making progress.

Some people have never seen a mountain they don't want to climb. I don't wish to climb mountains. I see a mountain and I think: That's pretty. I have no wish to climb that. What after all do you do after you climb a mountain? You climb back down. And you find a bigger one to climb. That repetitive striving does not appeal to me. Maybe it's because I get altitude sickness. Or maybe it's because I'm lazy. Or maybe it's because I prefer water. I see a body of water, and I want to swim in it. Maybe swimming is more like a mission—being immersed in a task in which you are held, surrounded by the task, inside consciousness, wading, forgetting everything but for the task—and scaling a mountain feels more Austrian and ambitious. However, I spoke to a rock climber recently and asked him why he climbs rocks, and he said it was for the same reason I like to be in water—because it puts him at the very edge of a moment.

So I must dispense with a metaphor that is beginning to sound essentialist, as if I'm speaking of watery vaginas and tall penises. And who cares about anatomy, really. Anatomy is tiresome. Men, women, women, men, women becoming men, men becoming women, and everything in between, I celebrate this, I say yes to this, and I think, yes, let's all become each other! But forget anatomy. Let's just be kind.

You, my mother, enjoy thinking. You like to contemplate, you are worried that death will be without consciousness, you worry about leaving it all behind. I wonder if your worry about mission is really a worry about leaving consciousness behind. What if consciousness persisted somehow? If that was not a worry, would there still be something you wished you had done? What would that thing be?

You have done so much but in your mind it does not add up. How many plays have you been in? More than a hundred, I'm sure. Joan of Arc, Peter Pan, Dull Gret—all these women and boys you've been for the sheer pleasure of doing it. Does it only count if you're in the midst? Does it only count if something is left behind? What is permanent? Words, works? Children? Education? How many young women have you educated? *The Odyssey* that you poured into young women's minds at Regina Dominican High School, the Dickens you poured into their often-disinterested minds? What of your PhD? Captured over the age of fifty, scaling the theoreticians while almost bowled over with grief over your husband's early death? Does that count? Does making sure your daughters grew up solid after their father died count? Would fame count? Everything perishes eventually; it's only a matter of degrees.

Apparently, we don't get to take anything with us. Not our children, not our fame. We go alone. Our sense of mission or ambition sustains us during our lifetime, and then if we're lucky, we go on to the next lifetime.

What if our mission was, as the critic Walter Pater put it, "not to sleep before evening"? He writes:

Every moment some form grows perfect in hand or face; some tone on the hills or the sea is choicer than the rest; some mood of passion or insight or intellectual excitement is irresistibly real and attractive to us—for that moment only. Not the fruit of experience, but experience itself, is the end. Not to discriminate every moment some passionate attitude in those about us . . . is to sleep before evening. With this sense of the splendor of our experience and of its awful brevity, gathering all we are into one desperate effort to see and touch, we shall hardly have time to make theories about the things we see and touch.

Does Pater's vision count as ambition or mission? You have done what Walter Pater asks your whole life, do you know that? You are probably doing it even now. Please don't be sad, Mom. You've had a mission all along.

Love,

Sarah

P.S. This is probably altogether the wrong kind of essay to write. It should be about women not fearing the word ambition *and telling our daughters to lean in. And I wrote of being suspicious of ambition and how to be content with death and how to stare out at a window with passionate excitement. Oh, well. Maybe I should also write to my daughters. If I were to write a letter to my daughters, I might say:*

Dear Anna and Hope,

When you were small children, there was a controversy in feminist circles about "leaning in" versus "leaning out." And I say to you, formidable creatures, don't lean in, don't lean out, stand up straight for God's sake! You're going to need all your strength and all your posture because you will be juggling planets and plates on a new historical stage in which women will have babies while running governments. You will have lots of new "of courses" that I didn't have when I was a girl. Of course women can be president. Of course women can marry women. (After the last gay wedding I came back from, you, my older daughter, Anna, seemed pensive. I started to explain to you that men can marry men, and you said, exasperated, I know all that, Mom, I'm just wondering, when do you think Mark and Todd will have babies?) So. Of course gay people can have children. Of course women can be president. But there will still be confusions.

You know your yellow Dr. Seuss book *My Book about Me*? I also had this book when I was a child. I filled in the blanks about myself. On the very first page, the book reads: "I am a boy" or "I am a girl" with two little boxes to check one or the other. As a five-year-old, I crossed out both boxes and wrote "P-R-S-O-N." "I am a person," or "prson." Spelling *person* with no "e" makes the word more vulnerable to substitution—add an "i" and you have *prison*. "I am a prison." But no matter. Somehow I knew even at the tender age of five that checking either one of those boxes was dangerous. I don't know whether or not I resolutely thought gender was a prison, or if I was just trying to be accurate in the way that writers are.

However, I kept my yellow *My Book about Me* and kept adding to it as I got older—a testament to the fluidity of identity over time, several words are crossed out, rewritten, revised. At around age six, I crossed out "prson," and in pen, I checked the box: girl. I am a girl—so, ipso facto, I am no longer a person. Person got crossed out. It took only one year for me to be schooled in the way of the world. Apparently, I could not be a "me" without also having a gender.

Eighteen years after the Dr. Seuss book, and after having written many poems, short stories, and the occasional play, I took a class in college called The Problem of the Woman Writer. I thought: What's the problem? Is there a problem? A problem with women writing? A problem with women? Or with women writing? I was compelled to take the class. It was a taught by a brilliant feminist scholar named Ellen Rooney, and at first I barely understood a word she said, so laden was her speech with words like *semiotics* and *phallogocentric*. I was desperate to learn her language. I was so intimidated by her that once, when we found ourselves next to each other at stalls in the bathroom, I could not pee and talk to her at the same time. Instead, I crumpled some paper to make it sound like I had some other purpose.

On the first day of her seminar, The Problem of the Woman Writer, we discussed an essay by the feminist theorist Luce Irigaray called "Speculum of the Other Woman." We spent a long time talking about the fairly abstract argument. Finally I raised my hand, an eighteen-year-old from Illinois, and asked, "What is a speculum?" One senior yawned, and a couple of the other women looked at me, curious. I thought it must be some philosophical term. I hadn't yet had my first gynecological exam. I was schooled that day. A speculum was no more, and no less, than a metal medical tool inserted into a woman's vagina, so that her insides can be seen.

It has been twenty-two years since I read the "Speculum of the Other Woman," and now I am hard-pressed to remember the substance of the essay, only that I was ashamed in front of other smart women to have asked what a speculum was. I didn't have the language for a concrete object that was to have opened me, made me seen, by a medical expert.

Since that time, my daughters, I have had three children including both of you, and I have lost all shame. When you give vaginal birth to twins, you become used to a roomful of people looking inside you, seeing what you cannot see. Gender when I was five years old was abstract—something that could be crossed out—*I am a prson*. Gender became more concrete at age six, when I wrote, "I am a girl." And then when I was eighteen, gender became abstract again—something to be analyzed, something that could be a philosophical problem. But gender when a male doctor is pulling a breech baby out of your vagina—that is very concrete.

I found it easier to be a feminist before I had children. Not the title, mind you. The negotiations. (By the way, I just put on three eggs to boil for breakfast.) There are multiple questions that must be asked every moment of every day: Do I do this or that? Or: Should my husband actually be doing this or that? How important is my work? If my child is vomiting, is that more important than my work? Yes. If my child has a weaving exhibit, is that more important than my work? Questionable. The: How can I write at all amidst constant interruption? Can I still think? Is thinking still a value? I believe that it is.

People sometimes ask me if I have trouble with being described as a woman writer. Many women writers don't like it. Virginia Woolf said in *A Room of One's Own* that an artist's mind should be androgynous. She writes, "Perhaps to think . . . of one sex as distinct from the other is an effort. It interferes with the unity of the mind." Woolf described Shakespeare and Coleridge as having androgynous minds, incandescent, the fusion of man and woman within one brain creating a sort of fusion in which, she wrote, "the mind is fully fertilized and uses all its faculties. Perhaps a mind that is purely masculine cannot create, any more than a mind that is purely feminine."

Virginia Woolf also said that "a woman writing thinks back through her mothers." She was very exacting with her punctuation and her spelling: She said "mothers," plural. Not just our own mother, but when we write we think back through our mothers. Did she mean our nonbiological mothers, our chosen mothers, our literary mothers? (For me: Paula Vogel, Toni Morrison, Marianne Moore, Jane Bowles, Jane Austen, Alice Walker, Elizabeth Bishop, and so on.) Or did she mean our mother's mothers? Or did she mean, in the Buddhist sense (and it's difficult to imagine Woolf as a Buddhist somehow, but still) that we've all been reincarnated countless times and that we have had many mothers?

There is a Tibetan Buddhist prayer in which you think closely about your mother. You imagine all the impossible tasks she did for you, all the ways in which she suffered for you, all the care and compassion she gave you to keep you alive. Then in your mind, you offer your mother all of your happiness, and take all of her suffering for yourself.

Imagine for a moment that you take all of your mother's suffering and give her (though she may be dead) all of your joy, and success. Then imagine that someday you will have a daughter. Maybe an actual daughter, or a literary daughter. Imagine that she is wishing you success, and happiness, and taking your suffering in order to transform it. Imagine that we are all connected, a rising circle, wishing each other well. Paula Vogel, my teacher, always taught me that circles rise, and I believe this. How to be ambitious about circles? Is this the feminist contribution to theories of ambition? That ambition can be a circle rather than a line?

I recently read a feminist critique of the idea that women's ambition must tend toward the collective and relational. And I realized that I have a confusion about the word *ambition* untethered to an object. Doesn't the nature of ambition change depending on the goal? It is different to be an ambitious capitalist, an ambitious peace-worker, an ambitious socialite, an ambitious pope. And what of an ambitious writer? The very phrase fills me with dread, vaguely makes me want to vomit. I suppose because the nature of ambition seems contrary to grace, and so much of writing is waiting for sentences to come. There is the ass-in-chair part of the writing, the doing of it, and then there is the other part, the part that comes unbidden. Is ambition a refusal of unbidden gifts? Or is a woman who refuses to admit to her own ambition nothing more than the woman who, historically, is not supposed to show her own desire?

What do I wish for you, my daughters? My mother, your grandmother, wrote me back after I wrote her that letter yesterday about ambition. She wrote me that when she was a child she used to pray to a Catholic God: "Please let me get one hundred on my test and be a nice person." Daughters, I hope that when you grow up you don't see any opposition between being smart and being nice. I hope if you get married that you marry men who are feminists or women who are supportive of your ambitions. I hope the two of you are friends. I hope one of you does not eclipse the other with blind ambition. Ah—is that what my fear of ambition is based on? That it would be unseemly to eclipse your sister, especially if you *meant* to? Does ambition eclipse sisterhood? Can we be ambitious about raising up other women?

Girls, do you remember the time when one of you was watching the other play soccer? Anna, your team was demolishing the other team. The other team seemed to have no one cheering for them on the sidelines. So, at one point, I cheered for the other team because I felt bad for them. "Good block!" I said. Hope, you were on my lap watching your big sister play. Hope, you turned to me with rage and said, "Why aren't you cheering for my sister?" "I am!" I said. Your brow darkened and you said, "*Then why did you say 'Good block'?* " I now want to print T-shirts that say: "Why aren't you cheering for my sister?" So focused were you on cheering for your own sister that my cheering for another team produced rage. Is ambition always predicated on competition—and what does it mean to cheer for our sister, and even on occasion, to cheer for the other team?

Maybe it's not enough to tell our daughters to be ambitious. We need to redefine ambition to include love. This new definition might have a new spelling: *ambission.* Ambission might include love for the world, love for work, love for our sisters, love for others. If ambition includes love, then, daughters: I hope that you do not fear ambition, that you do not see ambition as something that eclipses mission. That you see ambition as a mindful, skillful way of making concrete a mission you have found. I hope you find your mission. I hope the world is kind to you. I hope when I get old you are nice to me.

That word again: *nice*! Anna, your first word was actually two words: "good girl." For too long women have wanted to be good girls, and being a good girl meant not being ambitious. We had to be the guardians of virtue because there was so much rape

essays. Her pieces have appeared on numerous sites such as the *New York Times*'s *Well Family*, the *Washington Post*'s *On Parenting*, *Redbook*, *Verily Magazine*, *Role Reboot*, and *Elephant Journal*. She frequently contributes to local magazines and can be found in several print anthologies, including *Chicken Soup for the Soul*. She may someday write and travel, but she won't be a lawyer.

LAN SAMANTHA CHANG was born in Appleton, Wisconsin, where she attended public schools with her sisters Tai, Tina, and Ling. Her parents, Nai Lin Chang and Helen Chung-Hung Chang, emigrated from Beijing and Shanghai in the 1950s. Samantha is the author of two novels, *Inheritance* and *All Is Forgotten, Nothing Is Lost*, and a collection, *Hunger*. She has received fellowships from Stanford, Princeton, and Harvard Universities, the John Simon Guggenheim Foundation, the National Endowment for the Arts, and the American Library in Paris. She lives with her husband, Robert Caputo, and her daughter, Tai Antonia, in Iowa City, where she teaches at and directs the Iowa Writers' Workshop.

MARCIA CHATELAIN, a native of Chicago, is associate professor of History and African American Studies at Georgetown University. As a little girl, Marcia fed her intellectual curiosity with *Nancy Drew* books, and she dreamed of solving mysteries involving secret staircases and old clocks. After graduating high school, Marcia realized that she was too risk averse to pursue detective work, so she pursued degrees in magazine journalism and religious studies at the University of Missouri—Columbia. Storytelling and student activism introduced Marcia to the power of research and teaching, and she was led to Brown University's PhD program in American Civilization. Marcia is the author of *South Side Girls: Growing Up in the Great Migration*, an examination of the experiences of girls and young women during the historic movement of African Americans from the South to Chicago in the early twentieth century. Marcia is a proud Harry S. Truman Scholar, a recipient of the Ford Foundation Postdoctoral Diversity Fellowship, and has served on the Board of Girl Scouts of Western Oklahoma. When she isn't searching for clues, she enjoys hosting her weekly podcast, *Office Hours: A Podcast*, which features Marcia talking to students about the things that are most important to them.

ELIZABETH COREY is an associate professor of political science at Baylor University, in Waco, Texas, where she also serves as director of the honors program. She has received several awards for teaching and research and is currently a 2016–2017 Robert Novak Journalism Fellow. Her writing has appeared in *First Things* and the *Atlantic*, as well as in a variety of scholarly journals. She received a bachelor's in classics from Oberlin College, and master's and doctoral degrees in art history and political science from Louisiana State University. She is coeditor of the Radical Conservatisms book series at the University of Pennsylvania Press. Elizabeth's more popular writing generally concerns the question of what it means to live as a traditionalist in a progressive world—engaging social and political questions in a way that aims to be both charitable and critical at once. Most importantly, she is the mother of three children: Anna Katherine (eleven), John (nine), and Margaret (two). In her role as a wife and mother, she does a great deal of grocery shopping, laundry, reading books aloud, and generally enjoying the ability of her children to live in the moment.

CAMAS DAVIS has been a magazine editor and food writer for publications such as *National Geographic Adventure*, *Saveur*, *The Drama Review*, and *Portland Monthly*. She's the founder of the Portland Meat Collective, a meat school and agricultural resource, and the Meat Collective Alliance, a nonprofit. She has become a spokesperson for food system reform, and her work has been covered in national publications from the *New York Times Magazine* to *Martha Stewart Living*. She has continued to write about her experiences in the world of meat for media outlets such as *This American Life* and *Ecotone*, and she is currently working on a memoir (Penguin, 2017). She lives in Portland, Oregon.

ROXANE GAY lives and writes in the Midwest.

CRISTINA HENRÍQUEZ is the author of the novels *The Book of Unknown Americans* and *The World in Half*, and of the short story collection *Come Together, Fall Apart*. Her work has appeared in *The New Yorker,* the *Atlantic,* the *Wall Street Journal,* the *New York Times Magazine,* and elsewhere. She lives in Illinois.

JULIE HOLLAND, MD, is a psychiatrist specializing in psychophar-macology with a private practice in New York City. Her book *Weekends at Bellevue* chronicles her nine years running its psychi-atric emergency room. Featured on the *Today* show and CNN's "Weed," she's the editor of *The Pot Book* and *Ecstasy: The Complete Guide*. She's the medical monitor for PTSD studies involv-ing MDMA-assisted psychotherapy or cannabis. She is a harm reductionist well known for her cannabis advocacy work. Her latest book, *Moody Bitches: The Truth About the Drugs You're Taking, the Sleep You're Missing, the Sex You're Not Having, and What's Really Making You Crazy* has been translated into eleven languages.

PAM HOUSTON is the author of two novels, *Contents May Have Shifted* and *Sight Hound*; two collections of short stories, *Cowboys Are My Weakness* and *Waltzing the Cat*; and a collection of essays, *A Little More About Me*, all published by W. W. Norton. Her sto-ries have been selected for volumes of the *O. Henry Prize Stories,* the *Pushcart Prize,* and *Best American Short Stories of the Century.*

She teaches in the Low Residency MFA Program at the Institute of American Indian Arts, is a professor of English at UC Davis, and directs the literary nonprofit Writing By Writers. She lives at nine thousand feet above sea level near the headwaters of the Rio Grande and is at work on a book about that place.

JOAN LEEGANT is the author of a novel, *Wherever You Go,* and a story collection, *An Hour in Paradise,* which won the PEN/New England Book Award and was a Barnes & Noble Discover Great New Writers pick. Her fiction has appeared in numerous literary journals and anthologies. Formerly a lawyer, she has taught writing at Harvard, Oklahoma State, and Bar-Ilan University outside Tel Aviv. In 2014–2016 she was the writer-in-residence at Hugo House in Seattle.

AYANA MATHIS is a Philadelphia-born novelist and teacher. Her first novel, *The Twelve Tribes of Hattie,* was a *New York Times* best seller, and was chosen by Oprah Winfrey as the second selection for Oprah's Book Club 2.0. Ayana was the recipient of the 2014–2015 New York Public Library's Cullman Center Fellowship and a 2015 Bogliasco Foundation Fellowship. She is an assistant professor of English and creative writing at the Iowa Writers' Workshop, from which she earned her Master of Fine Arts in 2011.

NADIA P. MANZOOR is a British-Pakistani actor, writer, and producer, whose autobiographical one-woman show, *Burq Off!,* has sold out to audiences in New York, LA, San Francisco, London, Toronto, and Korea. It has been called a "gutsy, honest, hilarious must-see!" by Deepak Chopra, and "terrific" by the *Economist.* She is the cocreator and lead actor in "Shugs & Fats," a Gotham Award–winning Web series and was recently named one of the twenty-five new faces of independent film by *Filmmaker* magazine. Incisive and outspoken, Nadia has appeared on CNN, the

BBC, NPR, Al Jazerra, and CBC's Radio Q, and her work has been featured in *Elle India*, *Vogue India*, the *Daily Beast*, and the *Times of India*. She recently delivered a TEDx talk on the story of identity, and is a frequent guest speaker on panels that focus on women in Islam and the Muslim identity, and her writing has appeared in the *Huffington Post* and on India.com. She holds an MSW from Boston University, and to further fuse her passion for performance and social justice, she founded Paprika Productions, an all-female production company that produces works by brave, curious women. She lives in Brooklyn. For more information, visit nadiapmanzoor.com

FRANCINE PROSE is a novelist and critic whose most recent book, *Peggy Guggenheim: The Shock of the Modern,* was published by Yale University Press. Her previous books include the novels *Lovers at the Chameleon Club: Paris, 1932, My New American Life, Goldengrove, A Changed Man, Blue Angel* (a finalist for the 2001 National Book Award), and the nonfiction *New York Times* best seller *Reading Like a Writer: A Guide for People Who Love Books and for Those Who Want to Write Them.* She writes frequently for the *New York Times Book Review* and the *New York Review of Books.* She is a past president of PEN American Center and a member of both the American Academy of Arts and Sciences and the American Academy of Arts and Letters. She is a Distinguished Visiting Writer at Bard College. She lives in New York City.

THERESA REBECK is a widely produced playwright throughout the United States and abroad. Plays include *Mauritius, The Scene, Spike Heels,* and *Seminar,* which was on Broadway in 2011 starring Alan Rickman. In television, Ms. Rebeck has written for *Dream On, Brooklyn Bridge, L.A. Law,* and *NYPD Blue*, among others; she was also the creator of the NBC drama *Smash*. She recently finished her second feature film as writer/director, *Trouble,* starring

Anjelica Huston, Bill Pullman, David Morse, and Julia Stiles. She has published three novels, *Three Girls and Their Brother, Twelve Rooms with a View,* and *I'm Glad About You* (published by Putnam in February 2016). Ms. Rebeck proudly serves on the board of PEN International as executive secretary, and she is a longtime member of the Dramatists Guild Council. Ms. Rebeck is originally from Cincinnati and holds an MFA in playwriting and a PhD in Victorian melodrama, both from Brandeis University.

MOLLY RINGWALD is an actress, author, and singer. She began her film career at the age of thirteen with her Golden Globe–nominated performance in *The Tempest* and has worked with such directors as Paul Mazursky, John Hughes, Cindy Sherman, and Jean-Luc Godard. She is the author of the national best seller *When It Happens to You,* a novel in stories. Her writing has been published in *Esquire, Vogue,* the *Guardian,* the *New York Times,* and *Interview,* among others.

SARAH RUHL is the playwright of *Stage Kiss; In the Next Room, or the vibrator play* (Pulitzer Prize finalist and Tony Award nominee for Best New Play); *The Clean House* (Pulitzer Prize finalist, 2005, and the Susan Smith Blackburn Prize, 2004); *Passion Play* (PEN American Award and the Fourth Freedom Forum Playwriting Award from the Kennedy Center); *Dead Man's Cell Phone* (Helen Hayes Award); *Melancholy Play* (a musical with Todd Almond); *Eurydice; Orlando; Demeter in the City* (NAACP nomination); *Late: A Cowboy Song; Three Sisters; Dear Elizabeth;* and most recently, *The Oldest Boy* and *For Peter Pan on Her 70th Birthday.* Her plays have been produced on Broadway at the Lyceum by Lincoln Center Theater and off-Broadway at Playwrights' Horizons, Second Stage, and at Lincoln Center's Mitzi E. Newhouse Theater. Originally from Chicago, Ms. Ruhl received her MFA from Brown University, where she studied with Paula Vogel. An alum of 13P and of the New Dramatists, she won a MacArthur Fellowship in 2006. She was the recipient of the PEN Center Award for a mid-career playwright, the Whiting Award, the Feminist Press's Forty Under Forty Award, and a Lilly Award. She proudly served on the executive council of the Dramatists Guild for three years, and she is currently on the faculty at Yale School of Drama. Her book of essays on the theater and motherhood, *100 Essays I Don't Have Time to Write,* was a *Times* Notable Book of the Year. She lives in Brooklyn with her family. For more information, visit www.sarahruhlplaywright.com.

ERIKA L. SÁNCHEZ is a poet, essayist, and fiction writer. She is the author of the poetry collection *Lessons on Expulsion* (Graywolf, 2017) and *I Am Not Your Perfect Mexican Daughter* (Knopf, 2017). Her poetry has been published in *Guernica, ESPN.com, Boston Review,* and *Poetry* magazine. She has also been featured on "Latino USA" on NPR and published in *Please Excuse This Poem: 100 New Poems for the Next Generation* (Viking, 2015). Erika is a recipient of a CantoMundo Fellowship, a "Discovery"/*Boston Review* Poetry Prize, and a Ruth Lilly and Dorothy Sargent Rosenberg Poetry Fellowship from the Poetry Foundation. Her nonfiction has appeared in *Al Jazeera,* the *Guardian, Rolling Stone,* and many other publications.

YAEL CHATAV SCHONBRUN, PhD, is a clinical psychologist and assistant professor at Brown University. She has been awarded several grants from the National Institutes of Health to conduct her research on extending treatments to underserved populations. She is the author of chapters in several books on mental health conditions and treatment, has written thirty scientific articles. Dr. Schonbrun's nonacademic writing has appeared in the *New York Times, Elephant Journal, Kveller,* and *Psychology Today.*

Dr. Schonbrun also maintains a small private practice where she specializes in couples' treatment.

EVANY THOMAS has been pinballing around the tech industry ever since the late 1990s (Microsoft! Webmonkey! Friendster! Yahoo! TED! Wells Fargo! Facebook!), with a brief detour into the print world to write *The Secret Language of Sleep: A Couple's Guide to the Thirty-Nine Positions* (which has since been published in German, Japanese, Chinese, British English, and Italian). She now works at Pinterest and lives in El Cerrito, California, with her husband, kid, and their two fancy pet rats. For all the details, visit www.evany.com.

CLAIRE VAYE WATKINS is the author of *Gold Fame Citrus* and *Battleborn*, which won the Story Prize, the Dylan Thomas Prize, New York Public Library's Young Lions Fiction Award, the Rosenthal Family Foundation Award from the American Academy of Arts and Letters, and a Silver Pen Award from the Nevada Writers Hall of Fame. A Guggenheim Fellow, Claire is on the faculty of the Helen Zell Writers' Program at the University of Michigan. She is also the codirector, with Derek Palacio, of the Mojave School, a free creative writing workshop for teenagers in rural Nevada.

ACKNOWLEDGMENTS

First, I have to thank my contributors, all of whom carved time out of their busy lives to reflect and write on an issue that inevitably became more crucial and more complicated with every sentence they attempted. Working with them has easily been the best crash course in human experience and the artistic process available anywhere. Camas Davis, Julia Haslett, Ann Packer, Joan Leegant, and Martha Walters were great early readers and thought-shapers, offering encouragement as the project hit its various milestones. Don Waters helped me grapple with the subject on so many levels, in life and on the page (and is responsible for the title of my essay). My father, Richard Romm, has always been a fan and supporter. Thanks to my agent, Maria Massie, with whom I brainstormed this idea while living out of boxes in Iowa. And a special big-time dance-party-style throwdown for Katie Adams, whose devotion to this project was unfailing and whose mind is a quick and bright amazement.

"[AMBITION IS]
NEVER SETTLING,
ALWAYS STRIVING
FOR MORE."
—PUBLISHER, 35

"[I AM AMBITIOUS BECAUSE] IN ADDITION TO WO
AND RUNNING MY FARM, I SPREAD THE GOSPE
EATING AND LIVING SUSTAINABLY. I GIVE MY TIM
COOKING SKILLS TO TEACH OTHERS, AND DONA
TIME TO FEED THOSE WHO HAVE LESS."
—FARMER, CHEF, GRAPHIC DESIGNER, WIFE, ACTIVIST, 54

"[I'M AMBITIOUS BECAUSE]
IF I WANT IT, I WILL DO
WHAT IT TAKES TO GET IT."
—PRODUCER AND MENTOR, 36

"AMBITION IS NEVER BEING FULLY
WANTING MORE, AND TAKING A
WHATEVER THAT 'MORE'
—SOCIAL MEDIA MANAGER,

"[AMBITION] IS SIMPLE:
KEEP WORKING NO MATTER
WHAT HAPPENS. IF THINGS
ARE GOOD, KEEP WORKING.
IF THINGS ARE BAD, KEEP
WORKING. BELIEF IN
Y

"[I'M A

"[AMBITI
DO OR
THAT F
TALEN
— DIPLOMAT,

E ROAD THAT H
OF REJECTION
EVER REALLY GR
GOOD. IT WAS
THAT M

"I DO
I'M OF
SO, I
MAKI
D

ON IS SETTING
DARDS AND SUR
—TEACHER AND W

"[AMBIT
BARRIERS AND BREAKING THROUGH THEM, MAXING OUT
THE BEAUTY AND SATISFACTION IN LIFE."
—MEDIATOR, FACILITATOR, COMEDIAN, TEACHER, LAW SCHOOL HOPEFUL, SCIENTIST, 28

"AM
BURN
THIN